Every Contact Leaves a

ALSO BY CONNIE FLETCHER

Every Contact Leaves a
TRACE

Crime Scene Experts Talk About
Their Work from Discovery Through Verdict

Connie Fletcher

St. Martin's Press
New York

www.stmartins.com

Library of Congress Cataloging-in-Publication Data

Fletcher, Connie, 1947–
Every contact leaves a trace : crime scene experts talk about their work from discovery through verdict / Connie Fletcher.
    p. cm.
ISBN-13: 978-0-312-34037-7
ISBN-10: 0-312-34037-0
1. Criminal investigation.   2. Murder—Investigation.   3. Crime scene searches.   4. Evidence, Criminal.   5. Forensic sciences.   I. Title.

HV8073.F54 2006
363.25'9523—dc22

                                                            2006040372

First Edition: August 2006

10   9   8   7   6   5   4   3   2   1

This book is for Trygve, Bridget, Nick, and Julie.

CONTENTS

ACKNOWLEDGMENTS

This book was powered by the willingness of forensic experts to speak candidly about their work to an outsider. I owe a debt of gratitude to the eighty men and women who spoke to the science, but also to the art of crime scene investigation. They were clear in their explanations of forensic science, and often moving in their accounts of crime scenes and criminal investigations.

I owe a special debt to the following people, who guided me to other reliable sources, spoke with me numerous times, let me tour crime lab facilities, or kept checking in with me to see how things were progressing: Chief Tom Cronin of the Coeur d'Alene, Idaho, Tribal Police/criminal profiler; Chief George Carpenter and Deputy Chief Brian King of the Wilmette, Illinois, Police Department; Lieutenant of Investigations James Mackert and Detective Roland Jones of the Chicago Police Department; Chicago Police Superintendent Phil Cline; Kara Stefanson, DNA Resource Specialist, Cook County State's Attorney's Office, Chicago; Commander Joe Murphy and Lieutenant Dave O'Callahan, Chicago Police Department; Norm Gahn, Assistant District Attorney and DNA evidence specialist, Milwaukee, Wisconsin; John Juhala, Commander, Forensic Science Division, Michigan State Police; Vernon Geberth, Lieutenant-Commander, Bronx Homicide, NYPD; Barry A. J. Fisher, Crime Lab Director, Los Angeles County Sheriff's Department; Captain Ray Peavy and Sergeant Rich Longshore, Homicide Bureau, Los Angeles County Sheriff's Department; Sue Ballou, Program Manager for Forensic Science Research at the National Institute of Standards and Technology, Gaithersburg, Maryland; Dr. Sunandan B. Singh, Medical Examiner, Bergen County, New Jersey, and Deputy Medical Examiner Mary Ann Clayton,

Bergen County, New Jersey; Donna Fontana, forensic anthropologist, State of New Jersey; Detectives Bill Hamilton and Bill McIntyre, Atlantic County, New Jersey; Michael Camp, Crime Lab Director, Milwaukee, Wisconsin; Chris Plourd, defense attorney, forensic evidence specialist, San Diego, California; Richmond Riggs, prosecuting attorney, Genesee County, Michigan; and Director Frank Dolejsi, former Assistant Director David Petersen; Latent Print Examiner David Peterson, all of the Forensic Science Lab, St. Paul, Minnesota.

Thanks to my wonderful editor, Diane Reverand, and to my tireless agent, Nat Sobel, who have seen me through four books, making it fun each time. Thanks to the people at Loyola University Chicago, who freed me up to do the research: Chair Elizabeth Coffman and Dean Isiaah Crawford.

The backdrop to all this is my family: my husband, Trygve, my daughter, Bridget, and my son, Nick, who help me enormously just by making me happy. And thanks to my sister, Julie, who started the stories when she became a Chicago cop.

When you investigate a murder, it's like you're looking through a piece of cloth. And you come upon this red thread—that's something that you think will be an avenue of investigation.

So, you very gently follow that red thread. You keep following that red thread wherever it may go. It almost never goes in a straight line. It goes around, back, and loops in on itself; it crosses, stops and goes, and meanders along. Sometimes it's a big, wide red thread. Sometimes it's a tiny little thread. Sometimes it gets bigger. Sometimes it gets smaller. Sometimes the red thread just . . . stops. But then you start looking for the end of the thread again.

You have to follow where the red thread takes you. Always being careful not to put too much pressure on it, or it'll just break.

I tell new detectives: "Follow the red thread, wherever it takes you. But be careful."

—Sergeant Jim Givens (Ret.) Commander,
Cold Case Squad, Phoenix, Arizona

Every Contact Leaves a

INTRODUCTION

"It's not *CSI*." A few years ago, as forensic crime shows started splashing across TV screens like so much blood spatter, I started hearing this from cops I know in my family and their friends. I heard it from homicide detectives I'd interviewed for previous books. The cops always stopped, sort of mysteriously, at this three-word review whenever the shows were mentioned.

At the time, I didn't know any forensic scientists. I didn't know anyone who worked collecting and processing evidence at crime scenes. I didn't know anybody who worked in a crime lab. But I did keep hearing cops, when they talked about cases they worked on, give variants of this one-sentence critique of crime shows: "It's not *CSI*."

At first, I thought cops' distaste for crime shows might be some form of professional jealousy, a way of preserving insider status (I've found that cops tend to have contempt for all crime shows, with the exception of reruns of *Barney Miller*). I thought it might be, in the case of homicide detectives, a way of downplaying the importance of science at crime scenes, science that can be intimidating and exclusionary to detectives who do old-fashioned, shoe-leather police work.

Just as an occasional viewer, I found *CSI* and its minions sort of unsettling, rather than convincing. The tone of the shows, especially *CSI,* seemed too smug with the science and too in-your-face with body parts (granted, I hold my hands in front of my eyes, saying, "Jesus, Mary, and Joseph" over and over during horror movies).

But it seemed odd that four people would concentrate on one

case at a time, handling all the work from scene processing through analysis at the lab (and why was the lab always so dark?), on through smirking interrogation of suspects. It didn't ring right. First of all, who would wear designer suits, leather, and suede to places festooned with body parts? Second, what was with all the gloom? The detectives I know are incredibly skilled socially, fun to be with, and humorous, not at all like the grim, condescending troupe of *CSI*.

So I wanted to see if the cops were right about *CSI*. I had no way to do this except to contact experts about crime scene investigation, the ones who actually collect and analyze evidence. My resolve was not just to see how reality jibed with TV and movie portrayal, but to get an in-depth look at forensic science as it is now applied to crime scenes. I decided an oral history of as many people as possible involved in crime scene work was the way to go because oral history lets people talk factually, talk emotionally, tell stories, give opinions freely. I feel it's the best way to get a portrait of a different world, from the insiders' viewpoints.

The forensic science world is not an easy one for an outsider to crack. How do you find and then talk with a DNA analyst buried deep within the DNA section of a lab? How do you get an evidence technician, or a forensic anthropologist, or a medical examiner, to open up about what really goes on? How do you know who the players are? How do you know you've gotten to reliable sources? How do you know you're asking the right questions, rather than woefully ignorant questions?

I work with the belief that, for a project like this, the whole world opens up if you can find the right lever. What the outsider needs, as I learned in college anthropology, is a "key informant," a reliable source within a group who puts you in contact with other reliable sources. I was lucky enough to have several key informants going into this project. I talk about these people in the acknowledgments. As I interviewed them, one reliable expert would lead me to the next. Experts kept telling me, "Forensics is a pretty small world. We all know each other."

It's one thing for the outsider to get forensic experts to agree to talk; it's another challenge to the outsider to understand what they're saying. I'm of a decidedly nonanalytical bent. I was so hopeless in high school algebra, for example, that I thought they would tell us what x was in senior year. (I thought that it might be an apple.) What saved me in interviews was the fact that I represent the public, and forensic experts are well versed in translating for jurors when they testify in court. Also, scientists are used to working with detectives and attorneys, some of whom may be as English major-y as I am. And I've taken a personal vow to always admit ignorance, rather than pass it along to the reader.

What surprised me in interviews, besides the skill (and patience) with which forensic scientists made their material accessible, was how much they sounded like cops. I'm a great admirer of police as consummate storytellers. I never expected scientists to be, but here were DNA analysts telling gripping stories that hinged on a fleck of blood, forensic anthropologists waxing poetic about how you can see the traumas of a person's life in his or her skeleton, trace evidence analysts giving heart-stopping narratives about serial killers caught by a paint chip.

I learned something about their personalities, as well. If you know any latent print specialists with children, ask them about seeing their newborns' footprints for the first time. You'll get a sense of the wonder with which they approach their work. They also tend to be artistic, playing the piano or painting in their spare time. I thought DNA analysts would be dull as ditchwater, but they tend to have keen senses of humor (maybe because they can't talk at all in the lab, they're less uninhibited talking outside it). Trace analysts confess to being a bit obsessive-compulsive, a good thing when you're examining fibers, but potentially crazy-making at home. And unlike TV and movie portrayals of the crime scene processor as a totally unemotional machine, the men and women who work crime scenes can be haunted by them.

If you talk to enough forensic scientists, you'll never walk in the woods again without expecting to find a body. So many times, a forensic anthropologist would say to me, "When you find a body in the woods . . . ," and then tell me exactly what to do when I make this discovery.

Forensic scientists also tend to sound a little like chefs. Many, many times, I felt I was listening to a very bad recipe; for example, one anthropologist who examines skeletal bones in the lab instructed me: "First, put the skeleton in a vat and boil off the flesh. Then cut away any remaining tissue . . ."

Speaking to homicide detectives, fun as they are, can also be unnerving. When I met them in person, at any pause in the conversation, I'd notice that they'd fix me with a hard stare, the kind of stare that says, "We know what you did."

I ended up speaking with eighty forensic experts around the country: crime scene processors; members of the National Commission on the Future of DNA Evidence; DNA analysts; latent print specialists; trace evidence analysts; bloodstain interpretation experts; toxicologists; forensic anthropologists and forensic archeologists; entomologists; a forensic botanist; firearms examiners; homicide, robbery, and burglary detectives; cold case detectives; medical examiners; crime lab directors; and attorneys. I visited crime labs. And this is what I found out:

It's not *CSI*. The work is much more time-intensive and demanding ("Crime scene processing is a goddamn pain in the ass, if you do it right," said one New Jersey scene supervisor). Solving a crime depends more on a number of forensic sciences meshing with solid investigative work, rather than on one grandstand forensic play ("The thing about these shows—everybody thinks that you just run in and scoop up a bucket of DNA and you're done," says one evidence technician).

Just about every forensic scientist and crime scene investigator I interviewed had the name of an obscure (to the outside world) French criminologist, Edmond Locard, on his/her lips. Crime scene experts often refer to the "Locard principle." Locard took what the Sherlock Holmes stories advocated, the examination of microscopic bits of evidence, and built the science of forensics around it.

Locard's famous pronouncement, "Every contact leaves a trace," applies to all forensic science. The technology of recent years, not just in DNA testing, but in instrumentation across the sciences, brings the "Locard principle" into the twenty-first-century crime scene and courtroom every day.

And the work is much more innovative than the sci-fi applications of forensics on TV. For example, forensic DNA technology was advanced by the efforts of the Office of the Chief Medical Examiner in New York to identify the victims of the attacks on the World Trade Center. Bloodhounds are used in the South to sniff out trace evidence that criminals on the run may be dropping and picking up. Crime scene investigators in Alaska have adapted their methods to a state that has vast reaches and only one real road: Evidence technicians there carry the necessary scene processing equipment in backpacks, and travel to scenes by plane, boat, and snowmobile. The Los Angeles County Sheriff's Department runs a homicide school for detectives. They reconstruct inside and outside scenes in a hotel they take over for their sessions, using props such as mannequins, shot-up cars, suicide notes, stage blood, and severed limbs from Halloween shops to ratchet up the realism.

The format of this book is oral history. I let the experts speak for themselves (a credit after each quote lets the reader know what the specialist's job is) in the body of each chapter. Most of the people interviewed had to obtain permission from their department, agency or crime lab to speak with me. One of the conditions was that their comments be kept anonymous. A handful of people are identified by name, with their consent.

My goal is to keep out of the way of the experts as much as possible. I provide an introduction to each chapter, and then present the crime scene processors' and interpreters' comments and stories directly. Quotations marks, except as they occur within the quotations themselves, have been omitted.

Readers, however, need to know that these people are reliable guides. All the contributors to this book are listed and given biographical sketches at the end of the book.

This book moves from first discovery of the body through final verdict at trial. The experts talk about their specializations and about what they've seen and what it has done to them. Through them, readers will gain access to a world mostly fictionalized by *CSI* and its spin-offs, or made overly formal in on-camera interviews. If you're a student thinking of a career in forensic science, this book will introduce you to disciplines and techniques you may never have heard of. For people who protect, process, and interpret scenes, some new approaches and solutions might be found here. If you're about to enter your first crime scene, this book could help you avoid committing grave mistakes.

This is the experts' book: their words, their knowledge—and how they read the victims' stories in the traces left behind.

One

CRIME SCENE PROCESSING

Do it right the first time. You only get one chance. Once things have been moved, once things have been changed, once you lose that little window of opportunity, it's gone forever.
— Vernon J. Geberth, Commander, Bronx Homicide, NYPD (Ret.), Author of *Practical Homicide Investigation*

A crime scene investigator has to have a positive attitude. You've got to *believe* you're going to find the evidence. I just learned to play golf. It helps you search the crime scene. My ball goes into the woods. Every time. Now it's like a crime scene. I always come out with, say, six balls, when I lost two. The positive attitude is the same with golf and the crime scene: You don't look at the sand traps. You look at the green. Your objective is always to do your best at that crime scene.
— Dr. Henry C. Lee, Chief Emeritus and Director, Forensic Science Laboratory, Meriden, Connecticut

A DROP OF BLOOD ON A GYM SHOE. A PIECE OF FIBER FOUND on a stairway. The impression of a spade used to dig a basement grave. DNA picked up from a sneeze. A few microscopic traces of glass, blown back on the clothing of an intruder.

These have been the first threads of forensic investigations, discovered and collected at crime scenes, leftover particles from actions that have ripped the fabric of people's lives.

Before any investigation can start, evidence must be collected. The scene itself, whether inside, outside, or mobile, has to be gone over as if the processors were exploring a site on Mars. What's this? Why is *this* here? Why *isn't* this here? What does this all mean?

And—how do we get the evidence back to the lab without destroying it?

Generally, once the police call for assistance from the crime lab, crime scene teams consisting of evidence technicians and any forensic specialists needed—like blood spatter interpreters, trace analysts, firearms examiners—are sent to the scene. These processors start the chain of evidence that may stretch from the scene through the detectives' investigation, through the crime lab, all the way to trial. Processors and investigators have a term for the ideal: "keeping the chain tight." And they have only one shot at picking up the links left at the scene.

This chapter follows crime scene processors, presenting what they've found in their own words. Their comments are anonymous, but their expertise is indicated after their quotes (unless an entire section contains one type of expert, indicated before the section). Follow the processors and specialists as they work the scene from the outside in.

In late '81, they were training new crime scene team members in Minnesota. Of course, none of us was smart enough to ask, "Well, why is everybody who's been here for a long time getting *off* crime scene?"

We're all young and stupid, thinking, "This sounds great." Back in those days you started out as a crime scene photographer. We went through the whole course and had to demonstrate our proficiency.

Our final test was out at the stockyards in South St. Paul. We were in part of the stockyard that was unused, but there were cows waiting to become steaks kind of all around us. There was this large unused building. They made crime scenes in all these different rooms. They did footprints in snow, so we had to capture those. With crime scene photography, you take an overall picture, and then a medium-range, and then a close-up. So we had to take all these outside shots, in the old stockyards and out in the snow.

I can now appreciate the humor of the gentleman who put us through this whole process—he sat in the heated van the whole time, smoking—because here we are out there, documenting these crime scenes, in these smelly old buildings—they just reeked of cow manure and blood and dead animals. And he made us be out there all day long, doing this, demonstrating what we could do with our abilities on the camera. It was smelly and bad, it was January, which I didn't appreciate the humor of till later either, and our cameras were freezing up while we were out there, because it was about ten below outside all day long. So we became certified crime scene photographers.

I know now what they were trying to do with us that day. They were trying to get us used to what actual crime scenes are like. They're smelly. They're messy. And you're there for hours and hours and hours, processing them.

CRIME SCENE INVESTIGATOR

When the new people in the crime scene response team come on board, they're given a pager, and they watch the news, and then they look at their pager all night long, waiting for it to go off. They call me the next morning and say, "We didn't go on a crime scene!" And I said, "Well, there's a reason why you didn't go to a crime scene. First of all, somebody has to be killed. Definitely. Secondly, their local agency has to call us in. And thirdly, you have to be on call. If all three of those things fall together, then you'll go."

CSI is very much responsible for this. They're just so *eager*.

CRIME SCENE COORDINATOR

It's not like *CSI*. I think I've been in *one* crime scene that might even look remotely like something from *CSI*. Usually, the scene is in a trailer home, or an older home where there's piles of garbage around . . . You never get a nice clean scene like on TV.

I've got pictures of crime scenes I've worked on that I use in teaching. And trainees say things like, "Well, on *CSI* they can tell if there's been a struggle because the lamp's been overturned."

Well, at every scene I've been to, the lamps are *usually* overturned, and they're laying next to the eighty crushed beer cans laying on the floor—and the White Wolf vodka bottles. I show the trainees a picture of this. The trainee might say to me, "How do you tell there's been a struggle in this room, sir?" "Well, see how the garbage has been disturbed in *this* area, but not over here?"

EVIDENCE TECHNICIAN

I remember the first burglary scene I ever walked into. The house was totally ransacked. Stuff all over the place. And I just remember standing there thinking, "Where the hell do I start?"

CRIME SCENE SERGEANT

Getting to the Scene

The crime scene call comes in. You figure out, first of all, the type of crime committed, whether or not the scene is inside or outside, whether or not there's a victim still at the scene, and whether or not there's a suspect. Based on the type of scene, the manner of death, and the information from the desk officer, I put together a crew that covers the various disciplines of science that I would expect to find at that scene.

The call might be, "Hey, we got a crime. It's a double homicide, it's in a house, the victims have been shot, there's been forced entry, and it looks like they ransacked the place."

Based on that information, I would put together a couple of latent print people, because there's gonna be a lot of fingerprints to do, I would make sure there were evidence people to handle footwear and tire tracks and fibers, I would ask a firearms person to handle the shooting end of it, and we would pull in perhaps one more person to help with scene documentation and photographs. So you might have a crew of four, five people.

Then we pick up the equipment truck and take off for the scene.

SCENE SUPERVISOR

I think everybody's had a couple near-death experiences getting to scenes. Like the time we're doing seventy mph, trying to get to a scene quickly, and the tire blows out, it's completely shredded and we're on some back country road. If we were driving a Humvee, like they do on *CSI*, we wouldn't be in any trouble. But we're just driving these big old bread trucks.

CRIME SCENE PROCESSOR

We had just driven to a scene one time. We're standing around outside the scene, waiting for the search warrant to show up. This was not in one of the better neighborhoods. The evidence people and the cops are all waiting around outside the crime scene van. Our van is fully marked, you know, BUREAU OF CRIMINAL APPREHENSION in big letters on the side and everything.

Suddenly, you hear gunshots in the neighborhood, and all of a sudden, all the cops are gone. I'm standing there thinking, "This is not good. We're sitting here with this *beacon* almost—*Come shoot us.*" We evidence people don't carry weapons. And all the cops just grabbed their guns out of the van and ran off, leaving us there.

A lot of times, there'll be the sound of gunshots or news of a high-speed chase comes over the radio, and you can see—all the cops at the scene, supposedly there to protect us, they'll all come up and ask, "Can I go? Can I go?" It's a testosterone thing with them.

CRIME SCENE PROCESSOR

Getting to a crime scene in Alaska is unique in that, if a crime is reported, timewise it may take a while to get there. Our crime lab covers the whole state.

There's basically one road that runs up the middle of Alaska, and that goes along the railroad; it goes to Fairbanks and then there's a four-hundred-mile gravel road up to the North Slope, where the oil is, with essentially no real gas stations on the way up. Out in western Alaska, there are no roads except for maybe a few miles around a town. We have to use snow machines, Ski-Doos, a lot.

Our crime scene investigators have backpacks prepared ahead of time, with most of the essential crime scene processing items in them. Usually, you take commercial aircraft as far as you can go. Let's say you're flying to Bethel [about forty miles inland from the Bering Sea]. You take Alaska Airlines to Bethel and then you take a commuter flight from there, and then maybe you get picked up by a department, and from there you go to a remote area. It might be by a four-wheeler or a snowmobile, or by ferry, or small boat. The Department of Public Safety has some small planes also. The weather's a factor, of course. You can take off in a plane in a snowstorm and not be able to see the end of the runway.

We go to the remotest regions of Alaska. We went to a scene—flew Alaska Airlines out to Bethel. Then I was picked up by the state troopers there and driven to the Kuskokwim River, and then we took a boat five miles up the river to a fishing camp, where the natives dry fish and catch salmon. There was a woman missing who was finally found killed.

I remember one crime scene where the investigators flew to a southeastern area, like Juneau, and then they took a smaller plane from there with floats, and they flew to a little fishing village. Some of the floats on these planes have wheels also. This time, they had to put the wheels down

and go up a boat ramp to get up on land and get to the
scene.

FORMER CRIME LAB DIRECTOR

Securing the Scene

I was teaching crime scene investigation one time and a patrol-
man says, "I'm a uniform guy. I'm a patrolman. What does
this stuff got to do with me?" I said, "Thank you, *God,* for
asking that question." I said, "Stand up and ask it again,
son." He did. I said, "Contrary to what all the homicide assholes of the world will tell you, you're the most important
guy. That first uniform cop sets the tone, sets the stage for
everything that follows. If you do what you're taught to do
in the academy and do it well—protect that scene and protect the evidence—you're giving us a good start. If you
don't, then everything's lost. *You're* the most important guy
there. *That's* what it's got to do with you."

HOMICIDE COMMANDER

For forensic people, a pristine scene would be: Police are
called to do a well-being check at a house. A couple of cops
show up and see that the door's been kicked in. *One* cop goes
inside, sees an old lady dead on the floor, goes up and checks
that she is dead. There's no need to transport that person to
the hospital if she's dead. Why scoop her up and run her to
the hospital? A lot of important evidence is going to be on,
or nearby, that body. Then the officer withdraws, secures the
scene, and calls forensics to come and process it. Now *that's*
gonna be a terrific scene. And that's pretty rare. Everybody
wants to come and see what's going on at the scene.

HOMICIDE DETECTIVE

We've literally had scenes where we've asked the officer at the
scene how many people have been down to see the body in

the basement, and the officer will say, "One." Well, we'll get down there and dust up footwear impressions around the body and find that there's six or eight or ten pairs of shoeprints in a circle around the body.

FORENSIC SPECIALIST

If you get a crime scene in winter, snow on the ground, an effec-tive way to get rid of extra officers at the scene: Hand them a shovel and say, "Here, why don't you hold onto this with both hands and help me shovel here in a few minutes?" You turn around and they're gone because now they've realized they might have to work.

EVIDENCE TECHNICIAN

Working from the Outside In

What I love about doing this: Any scene you walk into, you have to use any knowledge, capabilities, skills that you have to try to decide, "What is the best way to approach this scene?" It's like—If you like jigsaw puzzles, it's like doing a different jigsaw puzzle every time you go in there. It's a brand-new puzzle each time.

CRIME SCENE TEAM LEADER

I get sent to a scene. I'll do a walk-through to see what I'm deal-ing with. My observations usually start on the outside, mainly because one of your main objectives when you're processing a scene is to identify your fragile evidence and take steps to protect it, to document and collect that first. So, anything outdoors obviously has the potential to be more fragile than evidence indoors, because of the weather and everything else. . . . If there's a footwear impression in the dirt outside, and there's a thunderstorm coming, that footwear has just become a piece of fragile evidence.

FORENSIC INVESTIGATOR

When I'm on a scene and when I train people, I always tell them, "You have to think like a crook." How did the suspect handle this? How did he get in?

Well, he got in by prying this window open. Okay. How did he pry the window open? Well, he took a crowbar and jammed it in the window, got it loose, and he used his hands to push open the window. Right there, what do you have? You have a crowbar and you have pry marks that might have a little gouge on it from the crowbar. We have a rubber cast for this; we can actually cast those imprints, and we have people in the lab that actually get paid to compare stuff like that.

Or you deduce that the guy used his hands to push open the window. Well, are there prints on the outside of the window? Now, the window's open. How did he get inside? The window's kind of high, so he probably grabbed up underneath the inside of the windowsill and pulled himself up. You want to look for prints there on the underside of the windowsill.

You wouldn't *believe* how many people are sitting in prison in South Carolina now because I went behind them and dusted for fingerprints underneath the windowsill and, lo and behold, there the fingerprints were—upside down. A jury sees that it doesn't take too much to figure out that the only way those fingerprints could get on there was the burglar was jumping in from the outside.

LATENT PRINT SPECIALIST

You have to have an extremely open mind when you go into these places. Nothing's off-limits. Let your mind wander. Think about it. Think about what this person did, how they did it, where they were, what would they do. You need that thought process to kick in.

For example, we had a homicide case in Kansas. There was a little back porch with a single lightbulb, which wasn't working. The latent print guy figured that maybe the killer unscrewed the lightbulb before he came into the house. So he took off the lightbulb, got some nice prints from it, and we got the killer.

LATENT PRINT SPECIALIST

There was a homicide in a home and a blood path in the snow, going away from the house. We were trying to figure out where the guy went. It was night, and dark, and out in the middle of nowhere. We actually sprayed Luminol—it reacts with blood and gives a kind of glow-in-the-dark effect—on the snow and we were able to pick out the blood trail.

This was a party. As soon as we showed up, everybody scattered, of course. So there were footprints all over the snow. But we were able to determine which path our wounded person took because of the blood trail that was next to the impressions.

CRIME SCENE PROCESSOR

I make up kind of a mental list as I go along. Sometimes, espe-cially if it's a more involved scene, I'll write down some notes about what I'm seeing and ideas for processing.

I start with the documentation process. Then I start photographing the scene—from the outside to the point of entry through to the crime scene itself. Still photographs for the majority of scenes, sometimes video for homicide cases. You get a feel for the scene before you start collecting anything.

SCENE PHOTOGRAPHER/INVESTIGATOR

Sometimes you may have to approach far enough into the scene to have a real good handle on what you're looking for. If a body, say, is in a living room, right inside the front door of the residence, you may wish to enter the house through a back door, and get close in enough to see if the person's been shot, or stabbed, or what's going on, and then go back and

process your way back into the house correctly, knowing now
the manner of death.

EVIDENCE TECHNICIAN

Moving Inside . . . Protecting Against Contamination of Evidence

Let's say you got a situation where—dead body in a house.
Baseball bat. With a whole lot of blood on the end of it, and
the guy's head is caved in. Cop goes in and, you know, clearly,
here's the murder weapon. So he picks up the murder weapon
by the handle and he puts it in a bag. Well . . . is the blood on
the end of the bat really that big a deal? No. Because—pretty
good guess where it came from. I mean, we'll want to do the
testing, but it ain't gonna be brain surgery to figure out that
the blood on the end of the bat comes from the dead guy.

However, what do we really want to get? We want to get
the skin cells that are left on the handle of the baseball bat.
Because it takes a reasonable bit of force to crush somebody's
skull with a baseball bat. There's gonna be friction. The
killer's gonna leave some skin cells on the *handle* of the bat.
That's the important stuff. Not the blood, even though it
looks like the blood is gonna be important.

It's like, "Look, boss, I got the murder weapon!" "Yeah,
and you also just contaminated the whole handle."

DNA EXPERT

The general rule for *everybody* at a scene is: Make sure you
know where you're walking. You want to avoid direct entry
and exit ways through doors. Walk on the outside border of
a floor. If the body's in the kitchen, for example, walk close
to the counters. Really straddle the common walking areas so
you're not obscuring footwear impressions or other evidence.

Other rule: Hands in pockets. Don't touch or pick up
anything. It's another instinct police officers have. When

they see a gun on the floor, they want to pick it up and look
at it. They're transferring their own DNA and prints over
whatever evidence is on there.

                                                    SCENE SUPERVISOR

With DNA technology, contamination has become a *huge* issue.
It's because—just in the past two to three years—we can get
so much more DNA from evidence than we ever could before, with smaller and smaller samples

If we can get DNA from a single hair, then a single hair
dropped onto a body from one of the processors can cause us
problems. Thirty years ago, we weren't worried about dropping a hair at a crime scene.

                                                          DNA EXPERT

It's hard to explain to cops that now that they have to take these
really insane, bizarre precautions that they *never* did before
when they went into a crime scene. So now we have to tell
everybody, "You want to remember: You want to keep your
DNA out of the scene as much as possible So—you have to
wear a mask. You have to wear gloves. And you don't want to
touch *anything*. And if you drop your hairs onto the scene,
we'll end up testing your hair."

We tell them, "If you want to talk, or cough, or sneeze,
you don't want to do it at the scene." Not *talking* at a scene?
That's really hard for cops.

                                                          DNA EXPERT

I do a lot of training of new crime scene team leaders. That's
when I teach them my little tricks of how to get rid of the
unwanted police officers, or people who just hang around.

It's sometimes hard to control a scene, because it *is* their
scene, and everybody wants to see it. Mostly, they like to
hang around. Or you go to some small towns and they'll say,
"Gee, we never had a homicide before." And the county at-

torney will show up, and the county attorney's family. . . . Everybody wants to see a dead body and a crime scene.

But when they won't leave—You know the alternate light source they show every once in a while on *CSI*? I used to always slap a big old LASER HAZARD sticker on it.

You know, "Watch your eyesight." And all I do is say, "Let's go get the light." And you'd bring it into the room and say, "Okay, guys. I don't have enough goggles for everybody. Apparently, this could cause you to go blind, but I've gotta turn it on now . . ." And they'd disappear.

If you have chemical processing, you just put a big BIO-HAZARD sticker on that chemical process and bring it in, or slap on a CANCER-CAUSING AGENT. That has a good way of clearing the room.

Or you—At some point the body has to be turned over. That releases all the pent-up gases. I've seen a lot of guys run out at that point.

CRIME SCENE SUPERVISOR

Everything you do at a scene is important. We had a homicide case in 2000 where a woman and her daughter were murdered. It was summer, and they'd been left in their closed-up apartment for a long time. When the paramedics went into that house, one of the paramedics got sick and threw up in the sink. And he was too embarrassed to say anything to anybody.

The vomitus was collected as evidence. It had to be analyzed in the lab. When the case went to trial, the defense attorney said that the guy accused of the crime was just an innocent person, wrongly accused, and that the *real* killer was the person who vomited in the sink.

The police officers investigated everybody who had ever been at the scene, talked to everybody. And I'm sure as soon as that officer came up to the person, he said, "Yes! I did it!" "We want your DNA." "Okay!"

That incident shows why it's really important—If the

paramedic had admitted throwing up as soon as it happened—"I contaminated your crime scene; I threw up in the sink"—they would have known it was his. That would have gone into their documents. They might not even have collected it. And the poor analyst at the lab wouldn't have had to analyze this paramedic's vomit.

The brother-in-law of the victim was ultimately convicted of the murders, but if the paramedic hadn't owned up to it, the brother-in-law could have gotten off. That could have been reasonable doubt for the jury.

DNA ANALYST

You have to be very adaptive and flexible. You can't walk in and say, "It happened this way." You weren't there when it happened. It might *seem* like it happened this way, but it can be completely different.

A crime scene I had last time I was on call: A dead body was found on the side of the road in a swamp in a rural area. Our crime lab supports the smaller agencies that don't have the money or the manpower to process a crime scene. So, by the time we got there, the local detectives, they already knew who the victim was, they knew who did it, and they knew where the suspect was, and all they were waiting for was for us to get there and process the scene so they could go arrest this guy.

We got there and started processing the scene. *They* were sure the victim was male. But, of course, we started looking around and, lo and behold, it was a female. She was fairly heavy and she was lying on her back, so her breasts weren't really that well-defined and she had on a coat.

They didn't get the perpetrator right, either. They had a missing person in the county, male, and they thought this was drug-related and that their suspect killed him. The truth was that it was domestic-related. The boyfriend killed her. It was completely different from what the local police had.

They had taken what they'd seen, and inserted their own facts into the situation, and arrived at their own conclusions based on those facts, which were faulty.

This was just a perfect example of tunnel vision, not just at a crime scene, but in detective work. They saw it. They knew it. That was it. It was over. Not even close to what the actual truth was.

CRIME SCENE INVESTIGATOR

One of the weird things about doing bodega robberies—which is what most of the groceries are in the neighborhood where I work—you go in after you get the robbery call and you'll see a couple of bucks in the register. And you think, "What the hell. Did the robber leave something?" Nope. It's Dominicans who run the bodegas, and it's like, "Okay, robbery's over. Back to work. Let me un-duct-tape myself and get back to selling lottery tickets." It's a great work ethic, but not good for the crime scene.

DETECTIVE

Identifying Fragile Evidence

The basic premise of all crime scene investigation: Somebody entered. Somebody left stuff. Somebody exited, and they took stuff with them.

SUPERVISORY SERGEANT

There was a burglary at a rather expensive home in Anchorage. It had snowed that night, nothing unusual. The burglar had wrapped the ends of his fingers with black electrical tape. After he left, at the side of his car, he unwrapped it from his fingers and left the black tape in the white snow.

We took that tape back to the lab. One of the guys in the lab, some time before, had been having trouble getting fingerprints off curved surfaces. If you photograph the curved surface, you would only get a partial print that was in focus. So he developed a device where you would rotate this curved surface and get the photograph with the open-shutter camera on film, and you could get the entire fingerprint.

So we used this method on the black tape the burglar left. We took that tape and put it around an object and then rotated it, and got all his fingerprints off that tape.

FORMER CRIME LAB DIRECTOR

You take care of the most sensitive evidence first. It's like when you get home from the grocery store, you put away your perishables first.

So, that means anything that's in a high-traffic area, or in danger of getting picked up by anyone else. It means footwear and tire tracks, shoe impressions, trace evidence: hairs, fibers, blood samples. Quite a ways down the list would come the firearms evidence, because the bullet itself is quite hardy. Powder particles stay put fairly well. The gunshot residue on hands and clothing can be collected. But before you get to that point, you're looking for very fragile stuff.

EVIDENCE TECHNICIAN

The definition of fragile may change, depending on circum- stances. DNA, especially in the form of blood, isn't necessarily fragile. But, certainly, if you've got a victim at the scene, then other types of transfer evidence, like hair and fibers, may be fragile, since they may disappear once the victim's moved. Or you've got a point of entry in a burglary, and there's a hair or fiber there, that could be lost, too, if it's not collected right away.

FORENSIC SPECIALIST

You mark and document evidence as you go through the scene. There's a general order we go through. First, photographs. Then, footwear impressions. More photographs. Then we mark the items we're going to collect, with a playing card, or little signs, or flags to indicate where it is, with a photo of the object with its number. Then we start collecting the items. We'll start powdering the walls and surfaces for fingerprints. If there's blood, we'll do serology before we process for prints in that area.

LATENT PRINT SPECIALIST

We like to mark the evidence as we go. It's kind of like how the referees put out the chain to mark yardage in a football game. We like to get a sense of how everything relates to everything else before we collect it.

EVIDENCE TECHNICIAN

We got a call. There's been a break-in and a murder of a man in his cabin. This is in the North Woods; there are still some cabins up there with no electricity. We go up there, and it's about ten or twenty below.

The first thing we had to do was build a fire in the old woodstove, to get the whole cabin up to heat. When it's that cold, you can't do any latent print processing. The reason is, if you put a fingerprint down in freezing temperature, the water you transfer, the perspiration you transfer, is going to freeze. And the fingerprint powder will not stick to that print. It'll run right off. You basically need a little bit of humidity in the air to process prints. If it's cold, you warm the area up, and, basically, what you're doing is, you're thawing the fingerprint out.

We spent the first four, five hours at the scene, building a fire and warming the place up, just so we could go through and process for fingerprints and collect everything else.

CRIME SCENE INVESTIGATOR

Sorting Through Chaos

The crime scene can be overwhelming at first. It took me a couple of cases to kind of get in the groove, to say to my-self, "Okay. There's always going to be a point of entry. There's always gonna be a point of exit. And there are al-ways going to be items that somebody had to have touched in between."

CRIME SCENE TEAM LEADER

There are different kinds of searches you can make of a crime scene. In a grid search, you separate your crime scene into grids and you search each grid. In a strip search, you search each strip back and forth. Then there's the spiral search. You start in the middle, which is the victim in a homicide, and you work outwards in spirals. What pattern you choose is up to you, really.

FORENSIC INVESTIGATOR

When you walk into a crime scene, probably seventy or eighty percent of being successful is just *observing*, identifying the areas that are likely to yield useful evidence, and *then* pro-cessing. There's no magic wand that you can wave over a crime scene and just have fingerprints jump out at you, for example.

With crime scene processing, you can have the greatest technology in the world to examine a crime scene with, but you still have to apply it intelligently. And if you can't figure out where you're gonna look for the fingerprints, then it doesn't matter how much technology you have.

Go back to Sherlock Holmes. Doyle made Holmes a mas-ter of observation. He had him using different scientific techniques, but the bottom line was, he was a master of ob-servation.

CRIME SCENE TEAM LEADER

What you have to do at a scene is get a sense of how the victim lived. Some people are incredibly tidy. Some people are just slobs. But even there, you can tell the difference between a room that had some recent activity in it versus the ones that didn't.

You look for the atypical. You have to remember that "normal" is established by the scene. Not by what *you* think normal is.

CRIME SCENE TEAM MEMBER

A gentleman was found dead in the bathroom of his apartment. The apartment was locked from the inside. His throat had been slit numerous times. He was lying on the floor in a puddle of blood. And there's a set of footprints leading away from the bathroom to the front door.

We do a lot of blood spatter interpretation, so they called us in to take a look. We were briefing in the crime scene van on the way there, and a guy goes, "Gee, I'm not gonna join you in there because I've been sick with the flu for the last couple days." I said, "Well, thanks for coming into the van and sitting with us."

We get to the scene and sure enough, there's bleeding of significant quantity. The man has several cuts on the neck. Actually, the knife was still in the neck. It was just a kitchen knife.

I'm looking at the footprints leading away, and the rug was a thickly piled carpet. It's not like you could get a nice clean footwear impression in this carpet, just kind of the shape. The prints walk away from the body and stop right at the door.

The interesting thing is, you couldn't lock the door from the outside because this was a deadbolt. It was just an internal throw deadbolt; there was no corresponding key on the outside. So I'm looking at it, going, "Well, nobody left. What's the story here?"

I spent a lot of time just kind of sitting in the living room and staring at those footprints in blood. His body was still there, in the bathroom. It looked to me like they were stocking feet or bare feet, possibly, because they had more of a foot outline than a footwear outline. And as I looked at them further, I could see there was kind of a darker area, triangular-shaped, leading *out* on the footprints. Let's say that was near the heel. And I could also see a lighter, triangular shape near the toes.

What we finally concluded: This gentleman had gone into the bathroom and tried to cut himself a couple times. Didn't work. So what he did was, he walked out toward the door, which was also where the telephone was. And I think he made the command decision that "no, I'm gonna go through with it." But what he did is, he walked back to the bathroom on his previous footprints. So that you only saw the footprints leading out because as you walked across the carpeting, you saw that the footprints got lighter and lighter. What I was able to demonstrate was that this triangular shape, which was probably a clot of his own blood that he stepped on originally, showed directionality out and then you could see that directionality and the fainter outline of the footprint on the way back.

That was our explanation. The family became comfortable with it. The medical examiner explained to them why there were so many different cuts on the neck, the idea that suicides often start with hesitation marks, rather than just one slice.

I was discussing the case with my boss, who had done years and years of crime scene work. First question out of his mouth was, "What did his closets look like?" I said, "Why?" He said, "I'd be willing to bet all the shirts were neatly hung up. Everything was totally in order." He described that guy's closet to a T without ever seeing it.

The suicide was a guy who was fastidious about keeping things neat and clean. And I think that drove him. When he retraced his steps going back to the bathroom, I don't think he did that to confuse us. I think he didn't want to put any more blood on the carpet, because that would bother him to no end. He finished killing himself in the bathroom. Nice guy, he does it on the tile floor because that will clean up so much nicer than the carpeting.

I've learned to look at the person's lifestyle, now, when I'm at the scene—to try to get a sense of what that person was like.

SCENE SUPERVISOR

A young Asian woman went missing in a very hot Maryland summer. She was in a common-law marriage. The woman had very close family ties. And her relatives hadn't heard from her in twenty-four hours, which was unusual. They started calling more often. The common-law husband gave excuses: "Oh, she's out shopping," or "She's visiting so-and-so." Finally, they really pressured him and he said, "Well, I really don't know *where* she is and I haven't heard either." He changed his whole tune, which kind of made them nervous.

After a few days, the police did get involved, and the crime lab team went to the home.

The husband was the suspect because, just after her disappearance, he withdrew a large amount of money from her bank account. And he had major gambling debts.

The investigation was, Okay, where *is* she? Her body wasn't in the home. Is she buried in the yard? So any place in the yard that looked like it had been recently disturbed, we spent time digging and checking around only to find nothing there, other than freshly planted flowers.

We had the relatives walk through the house. "Does anything look like it's missing?"

And what they noticed was that a sleeper sofa down in the basement was missing. In the summer months, she would routinely go downstairs. And she'd lie on the sleeper sofa, watch TV, do whatever, and sometimes even sleep down there if the evenings were really hot.

And that sofa was missing. When that was found out, I applied Luminol to the area, sprayed it, and—son of a gun!—with the lights turned out, and with this chemical liquid sprayed all over everything, what showed up was luminescence of the wall outlining the back of the sofa, on the floor, outlining where the sofa would have been if it was pulled out, and then showing other luminescent marks going right into the bathroom in the basement. And also, partially, going up the stairs.

With that, we thought, Perfect. Something happened to her, or somebody, where we suspect blood. I took other chemical tests. I touched the areas that were luminescing to transfer the fluid onto a cotton swab surface. And I applied other chemicals, which also reacted—*another* strong indicator that it was blood.

We had a very, very good indication that all of this reaction was from blood. And it was consistent. If that sofa was open, and a person on it was being attacked, then you'd get this cast-off pattern of blood as it was occurring, with the sofa blocking a certain area, so when the sofa was gone, that area was clean, and then everything else around it was luminescing.

The pattern went into the bathroom. When we sprayed in there, we got a very strong reaction in the tub drain and also on a bathroom stool. And when we searched the stool a little bit more—it was like one of those old-fashioned stools in a fifties soda shop—we noticed a lot of fluorescence around it.

We flipped the stool upside down—I remember this exactly—there was a bit of tissue stuck in blood on the underneath of the stool. Here's something you wouldn't ordinarily see. The bathroom looked clean. The person did a great job cleaning it up. But when we flipped it over: "Oh, this is incredible! Collect it."

And then we went to the tub drain. We unscrewed the cover plate to the drain and opened it up, and there were some more tissue pieces stuck. We're talking some pretty good-sized tissue. Of course, to me anything above a speck is pretty good-sized. But this was like, say, the tip of your little finger. So we had a small clump of tissue stuck on the sides of the drain.

The killer probably moved the stool, not even thinking that where he was grabbing underneath would be a transfer. And the pieces in the drain just weren't thick enough to keep going down through the other parts of the drain. So they adhered really nice to the area.

We combined everything we were finding in there to give the lab enough sample. They were able to run enough samples on the DNA to show that it was consistent with DNA from a family member.

We had that strong evidence. What really put the clincher on the case was the detective work. They started just talking to people who had a reason to come to that house within a certain period of time. And they came upon a trash collector who was one of those private hires you call if you have unusual things—like a refrigerator, or whatever—you want collected at your home. He said he was contacted, went out there, and he was shown this sofa that the husband wanted to dispose of. He said, "You know, I should have thought something was odd, because the sofa looked like it was in great shape. It was in its entirety; maybe had a few tears here and there. The design of the fabric was the same as what I have in my home, so I was thinking I'm just gonna take this home. I can't understand why this guy wants to get rid of this." And the trash collector said to the common-law husband, "If you don't mind, I'll just take this home." But the man said, "No. I want this taken to the dump. I'll pay you extra." And the guy's like, "What the heck, I'll make extra money." He took it to the landfill. Of course, when the detectives went to the landfill—this was maybe a week after the event—there was no *way* they could find it.

The trash collector also said that the sofa was much heavier than it should have been. So we're putting together what happened—he must have killed her. We're speculating that he cut her up, maybe in the bathtub, and then put her in the sofa, and then tied the sofa seat down, and then had the trash collector dispose of it.

All through trial, the common-law husband never said anything. Even after he was convicted of murder, even without the body, he still would not say anything to the investigators as to where she was.

And wouldn't you know it? He won an appeal. So we had to go to trial a second time on this case, two years after the first trial.

The home was sold. New residents moved into the home. They decided they wanted to use the fireplace on the first floor. They stoked the fire. And even with the flue open, the smoke came back into the room. So they called in a chimney sweep. He found a small machete wrapped in Asian newspapers stuffed up into the chimney itself. Unfortunately, because the new occupants started a fire, the initial flames burned the date off of the newspaper and some other identifier words. They were hoping to search the paper for any topics that would identify a date.

I got it into the lab and, literally, it was so charred, it was just falling apart in my hands. Then, when I was looking at the machete, it, too, was so clean, and it was so subjected to the burning, that when I applied chemicals to it, it just wouldn't work, because everything was decomposing. All I could tell them was, "Yeah. Indication blood was present on the machete." There wasn't enough to even think about doing DNA on it. And, of course, if you even say the word "blood," the defense will say, "Well, they could have used the machete to cut some meat up, or chicken, or whatever." And you have to say on the stand, "Well, if that's what they do, then that's what they do. And, yes, that's how the blood could have gotten on the machete."

That answered the question, possibly, of what was the murder weapon.

And then the new people—these poor people; I'm surprised they bought the house anyway—but there was a crawl space off of the basement rec room area. They happened to go in there to clean up the space. And they found a few boxes, way, way back in a corner that were empty. But tucked behind the boxes was a strip of fabric that looked like it was stained.

That was what the detectives brought to me to analyze back at the lab. The fabric matched what was described by the relatives as the sofa fabric. And it was stained with human blood, all across. It looked like one of those little skirts that would cover the bottom of the sofa. I wondered if—Maybe putting her body into the sofa, too much got stained down there. And he's thinking, okay, I don't want anything loose. For now, I'll just pitch it in the crawl space. And I bet you he probably threw it back in there and thought he'd get back to it later. And he probably just totally forgot about it.

From that little skirt, we were able to get DNA to confirm again that the blood was from a family member of the relatives.

With that added evidence that we brought into the second trial, we got him sent away.

CRIME SCENE PROCESSOR/FORENSIC SPECIALIST

Assessing the Body

It's the paramedics' job to try to save the victim's life, if they're not dead at the scene. That effort can wreck a crime scene. Through the treatment, it can mask or damage physical evidence on the body. It can get rid of DNA evidence. Medical treatment can cause problems for us. Obviously, we're not going to demand that it not be done.

Same thing with firemen. Very often a fire is set to destroy a crime scene. Firemen are gonna go in and put out the fire. That often hurts us because they're washing our evidence away, as they *have* to. These are agencies with their own missions, and necessary ones, but it often makes it harder for us.

EVIDENCE TECHNICIAN

Everybody always talks about how the paramedics came in and ruined the scene. Well, their job is to save lives, and if they can work on somebody first, that's the priority.

I can easily tell the difference between what was placed there by the medical team and what was placed there by the crooks. Usually, you don't get little sterile pieces of paper that say Johnson and Johnson on them from the criminals breaking in.

The only thing I ask the emergency team is, once they've done their action: Don't move anything. If you have to pull a guy, move a guy, throw stuff around, leave it there. There have been cases where they've cleaned up their medical stuff and a piece of tape grabs a cartridge case. We've actually gone through the bag of stuff that they've cleaned up and found evidentiary items. So we just ask: Just leave everything there. And if you touch something, just let us know. We're gonna find out sooner or later, anyway.

The body is the last thing we're going to look at. Once the paramedics, or whoever, have determined the victim can't be saved, there's no point in rushing up to the body. It's not going anywhere.

SCENE LEADER

The body itself is a wealth of information. There may be evidence in the body, on the body, around it, under it. Bullet holes. Exit holes. Gunshot residue. Knife wounds. Blood spatter evidence. The body has a ton of probative evidence. Unless the victim is slightly breathing, we never let them move the body until we can get a good look at it.

FORENSIC INVESTIGATOR

We photograph the body. First, we take long shots of the body, to get the position relative to other objects in the room, or evidence that may be in the room, like bullet holes or blood spatter. Then we take close-up photographs—of the face, for identification purposes, of any wounds, and of any identifying marks, like tattoos.

EVIDENCE TECHNICIAN

At the scene, you're looking for bullet entrance and bullet exit on the body. The body, at some point, is going to get rolled over at the scene and, oftentimes, after everything else has been collected, an ET [evidence technician] or the firearms examiner, will be looking for bullet holes. I'm also looking for powder particles adjacent to that hole to see how close the shooter was to the victim. That helps me establish how far the line of flight might be. If they're struggling over the gun, then both the shooter and the victim are going to be very close and perhaps I'll have bullets sprayed in different directions.

FIREARMS SPECIALIST

The body tells its own story. Let's say someone is shot or stabbed and they die on the living room floor, on a carpet. And blood is running out of their wounds for several minutes or hours. That blood will seep into the carpet all the way down into the padding and into the floor below that.

The killer might remove the body and then steam clean

the carpet or spray something on it. He'll clean the surface to the extent that, "Hey, lookit! It doesn't look like there's any stain there!" But there's still a large amount of blood that's gonna be in the padding and on the subfloor below. We *will* find the blood.

It's all about thinking about what you need and then going the extra mile to get it. There might be blood in a bathroom or under a carpet, but people miss it, because they're not looking in the right place. The tile, the grout in a shower stall—if the blood is wet and it's allowed to move, it's going to absorb into whatever it can, and it goes up underneath a tile, or a wood floor, or a carpet, or a sofa cushion, or the threads of a garment. You just gotta get all in there and try to find it.

DNA ANALYST/TEAM MEMBER

Reconstructing the Scene

You use your observations to try to determine what occurred, in what sequence, and the positional location of individuals and objects at the scene. Bloodstain pattern analysis. Blood patterns on the clothing of the individuals involved. Objects that are knocked over. Other damage. Bullet holes.

It's basically trying to bring everything together to offer a logical sequence of how events occurred and the position people were in when they occurred. It can be as simple as going back to, let's say, a living room. If you were to lift up your chairs or your couch, if you have carpeting, it leaves indentations as to where the feet of those objects are. You can tell if an object has been moved or repositioned, based on whether those marks are directly under the feet of the chair or the couch, or whether they're next to it. Even something as simple as that may be a good indicator.

Even dust on a table—that's another good indicator. If you get good light, and there's a little bit of dust in that room, you can tell if a lamp, or a bottle, or a figurine, or a planter has been relocated from where it usually is, based on the dust pattern on the top of that object.

These objects can tell what really happened. They might have been used as weapons. They might have been knocked over in a struggle. And the suspect is denying that anything occurred in there. Or they're saying that things happened a certain way. The location of that object in the living room may directly contradict the individual's statement.

SCENE LEADER

Rule number one for people who conduct reconstruction: Keep an open mind. Don't develop a TV syndrome, where you think, in two seconds, "Okay. I've got it!" Reconstruction is not that straightforward. It's not always a black-and-white issue. Presence of evidence is important. *Absence* of evidence may be equally important.

CRIME SCENE RECONSTRUCTIONIST

Bloodstain pattern analysis. Typically, you look at three things: size, shape, and distribution of the stains. Stain size relates to how the stain was most likely formed. Distribution tells you where the blood-shedding event started and where it continued. Early areas of bloodshed will have fewer numbers of stains. The later areas of bloodshed will have a greater number of stains. You can tell the beginning point versus the ending point. Shape of stains will tell us if the stain struck the surface at an angle, or if it struck the surface straight on.

What has been found over the years is if you take a stain that has struck a surface at an angle, and you measure the length and width of it—because it's always going to have a elliptical shape to it if it strikes the surface at an angle—and you plug those into some mathematical calculations, essentially trigonometric calculations, you can determine the approximate angle that the blood drop hit the surface at. And with enough stains originating from the same blood-shedding incident, you may be able to calculate the area that those stains originated from. That can help us position the location of the victim. It may, under certain circumstances, help us position the location of the offender.

The best example I can give is, if someone is standing up and is struck in the head to the point where they've got an open injury, and they're hit again, blood is going to come off that injury. If they're close to a surface, like a wall, that the blood could land on, that's going to give us a pattern on the wall. And we might be able to say something like, "Okay, at the time this blood spatter originated, the source was five feet above the ground and three feet away from the wall." That may be significant because that may go to the story we're being told by the offender or a suspect.

BLOOD SPATTER ANALYST

It can be hard to sort out. The math applies to a certain type of stain, typically, your forceful-impact, spatter-type stain. But there's a *lot* of stains that you can see at a scene. Bloody footwear impressions, blood dropping on the floor, blood that gets flung off the weapon as the weapon's being swung. You may have other patterns in the blood. Obviously, if somebody walks in the blood, you're going to have footwear. If somebody kneels down in the blood, you're going to have fabric impressions. Somebody puts their hand down in the blood, you may have fingerprints or palm prints in the blood. You may have one pattern on top of another pattern. There's actually a lot there to process.

BLOOD SPATTER ANALYST

Especially with bloodstain evidence, if there's a lot of it, a big part of the final evaluation is just sitting there and absorbing the patterns that are present. Maybe running into some hypotheses about how they were formed. And just trying to take it . . . *one* section at a time. "Okay, this happened here. This happened here. What happened first?" Just take one piece at a time.

SCENE LEADER

In the beginning, blood was something you cleaned up. People didn't think it had any forensic value at all. We've come a long way.

EVIDENCE TECHNICIAN

Firearms analysis at the scene works sort of along the same lines as blood spatter analysis. But we use two points of reference: Where the bullet enters an object and where it exits, or if the bullet passes through an object, for instance, a wall or a window and a screen, we can use those two points of reference, those two lines in space, and draw a line between those and extend that line out, back along the path that the bullet took, to establish a relative line in space along which the gun had to have been located when the shot was fired.

FIREARMS SPECIALIST

Single homicides are not a big deal to process for firearms evi- dence. Doubles—I've been on many, many of them. Triples—I've gotten. A six-person homicide—that's the most bodies at one time that I've walked into a house on. That one was a challenge to reconstruct.

This happened in Flint, Michigan, about 1987. It was a drug house. A vie for power was going on within this drug family. A fellow who was presented to us as a lieutenant in this organization, he was an enforcer, for whatever reason, turned on the family. It was probably over money or drugs.

The way we reconstructed this scene was, there were two people when the shooting first started. The suspect killed both of them. One is a male; he's next to a bed in a back bedroom. There's a female that is naked, and she's in a bathroom, slumped over the bathtub. She'd been shot at very close range, center of her back, with a shotgun.

After that, two people enter the house: A female who came in with her coat on. She makes it as far as the dining room, which is about halfway into the house. Lying next to her is a black male, who also has his coat on. Then there are two more, closer to the front door, that are shot. We could figure out what happened from the relative positioning of the bodies. It's difficult to shoot six people in a house and not have the other folks aware of it. The bodies were in positions where they had obviously been surprised.

The suspect was killing them in pairs as they came into the house. Two people in the house, and then two more pairs of people coming in.

The scene took us hours and hours and hours to process, because we had to do each body as we worked our way into the crime scene. The suspect had used guns from the house. Ultimately, I found bullets, not only used in the shooting, but many, many bullets that had been fired at cockroaches and other things in the house. I went down to the basement, for instance, to look for a bullet that we knew had passed through one of the victims, only to find many, many bullets laying on the basement floor from previous shootings in the house.

There were several weapons, a handgun and a revolver, that were used. They were reloaded several times during the shooting incidents; there were groups of cartridge cases ejected out of those two guns in various locations. A shotgun was used to kill one of the victims. That was recovered. Literally hundreds of items of firearms evidence were collected from this scene, all inside the house. We used strings to get the flight paths of the bullets. We got firearms residues on various people's clothing, and on the center of the female victim's back. Those were measured and we could determine the distance from the shooter to the victims based on this.

What ultimately led to the shooter's capture: There were fingerprints on a shotgun. This was one of the exceptions to the rule that guns aren't good for picking up prints. This was a smooth shotgun that had good prints.

Police officers figured out who the suspect was, from the fingerprints and from people on the street, and found out where he stayed—it was in another drug house. They enacted a raid on the house, and got him. This guy was a member of the family. A bad guy killing other bad guys.

DETECTIVE

We've had scenes where objects are placed in hands to make the victim look like they had the weapon, after the fact. And we've had scenes where, after the fact, the murder weapons are moved, repositioned, wiped off, cleaned, put away. That happens, not on a regular basis, but pretty often.

DETECTIVE

We went to a scene where the husband shot his wife. The story that he gave was that she came at him with a knife and tried to stab him. So he was saying he killed her in self-defense. But there were a couple things that just didn't make sense.

There *was* a knife in her hand. But it was in the wrong direction to be used as a stabbing-type instrument. It was very apparent that he had placed the knife in her hand after he shot her and, probably in his panic, he had it facing the wrong way.

There was blood on the palm of her hand where she had touched the entrance wound when she was shot. The normal reaction is to grab where it hurts. And she *did.* And she had blood on her hand, but there was no blood on the knife. That was a staged afterthought.

CRIME SCENE RECONSTRUCTIONIST

Collecting the Evidence

You've got to do it right, or everything down the road, investiga-tion through trial, is tainted.

We generally save evidence collection for the end—except for the most fragile evidence. *That* we collect as we find it. But, with other evidence, it's important to get position and location first.

So, once the photography is done, and items have been identified as needing to be processed, maybe for fingerprints, or footwear impressions, or blood evidence, whatever—you just start doing the collection.

CRIME SCENE INVESTIGATOR

How **you touch objects is crucial. I always tell detectives: When** you're collecting evidence from the scene, and you know how a person would usually pick up an object—like picking up a wineglass by its stem, say—then pick it up in a totally *different* way, so you're not going to touch any prints. And secure it in a box, so the whole surface is protected and isn't going to move.

LATENT PRINT SPECIALIST

When I teach police about collecting blood, I always say, "If you learn one thing from me today, it's paper, paper, paper." When you put a bloodied object into a sealed plastic bag, that's a sealed environment. If there's humidity or moisture on the garment—and you know half of blood is water—that water cannot evaporate off, and it creates a very humid environment in that plastic bag for the microorganisms to multiply. But paper is porous enough—there's enough air infiltration in and out of the bag in between the fibers of the paper—that some of that moisture can get outside the bag. It evaporates off. Once the blood is dried, it's much, much more stable than if it's in a moisture-humid environment.

DNA ANALYST

The most difficult things to collect are, of course, the smallest things. And if offenders have tried to clean up. If they're trying to hide the crime scene, offenders will clean it up to the extent that *they* can't see it anymore, and they think that's good enough to get by.

I look at blood at scenes all the time. Even cleaned-up scenes. Most people don't do a good enough job to put one over on us. We can usually find trace amounts in cracks or in places the blood got so thin when they were cleaning it up that *they* couldn't see it. But because of chemical enhancement techniques, like Luminol, or you can use Hungarian Red, Luco-Crystal Violet, Malachite Green—there's a plethora of them—or because of the use of optics, or alternate light sources, we can still find the blood at crime scenes.

I always tell people: Although this stuff is great for *CSI,* that is a last resort. Because any time you add a chemical in an enhancement technique to a surface that may have blood on it, you are diluting any blood sample that is there because you're adding a chemical to it.

You want to get down on your hands and knees with a microscope—literally, like Sherlock Holmes—and look for blood that has been pushed into cracks and crevices or into the grain of wood floors.

FORENSIC INVESTIGATOR

We had one case where we had a murder where the guy cleaned up afterwards, and we had a faint image on the faucet handle. We made six lifts off of it. We identified who he was from the bloody impression. It was funny—somebody had identified him as having lived in the area. So the detectives were bringing him in to be interviewed at the same time that we got a hit on the AFIS (Automated Fingerprint Identification System).

This case was pretty bad. Here was a young mother who owed money to her neighborhood dope dealer and he used a hatchet and a couple of knives and tried to decapitate her. And he left her there and stole some things out of the house.

The girl worked in a casino. When she didn't come to work, some friends and family came looking for her, and when they opened her apartment, they found her eighteen-month-old child curled up in her arms. Not very pretty.

He had stolen her car and this dumb jamoke took a trip out of state for a couple days. We examined the car, and here he had receipts for every place he had been and we had an actual time line, based on the receipts he threw in the car.

DETECTIVE

If you walk into a place where there's been a crime scene and you smell bleach somewhere, we're gonna get the Luminol out because somebody's tried to clean it up.

Some things will give you false positives. Metal pipes and lead, for example, will light up like a Christmas tree, but it's not blood. I've used Luminol to spray the bed of a pickup truck. You get an overall glow, because it's metal, so you just have to let your eyes settle on that, and if there's anything brighter than that, that's what you're going after.

Luminol is used in a completely dark environment. Except on *CSI.* They like to use it in broad daylight.

CRIME SCENE INVESTIGATOR

This was a case in Kansas. This guy was beaten to death, he was face up on the kitchen floor. One of my partners had done a blood spatter analysis and agreed that, yeah, the guy was kicked right there where he was lying. And then it looked like there were a couple of bloody shoe prints leading away from that area. We used the Luminol later that night.

This turned out to be pretty creepy. The guy had a spiral staircase that went up to a loft bedroom. Now, think about the offender. He's probably got his left foot planted on the kitchen floor and he's kicking the guy with his right foot. Now he goes walking through the house. So, as he goes up those stairs, every other step lit up with the Luminol. To enough detail that we were able to photograph it in the dark and get a shoe pattern. It was like following a ghost walking up the stairs.

LATENT PRINT SPECIALIST

I remember a case in northern Michigan. One roommate had shot another in the kitchen and then transported him and buried him behind his dad's house. The shooting was at a party, and a witness finally came forward. We went to the house, looked at the kitchen, and it had been cleaned up.

The suspect had even painted the wall. But because the witness could tell us so precisely where it happened, I could go over that area with a fine-tooth comb. And the baseboard, the trim along the bottom of the floor, stuck out, just a little bit. And the paint hadn't been able to go into that little crack there. Some of the blood had run down the wall, from the shooting, behind that crack in the baseboard. I was able to pull that back and find blood. No problem. A large amount of blood.

EVIDENCE TECHNICIAN

Latent print work, especially with nonporous items or surfaces in a house, is the *last* thing we do at a scene, because once we start throwing powder around, we're basically going to destroy that place. We're going to be tracking powder everywhere and it gets to be a real mess. I did a house, took a day and a half, I used all black powder, and that's why they call me "Dusty."

LATENT PRINT SPECIALIST

I was at one scene where there were eight bullet holes in a wall. A man had shot his girlfriend six times, three times while she was standing up, and then three more times while she was lying on the floor. The weapon found was a six-shooter. I couldn't figure out what was going on. There was no reloading or anything. I finally talked to one of the locals and he said, "Oh, you can ignore two of those bullet holes. That was from last year." I was determined not to miss any bullets.

That was the one where my crime scene partner and I had to climb down in the pit and kill the snakes. There was a crawl space under the floor. The whole crawl space was just covered by garter snakes. I absolutely hate snakes. I am deathly afraid—I mean, I'll kill anything with my hands; I'll pick up most anything, but snakes I cannot stand.

I asked my counterpart if he'd mind going down there and collecting the bullets for me. I found out he hated snakes almost as much as I did.

We made the agreement to go down there together. This was just like *Indiana Jones and the Temple of Doom.* We're crawling through this, and these snakes are all over the place. He'd dig for a while and I'd circle around and kill snakes as they were advancing on us—that's one advantage to having those really heavy flashlights. Then I'd dig for a while and he'd kill snakes.

We knew we had to get those bullets. At one point, a snake fell on my partner's back and I felt compelled to pull it off. If it was anything else, it wouldn't have been a big deal. But it had to be snakes. We did find all three bullets.

CRIME SCENE TEAM MEMBER

Collection is just as important as any other part of the process. The best way to describe it is, junk in, junk out. If evidence isn't collected properly, or packaged properly, or transported properly, the scientists are going to be limited as to the opinions they can give about the evidence. But if the chain from beginning to end is preserved, the opinions in a trial are going to be much more informative.

SCENE LEADER

Crime scene processing today is a *gigantic* pain in the ass, to do it right. If you do it right, you could be at a crime scene ten hours, twelve hours, not unusual at all.

SCENE LEADER

The most important thing? Making sure you leave the scene with all the evidence.

We had a married young woman who was murdered in a garden apartment. Her throat was slashed. She was nude from the waist up. And she was in the bathtub. The tub was partially filled with water. Her husband came home and found her only about an hour or so after she had been killed.

So, there's blood all over this bathroom. We're in there taking our pictures and we collect some blood samples and make some fingerprint examinations on the doors.

Then we remove the body. And we're packing up our stuff. We're just about to leave.

But, just as we were leaving, I noticed that we didn't look at the toilet seat very carefully. And I said to my partner, "We better take another look at that before we leave."

We went over and looked at the toilet seat. We lifted it up. And here's two bloody fingerprints on the bottom of the toilet seat, and they were pointing toward the bathtub. I thought, "That's probably . . . the victim's trying to hang on to this when the guy was putting her in the water." We took the bolts out and we took the whole toilet seat with us.

We almost left that at the scene. Almost. But we didn't. And guess what?

They were the offender's prints in the victim's blood, which is the best evidence you can have. He was the husband's cousin. He went there when the husband wasn't home. It started off as a sexual assault. He didn't complete that part of it. But he murdered her, with a box-cutter knife.

FORENSIC INVESTIGATOR

Effects of the Scene on Crime Scene Processors

I was called to process a scene with four people dead inside a home in a Seattle suburb, about '97 or '98. I had just gotten back from a crime scene two hundred miles away—this is a large state. So I'd been at this scene near Vancouver where I was way up in the mountainside, covered in mud, in January, pouring rain, just miserable. I got back about eleven A.M., after being up all night. At four in the afternoon, I got another phone call to go to this homicide. This was the first really big scene I went to.

There was a family of four found dead: the mother, father, and two daughters. The older daughter had actually been found in a park about a quarter of a mile away, strangled. When the police officers went to the house to inform the family, they walked in and found that the mother and father and the younger daughter had been beaten with baseball bats and stabbed. There was blood in every room in the house. The amount of blood was startling to me; I didn't anticipate seeing so much. Now, of course, I've seen much worse. This was the first time I ever came home and said, "My God!"

It was like a three-thousand-square-foot home. I did one of those classic—which is what we all do—"Oh my God, where do I start?"

And then your training takes over. The whole thing is, "Wait a minute. This whole thing needs to be documented, photographs, notes, sketches, whatever. It all has to be done."

There's only one way to do it. You go outside and form your team. I was in charge of that.

You basically treat each room like a cube. You think of the room as a six-sided box: You've got ceiling, floor, north wall, south wall, east wall, west wall. You draw diagrams of each wall, the ceiling and floor, you mark it, you photograph it, you take notes. I was there for something like four and a half days.

The killers got rid of everything. We never found the

clothing the killers were wearing. They cut their hair immediately after the event. They wore T-shirts over their heads,
to cover themselves in case blood came on to them. We
found one of those in the bedroom that had come off. They
wore socks over their hands.

The only thing they didn't get rid of was one pair of
shoes that we found at the house of one of the suspects. I
noticed that on one of the shoes were six areas of blood
staining of different types. There were some smears, there
was some general stuff. But what was really important—
there was some blood spatter which was indicative of expi-
rated blood, which is blood that has been coughed up
through the lungs. You can recognize it by three things: One,
it's got a mixture of sizes, some big, some small; also, it's a
little bit diluted because it's coming through the mouth, so
it's mixed with the saliva; and then, thirdly, it has the property of having air bubbles in it. It's like a soap bubble. When
you pop it, you can still see the ring left behind.

One of the killers had these on the ankle of his shoe and
it was perfectly circular. That means it can only come from
directly horizontal to that shoe. In other words, he was
standing close, and the victims coughed blood onto him
when they were dying. The DNA turned out to be from the
younger daughter. The other blood on the shoe came from
the father. So we had blood from two of the victims on him.
I want to give credit to a guy we consulted, a bloodstain expert, Ross Gardner, who helped us wonderfully.

What had happened: The older daughter had two friends
who killed her. One of them owed money to her and she was
asking for it back. These were two young guys who deliberately did it before they were eighteen, because they didn't
want to get the death penalty; they'd already discussed that.
Couple of dropout kids. They wanted to know what it was
like to kill somebody.

There were three trials. They were tried separately; the

second guy was tried twice. They eventually were both convicted. They're in jail for life. Absolutely.

One of the prosecutors told me this: One of them basically kept saying, "We did it." He wouldn't tell them who
the other guy was, even though we all knew it was his best
friend. He told the prosecutors that if he was ever convicted,
he would tell them.

So the prosecutors went out to visit him about six months
after he was convicted. He was there for life. And they found
out that he had gotten engaged to this girl who was in jail in
Texas. They had become pen pals. So now he's engaged to
this girl who's in jail in Texas for life for killing her mother.
And this kid—this is after he'd been convicted of brutally
killing, with baseball bats and knives, a family of four, and
strangling the older daughter—he said, "Wouldn't you know
the first time I fall in love it has to be when I'm in jail for life
and so is she. I must have done something terrible in a former life."

The prosecutor told me he and this other prosecutor with
him just stared at each other, like, "What?"

CRIME SCENE TEAM MEMBER

The one I remember the most: This little girl, she was about
seven, she disappeared and they were searching for her, and
they found her in a dumpster. Since I was a young investigator working with an old-timer, I had to take my camera
and go in the Dumpster and take pictures of her laying in
there. I can remember that like it was yesterday. The
Dumpster was about half full of trash. And she was laying
in there. I had to move a couple of things around to take
some pictures of her. But I was always lucky—when they
had other child murders like that—I didn't get them.
Somebody else got them.

CRIME SCENE PHOTOGRAPHER

People always talk about what homicide detectives must go through, seeing all the horror. They never think of the evidence technicians and the specialists. And we see everything close up.

I've done four or five hundred crime scenes. And I'm thinking to myself, "Should I be upset by this?" You hear about critical incident stress syndrome and all that kind of stuff. Should I be getting it?

I've seen things that the average person shouldn't be seeing and I've seen lots of it. And I'm just wondering, should I be feeling upset? It worries me that I—*don't* get upset.

I went to a psychologist on staff with our state patrol. I went to him and said, "Should I be experiencing some of this stress syndrome?" And he said, "Do you get flashbacks?" "No." And he said, "Well, but you go to these scenes and they never come back to you?" "Well, when I'm writing my report, I have to look through all the photographs every single time." He said, "Wait a minute. You go to your crime scene, *then* you have to look at all the photographs again?" I said, "Oh, yeah. Repeatedly." "How many times do you do that?" "About fifty times a year."

He said, "Oh my God! If this isn't affecting you, then it isn't affecting you. Some people it does; some people it doesn't." So that was it.

I had a person who worked for me, she was a very, very good forensic scientist. She still works in the crime lab. She'd go to crime scenes with me. She was wonderful at the crime scenes, but then she would come back and think about it a lot and say things, like, "I wonder what the last thing the person saw was," and stuff like that. That was kind of a warning sign for me that maybe she shouldn't be doing this.

It's funny—there's a very well-established procedure for police officers seeing things, to have psychological support, but for the people from the crime labs who process the scenes it's considered, "Ah, it's just something you do. Don't worry about it." They think what we see shouldn't bother us because we're scientists.

FORENSIC INVESTIGATOR

The thing is, when you're dealing with homicides, especially when you're on the actual forensic team, you relive the actual last moments of this person's life. You see the struggle. You see the fight. You see the capitulation. And that kind of sticks with you.

CRIME SCENE RECONSTRUCTIONIST

On the Aftermath of Scenes

When I come home from a crime scene—and I've talked to all my colleagues who do this and they all say it's *exactly* the same for them all—when we come home—say we go out at ten o'clock at night and get home at three o'clock—there's no way on God's earth, even if you're tired, you can ever go straight to sleep. All of us do the same thing. We immediately come home and shower. Or we change our clothes in the garage before we come in. Even if you don't get anything on you, it's kind of like a cleansing thing. Even if you know you're not going to take anything in with you, you've taken all the precautions, you still do it anyway. It's just weird.

But all of us do the same thing. We all sit and watch TV, even mindless TV. We're watching reruns of the *Three Stooges* or something, three or four o'clock in the morning. We probably couldn't even tell you what we watched. But we know that if you go to bed and close your eyes or whatever, you will look at the ceiling, you know that your mind will still be going a hundred miles an hour from the crime scene.

CRIME SCENE INVESTIGATOR

Two

CRIME SCENE INTERPRETATION— INSIDE SCENES

Something that always gets me. I go into these homes, where there's a crime scene—I always go to the refrigerator. I know this is weird. I go to the refrigerator and, especially if children are the victims, as they often are, and I look at the little things they've done for their mom, and they have them up on the refrigerator. "Mommy, you have to go to school with me on Monday." Little notes and stuff like that. Little drawings that they've done. And I think, "Man. You know, that little kid, the last thing he thought when he was drawing this was that his mother was going to be dead, or he was going to be dead." It just kind of . . . it has an effect.
   —Homicide Detective

My wife's an elementary schoolteacher. She teaches third grade. I'll come home and say we were at a scene and a dead body was there. She always goes, "A *real* dead body?" "No, honey. Just a fake one. They always put a fake one in there for us. They don't want to disturb us." She doesn't know that part of my life. It's so foreign to her.
   —Homicide Detective

IN 1973, A RESPECTED LOCAL BUSINESSMAN AND PRECINCT captain in Chicago was suspected of kidnapping and murdering several teenagers. Attorneys blocked police from obtaining a search warrant on John Wayne Gacy's house. On a chance, one detective on surveillance on a cold December night knocked on Gacy's door and asked if he could use his bathroom. Gacy let him in. As the detective used the facilities, the heating system started up, and, with it, a smell came through the bathroom's ventilation system that was instantly and sickeningly recognizable to the cop. *Now* there was probable cause for a search warrant. Police discovered the bodies of thirty-five young men buried in the crawl space underneath Gacy's home.

Crime scene investigation doesn't proceed in a straight line from discovery through collection and analysis to the solution of a crime. Sometimes the scene itself must be discovered through arduous detective work. Sometimes the first responders to the scene write a death off as accident or suicide, and detectives work to get the scene reopened. Even in straightforward crime scenes, detectives interpret and reinterpret, using both their own reading of the scene and the information given them by crime scene processors and crime lab scientists. And then it's a constant back-and-forth collaboration among forensic investigators, detectives, and prosecutors, as the detectives develop crime scene information and test it against witnesses' and suspects' stories. This chapter shows some of the intricate footwork involved in that dance.

For an overview of the obstacles to crime scene interpretation, we start with a look into Homicide School, a training program for new and returning homicide detectives that is presented jointly by the Los Angeles County Sheriff's Department and the Los Angeles Police Department, as described by Sergeant Rich Longshore of the Los Angeles County Sheriff's Department's Homicide Bureau.

What we do—and this is a work in progress, we're constantly changing it—we hold it at a hotel. There's a former LAPD investigator who does four hours on crime scene management. While she's doing that, I go out and I set up various crime scenes in the hotel. There's also a big empty lot next to it. So we're able to go out and replicate certain crimes.

We believe—and we got this from our driver training people—you should let people go out and see what they did wrong, and this will spur the interest in the remainder of the class. In emergency driver training, on day two, they say, "Okay, get your helmet, strap in, let's go." After you've been in *x* number of simulated crashes, you're a lot more attuned to the learning process. So that's the process we use in the Homicide School.

Classes are limited to twenty-five people, so we break them up into random groups of five. I go out and set up crime scenes. It may be a "Dead Consuela" case, where it's a maid that is found dead in the back of the hotel. And the scenario is something like: Her husband and she had had an argument about her wanting to have kids, and he went to find her in the break area of the hotel, and he found her dead. We build in little twists, like the patrol officer who's there will tell the detectives that, according to the paramedics, she took a shotgun blast straight in the face. Except it wasn't a shotgun blast at all, it was blunt force trauma. This is not unusual, because you're always getting conflicting and erroneous information on your initial response. So we build this into the scenario. If the husband is interviewed, we will build into it the fact that he's on parole for domestic violence. And if they get so focused on him and start pressing him, he'll just ask for a lawyer. But the murder had nothing to do with him; he's just a witness. This is to show how easily you can get channeled into the wrong direction and not keep an open mind.

We've built in situations where we've had a gunshot victim in a car in the parking lot, an apparent suicide. As the officers begin to investigate this, they find there's a letter inside the car, there's a bottle of liquor inside, a gun, of course, and a patrol officer will have taken the gun out of the car and put it in his own car, for "safekeeping," as they say, which is a big no-no at a scene, but you find that all the time. They'll find a letter from the guy's wife that says, "Why can't you just leave us alone? Please. Get out of our lives. You promised you'd leave." And then you find a letter from a fictitious police department to this individual, who is a detective from this department, announcing his termination for alcoholism and domestic violence.

Then, if you follow up and go to the residence, to make

notification to next of kin, there's a secondary crime scene because he's also killed his family. We'll have the victim in the parking lot already evacuated to the hospital by the time the detectives arrive on scene, which is a common scenario. This is attempt suicide, so they go about their business, doing the investigation. They're told that it's a police officer who tried to kill himself; they learn that through their investigation.

We have a very realistic infant mannequin, and we make it one of the victims, and I'll put that at the foot of the bed and cover it with blankets. That's been missed a couple times. One of the guys who missed it—this was five, six years ago—and whenever I see this guy at a real scene he says, "You know, I'll never forget missing that baby. I won't miss another one."

Throughout the scenes, when we use blood, we use stage blood. I'll put stage blood around and I'll put spatter. We went to a Halloween store for help. We do one that's a home-invasion robbery. We'll sever an arm and put it in the bathtub next to the mannequin, with blood dripping down. On some scenes, I'll use mushroom soup, generally, to simulate vomit. Put a little stage blood in it, it's pretty realistic-looking.

For scenes inside hotel rooms, we'll open a phonebook, for example, to an airline. And then on a pad next to the phone book, we'll write down a flight number, but tear off the top page, to make sure they're looking for the impressions. We'll tape mock narcotics underneath the toilet lid. I'll turn up the heat in one room to ninety degrees on a hot day, and see if that distracts the investigators. Also, they have to note that because it adds to the decomposition of the body and it throws off your liver temperature and everything else. We'll pop popcorn in the room and spit some of it out, see if they'll check that for DNA. You want to be as realistic as you can without damaging anything, or the hotel will throw you out of there.

What we're doing now— One's a burned body case because we have a lot of those out here. We have a foam-rubber mannequin, we'll have it all charred, and put it in the bushes like a body dump. We'll burn some evidence around that.

We have another one, where I got an unmarked car, and I had it shot full of holes so I can use that to simulate an officer-involved shooting scene. We set up a scenario where the vehicle is shot full of holes, and the two suspects have fled after an exchange of gunfire with the officers. One suspect is dead at the scene; the other has escaped. We'll put blood on the wall, that type of thing, dump handguns in bushes. As they get through this thing—this is a pretty elaborate crime scene—we're running into this particular problem. Two of the three times we've done this, the officers have said, "Okay, we'll just go ahead and take the suspect's vehicle to the lab or the impound garage and we'll get a warrant and search it tomorrow. We've done a cursory search of the inside and that's good enough for us."

Well, there's a body in the trunk. The body is dead and the gunshot wound in the head lines up perfectly with one of the officer's return of fire.

Sometimes we get local media to come down and play the parts of reporters. We'll make them as obnoxious as possible, the things that reporters have to do. We'll build into it that a witness will tell a reporter some salient fact that he won't tell the officer. If the officer or officers are jerks to the media, the media won't pass this on, they'll pass it to themselves. You want to build a rapport—"Hey, I talked to this guy over here. Here's what he told me."

At the end of two weeks, at the end of the program, each group is required to put on a PowerPoint presentation about their particular problem, with their photographs, what they encountered, and how they would handle it differently next time.

Cop humor: There was one group that missed the baby at

the foot of the bed in the scenario of the officer who killed his family before his attempt suicide. When this group did their PowerPoint presentation at the end of the course, they had The Dancing Baby from *Ally McBeal* throughout the whole thing.

This last class, a group of them missed the body in the trunk. The last three images of their PowerPoint showed the group of them at a local restaurant planning their report. Their voice-over says, "Five investigators for this exercise: *x* number of dollars." Then they show the shot-up, bullet-riddled car. And it says, "One Crown Vic shot to shit by the cops: four thousand dollars." And then it shows them opening the trunk. There's the mannequin, and the voice-over says, "Missing the dead dude in the trunk: Priceless."

HOMICIDE SCHOOL SUPERVISOR

Rating Crime Scenes According to Difficulty

In the NYPD, we say there are two types of murders: ground balls and mysteries. The ground balls are just really, really obvious. The mysteries are the ones that challenge you.

HOMICIDE COMMANDER

Ground ball—most often it's domestic. You know, sometimes the guy's still there with the bloody knife. That's a ground ball. It's not a body in a field. It's not a drug dealer on the corner shot from a passing car.

One of our most recent ones was two guys who lived in a shelter. Well known to each other and didn't like each other. One of these guys stabbed the other forty-nine times with an ice pick. One of the women in the shelter was there when it happened and ran down the hall and hid in the closet in somebody's room.

So the story was immediately there and the perp was there and everything we needed to know was wrapped up within hours afterward. There was no finding witnesses and coaxing people into talking and dumping cell phones and trying to get video cameras and sending samples to the lab for this and that. It's just—You know, forty-nine times, it's not an accident.

DETECTIVE

We had a rape case. When the person dropped his drawers to commit the rape, his wallet fell out, he didn't realize it. So the wallet with the driver's license in it was left at the crime scene. Kind of simple.

DETECTIVE

Mysteries

A baby was kidnapped from the Greyhound Bus Station in down-town Chicago on Christmas Eve, 2001. We didn't have an actual, physical crime scene, like there is when you have an altercation. This was a situation where a woman conned another woman into giving up her baby while she exchanged tickets at the counter. She told her she'd watch her baby while she did this. The mother turned around and the woman was gone. She took the baby back to her own family, whom she hadn't seen for some months, and passed it off as her own.

The kidnapper didn't touch anything. This encounter took place in the middle of a Greyhound Bus Station waiting room. As the victim went up to the counter to exchange tickets, the other woman just stood in the middle of the room. So there are no glasses to dust for fingerprints; she didn't touch a counter; there was no physical exchange between the two of them. Nobody struck anybody, so there wasn't any blood, saliva, anything like that. There was nothing of evidentiary value there. It was totally clean.

When you have a stranger kidnapping, there's really nothing that the victim can give you that can help you go backward and try to find out connections. Up until the time they met in that bus station, these two women had had no inter-action together. So there was nothing for us to go back on.

And surveillance cameras couldn't help us here—the sur-veillance cameras were trained on the employees.

The forensics in this case was this: That baby was put into a van outside the bus station. So, hopefully there would be some type of transfer evidence there, like fibers from the van or fibers from the baby's clothing. When the mother of the kidnapped baby called, she gave us a snowsuit that the baby was wearing that night. So we had the name of the kid-napped baby written in the back of the neck, plus we had fiber and DNA evidence.

The big thing was, the family of the kidnapper was cele-brating Christmas. They took lots of pictures, pictures with the victim of the kidnapping in them. The kidnapper didn't want any pictures taken, but her mother said, "What do you mean? This is my granddaughter! I'm gonna take lots of pic-tures." This produced a lot of evidence.

On a case like this, you have to have the help of the me-dia. We did. The picture of the baby was in the papers, on TV; it was everywhere.

The grandmother got suspicious. People who came over to the house over Christmas kept saying to the grandmother, "That baby looks a lot like the baby that was on TV."

So the grandmother rushed to get the photos developed. Then she compared the photos and said, "Yeah. It *is* the same baby." And that's when she called the police.

A lot of people would have been in denial. "Nah, nah, that's not the baby." But that grandmother was sharp. And the evidence here came from pictures—the ones the real mother gave the media and the ones the kidnapper's family took at Christmas.

With this case, we had two victims, neither of whom de-served what happened. First, you had an innocent baby. And the mother, she was innocent, too. She was duped, under a stressful situation, into giving up her child. There's always satisfaction when cases end like that.

A kidnapping presents a special challenge. You can't just get tunnel vision and think, okay, there's no crime scene. When you have a kidnapping you have a mobile *and* a continuing crime scene. Every place the victim goes, there's a chance that evidence is going to be left. You never know what the evidence is going to turn out to be.

CHIEF OF POLICE

The most difficult scene is a sex murder inside. I'm not unique in this at all, police around the country will say the same thing. I've spent three days at that kind of crime scene, or more, to make sure you can get every bit of evidence you can out of that place.

CRIME SCENE PROCESSOR

A very, very attractive little eighteen-year-old girl was living with this guy who was completely dominating her. He was insanely jealous. She was not allowed to dress up during the day for fear that she might meet somebody. If she was driving, she had to keep her eyes down to the floorboard when she came to a stop so she couldn't catch somebody's eye. She wasn't allowed to talk on the telephone when he wasn't home. Many, many calls of domestic violence to the place.

Her family tried to get her to leave him. She wouldn't do it; she was totally in love with this guy. You've heard this story before.

She disappears. Her family went to the local police and reported her missing. They sent a patrol cruiser down to talk to this guy. "Were you planning on reporting Elizabeth missing?" "Oh yeah, I sure was, when I get a chance, but I'm eating dinner right now."

"Well, do you mind if we look around the house?" "No, not at all."

The officers look around and one of them goes out and looks in the garage, notices that the garage door opener is unplugged. He's just kind of walking around, and notices that mashed between the washing machine and the water heater is a lump of clothing. He kind of taps it with a flashlight and it hits solid. There's Elizabeth.

She's been strangled and sexually assaulted. The local police arrest the boyfriend and they end up calling us. I had a huge fight with our crime lab about wanting to do an alternate light source examination of the body at the scene, not transfer it to the coroner's office first, and I prevailed. The D.A. told me that if we had moved the body from the scene and not done the alternate light source, we probably would have got nothing.

As it turns out, this guy ends up failing two polygraph examinations. I could have easily convicted this guy. History of domestic violence, failed two polygraphs, uncooperative, unconcerned, the body in his garage.

We took the extra step of doing the DNA, expecting it to be his. It wasn't. The DNA belonged to his best friend. The whole story was, my victim had an identical twin. The boyfriend's best friend impregnated the twin and dumped the twin; he was married. My victim hated him. So, every chance she'd get, she'd say, "Get out of my house, I don't want you here, you're scum, I don't want you near my boyfriend."

He got tired of being dissed. He came over one morning after the boyfriend went to work at five in the morning. He got in the house because he had a key; he lived there at one time. He raped her. And he said, "I want more. I'm coming back. This is going to be our little secret." And she said, "I'll tell the world." So he killed her.

When he finally confessed, he told me that he figured we would get enough evidence on the boyfriend, based on his history, that we'd just go ahead and convict the boyfriend and *he* would never come to light.

HOMICIDE DETECTIVE

Ones That Nearly Got Away

There was a death of a four-year-old in western Michigan in 2000. The mother said there was a shotgun lying on the bed and that the little girl was playing around with the vacuum cleaner that had a narrow-shaped tool for getting in corners on the end of it. The mother said the four-year-old poked that tool into the trigger area of the shotgun and pushed it and the shotgun discharged and killed her.

Simple accident, right?

The responding investigators bought the mother's story. They didn't call the lab. The case was written off as an accidental death.

Some months later, one of the detectives was at an area detective meeting with one of our lab scientists, the head of our fingerprint unit. The detective told our guy about the case and said, "I have some feelings, some nagging feelings, about this case. Would you mind looking at the photographs from the scene?"

Our people looked at the photographs. They agreed there's something wrong here. Logically, they should have already had huge reservations with this. They said, "Can we go to the scene? Is it still there?"

Well, it was. So they went and started processing the scene. When they started moving furniture, they discovered a bullet hole in the wall. This had not been found previously. And from the angle and height of the bullet hole, they could tell that that gun was not fired on the bed. It was too high, and it was going down. It passed through the little girl's body and hit lower on the wall. So it couldn't have happened the way it was described.

If you think about it logically, if you know anything about shotguns—if the shotgun had discharged on the bed, you would have huge burn patterns in the bed surface from the muzzle blast; the blankets would be all shredded; the gun would have recoiled backward, been thrown off the bed. The pictures showed the gun lying on the bed still.

We then got the mother to take a polygraph. And after a number of hours, the mother confessed to killing the girl. Her reason for it was, she was married, but she had a boyfriend. The boyfriend wanted to move to Florida and wanted her to go along. But he didn't want the little girl along. So she killed the girl to get rid of her so she could run off with her boyfriend.

So she took the shotgun and just put it at the little girl's chest and—shot her. Gruesome case.

Almost went as accidental. The cops bought the mother's story. But, in the investigators' defense, you have to remember. You're in a terrible, tragic situation. Very few of us can accept the fact that a mother would put a shotgun to her daughter's chest and pull the trigger. You just can't buy that.

This case was solved because one detective was haunted by what happened. And he kept following up. You have to look at the factual evidence. And the story and the evidence have to jibe. And when they don't, then you have a problem.

The thing is, we never give up. We never, ever give up.

CRIME LAB DIRECTOR

We had one guy kill a woman and make meatloaf out of her. Oh, yeah. That was a funny case. It was not *funny*. God forbid— it's not *funny*—the poor woman got all— But it was a *bizarre* case. That woman might *never* have been found if we didn't bother to look.

It was a Friday afternoon and, you know, it was nice and warm and everybody was kind of skating out of the office. I'm a lowly officer in the major crimes squad at the time. One of our sergeants came to me and she said, "You busy? I need you to help me with an interview. I got a couple of people who want to talk here. These two women—their mom's been missing for seven months. One daughter went to the cops.

They blew her off. She got mad. She went to the state police, they blew her off, and then she came to us." So the sergeant talked to one daughter and I talked with the other daughter.

So I said, "What can I do for you?" She said, "Well, my mom's been missing and she lives with this guy George. I never liked him, but my mom took up with him. He's a cook at a motel and he lives on top of this newsstand." This is a newsstand right across from a county courthouse. Pretty busy intersection.

The daughter said, "I went there looking for my mom and she wasn't there. Her suitcase was there and I opened it up and there were these bones in there." So I'm looking at her and I say, "You mean, like chicken bones?" She says, "No, these were big bones." And I'm like . . . ohhh.

I said, "Well, where did George tell you your mom was?" "He said that my mom was in the Harrisburg Hospital." I called the Pennsylvania State Police and they told me there was no such hospital. I said, "Do me a favor. See if this woman's been a patient in any of your hospitals in the past year." The guy calls me back in ten minutes. "Nobody's ever heard of her in any of the hospitals here." I said, "Ahhh, this is not good."

So I get off the phone and I turn to the daughter sitting there. "All right. Tell me about the bones." We pick up the phone and we call our homicide unit. They weren't real keen on it at first. They said, "We're available, but you handle it first. Let us know if there *is* anything."

Some of our guys went out there. They interviewed the girls who lived downstairs from the guy and they said, "Oh, yeah, the cook. He used to make us meatloaf and bring it down all the time."

Up in his kitchen, there were cooking pots with big fleshy parts of thigh in them. And in the refrigerator. In the oven. He cooked down the body parts.

This guy was a butcher by trade. He actually killed the

poor woman, dismembered her, and . . . and, you know, made stuff with her, and *buried* her out back in a shallow grave, on a main street.

And right across the street was the county courthouse. I don't know how that guy did it. But he did it. He did it. I mean, *oh*, he was a bad guy.

And then the poor guys at the scene had to tell the girls downstairs. The poor buggers, when they found out what they had ingested. It was like—running and screaming into the night.

Then we called Homicide—"Guys, I think it's *time*. We've got body parts in pots here. You might wanna come up now." Well, the whole damn squad came up then, you know, after we had solved the case for them.

And they interviewed the guy, George, and he was like, "Yeah, she was a pain in the ass and I beat her and, you know, I finally cracked her over the head and she died. I didn't know what the hell to do with her." Well, Christ, George, I mean . . . Couldn't ya—give her a Viking burial or *something*? You didn't have to cook the poor woman down like Martha Stewart, for God's sake. For meatloaf.

I love meatloaf. I do. But I was off it for a long time after that.

HOMICIDE DETECTIVE

Interpreting the Scene

I play this game. If I'm called to a homicide— First, bear in mind, the first information that you get from the dispatcher is always inaccurate. Oh, yeah. It's inaccurate sometimes about the manner of death, it's inaccurate sometimes about the number of victims, it's inaccurate . . . because there's so much confusion at the initial crime scene.

So usually, as I'm driving there, if it's like a dumped body case, I go over in my mind—"Who the hell would dump a body at that scene? What connects *anybody* to that victim?" I try to go through every single thing in my mind that could be a possibility, even if it sounds completely stupid or remote.

SUPERVISORY SERGEANT

You want to record all your impressions, from the moment you get there. You never know what may become important later.

When you get there, it's a lot of sensory overload. But if you take the time to stop and look and analyze . . . the scene will talk to you. It'll tell you what happened. It'll tell you the sequence of things. It's just a case of taking the time to look at it and listen to it.

In some cases, it's just a whisper. Other cases, it's yelling and screaming at you: "Look at this! Over here! Over here! Look at this!"

And it's a case of the investigator taking the time to look at it, analyze it, and take it all in. And then look at it and put it in a logical perspective. I mean, it's all there. If you just rush through it, and be like a vacuum cleaner and just pick up everything, you miss everything.

But—it'll tell you *everything* that's going on.

I've had a lot of cases like that. I had one case where a woman was beaten to death with a hammer. An old woman. We got in there—and there was something wrong with the scene. It was *screaming* at me. And I couldn't figure it out. It took me probably half an hour before I finally figured out what it was. There wasn't enough blood. The suspect had cleaned up the blood. We came in there with Luminol later on that evening and I could tell the guy was left-handed. And he had cleaned up the blood—everything. When he was confronted with all this, he confessed. Plus the fact that I found his fingerprint on the side of the hammer. The print was in the victim's blood.

EVIDENCE TECHNICIAN

We had a narcotics rip-off thing. And there was one, two,
three—I'm trying to remember where the bodies were—I
think there were three, maybe four bodies in this little tiny
motel room. And these guys— One body's spread out on the
couch, one body's laying down on the floor, one body's laying in this little kitchenette area. I think there was another
body in the bedroom.

It was like a little kitchenette motel kind of thing. Real
rundown place. Summertime.

And the flies were all over the blood on the bodies and
you're constantly swatting at the flies to keep them away
from you. And, uh, just the smell . . . You walk into a place,
you smell the blood, and you truly can smell death.

And you look. The TV's still on. You can see what they
were watching on TV. The food's still cooking on the stove,
you know, the stuff they were doing when these guys came
in and just—took them out.

When you first get to a scene like this, you look around,
and there's very little to go on. But this one— You look at all
that stuff and you think: Had to be somebody they knew.
Otherwise, they wouldn't have been sitting around in these
positions. They would have been in some type of defensive
stance when they were killed. You know, the little stuff like
that kind of sticks out.

HOMICIDE COMMANDER

You *gotta* think things through. You *gotta* go back to scenes.
I used to love to go back by myself. We padlock scenes,
but once everything was collected, I'd go back by myself and
look. What happened here? By myself. I had to be by myself.
Not that I had any kind of special power.

Sometimes, I'd just sit in a chair. And I'd look. "He
came in here and he did this and he did that." And I've
seen it on TV. It looks hokey as hell in some of the shows,
but you do it.

And you gotta take notes, notes, notes. Because you forget things. So I'd go back with a tape recorder: "Okay, I'm back at the scene again. What the hell happened here? There's blood up on the top here, there's blood down there. How did it get there?"

And, sometimes, you'd go back, and you would say, "You know, we were *wrong*. It happened *this* way." Or—what would happen to you—an *anvil* would fall on your head and you'd say, "Oh. It happened *this* way." And once you see how obvious it is, you felt stupid. And you bring a boss back and tell him, "It didn't happen the way we thought. It happened this way."

You learn to do it. You gotta learn to think that way. If you don't want to think, you're not gonna last in Homicide.

HOMICIDE DETECTIVE/FORENSIC INVESTIGATOR

Pattern Analysis

You've got patterns within the scene itself. You might have blood spatter evidence, say, or patterns that show the path bullets took.

Some of the patterns extend out from the scene. You can look at some of them and figure out what kind of suspect you're looking at. You have to ask things like: "Why *this* victim? Why here? Why this time of day? What's different on *this* day as opposed to any other day?"

With pattern analysis, a lot of times, it's based on behavior or omission of behavior.

CRIME SCENE RECONSTRUCTIONIST

There's something known as "The Rule of the First Victim." Criminals will usually commit their first offense near where they live or where they work. They're comfortable with the area. They know how to get around. They know how to get back. So you start looking and asking questions around the immediate area of the crime.

There was a series of gas station robberies where force was used. They all occurred at six in the morning. We would go back to the first detectable robbery because chances are great that that one would be closest to where the suspect either lives or hangs out.

CRIME SCENE TEAM LEADER

In my experience, a burglar doesn't go out to target a specific *house.* A burglar goes out to look at a certain *area,* one that he's comfortable getting to and getting from. And then a target makes itself apparent.

Burglary has always been one of my favorite things to work. You should be able to walk into a burglary and figure out the level of planning, how comfortable the offender was at the scene. You always look for the reason behind the way the scene appears.

CRIME SCENE RECONSTRUCTIONIST

Cat burglars are actually pretty smart. We had one guy—we called him the Flatware Burglar. He was a junkie, but, boy, he knew silver and flatware better than anybody. He went into houses, and if they had nice flatware, that was the only thing he'd take. He took one piece that was valued at around $60,000. If it was crappy flatware, he would have it all lined up on the dining room table, almost like he was criticizing the owners' taste.

He operated in the summer months. The neighborhood would get hit three, four times in a short period; we'd throw a bunch of patrol cars in there; and the guy would disappear. As our activity level drifted off, he would come back. As we kicked it back up, he would disappear.

One time, we actually had eight patrol officers in the neighborhood we had predicted he'd hit—they're using night scopes—and he hit four houses on us and we never saw him. Aaagh, was I pissed.

What does that tell you? You know, if a neighborhood is hit that many times that repetitively, the burglar is somebody who fits in the neighborhood. Not only that—we were able to determine that if the guy hit north of a certain area, a bicycle would have been stolen from a garage within two blocks of the crime scene. What does that tell you?

He stole the bike because it was too far to walk.

It took us six months to get him, once we figured out the pattern. We finally got close enough to him that a detective stopped a guy riding a bike seconds after a call came in of a burglary nearby. He dropped his bike and lit out. He also dropped his backpack that had his identification in it. My supervisor told me, some months before this, that I was on a wild goose chase and should abandon all effort. So we'd go out and work on it anyway. And we got him. We got him.

Ten years he'd been burglarizing. He was very, very prolific. We cleared three hundred and eight-five residential burglaries on him.

The night we got him, he had hit three houses. The first house he hit, he took flatware. When he went to the second house, they had *better* flatware, so he left the first flatware at the second scene. He knew his flatware.

SUPERVISORY SERGEANTS

Interpreting Behavior Patterns at the Scene

If you've done any reading about serial killers, you know about organized and disorganized behavior. Serial killers get better as they go along; they get more comfortable, they experiment more, their behavior becomes more and more planned and organized.

Crime scenes are the same way. If it's a disorganized scene, that tells you something.

Maybe whoever went in there *didn't* go in with the intention of murdering someone. Maybe it was a robbery that got out of control or an argument that escalated.

A disorganized scene looks sloppy. But in an organized event, the person brings everything he needs to kill the victim—it's just much more well-planned-out.

And the scene will tell you that, just by looking at it.

CRIME SCENE INVESTIGATOR

We had one murder in Kansas where you could see— All around the body were vacuum cleaner marks. When you see something like that, you know you're looking at somebody who really knows how to plan.

LATENT PRINT SPECIALIST

Scenes can change. Scenes can deteriorate.

We investigated a gas station robbery-homicide a few years ago. The victim was a young man found injured at the scene. When I say "injured," he looked as if his head had been bashed in. He was also shot in the back. He died at the hospital.

We were convinced that the victim had been shot with his own gun, taken from him by the offender. The victim had taken a gun pinch [an arrest for gun possession] about four years before for a small-caliber handgun, and that's what he was shot with.

The owner of the gas station was an older gentleman with MS, something like that. He couldn't go to work on Monday, so he called his godson, Jimmy Pappas, a twenty-six-year-old first Gulf War veteran, to open up for him. He did, at six in the morning. This is the guy who became the victim.

We had a witness who went in for a pack of cigarettes. She looks over the cashier's cage, and sees the offender standing over the body, the bloody mess of the body of

Jimmy Pappas. The offender looks back at her. Their eyes meet. She runs screaming out of there and the bad guy runs out as well.

This was a very bloody scene. And it was disorganized. The killer thought the old man was going to be behind the counter. He went in with the intention of overpowering the old man, which he certainly could have done; he was a bruiser. But, instead, he meets this twenty-six-year-old Gulf War veteran. The initial altercation involved a fire extinguisher with the victim being beat in the head.

Now, who does a gas station robbery and uses a fire extinguisher as the weapon? A guy who hasn't planned it out ahead of time.

Or maybe he had a different plan. The fact that the old man was supposed to open up—and he didn't. The cage used to be open in the morning, because the old man would go out and make coffee. Not this day, with the old man gone. So this was an organized crime in respect to the planning of it; it became disorganized as it continued. It turned into a frenzied scene.

We were out there working the crime scene and we saw this one guy walking around, just walking around the lot, back and forth. He looked like he was carrying the weight of the world. We questioned him. He was a store employee; he admitted that he had set up the robbery, and we charged him.

But it took us two years to the day to get to the second guy. The witness said she couldn't identify the offender. Turns out, she knew him. His girlfriend's grandmother owned the building that our witness's sister lived in. And our witness used to bring her kids there for the sister to babysit while she went to work. She knew the killer; she just didn't want to say anything, She finally agreed to identify him and he ended up getting natural life.

CRIME SCENE TEAM LEADER

We get a lot of calls where the person is murdered at home, but is not found for a period of time. And so the animals have already started to take the body apart because they haven't been fed in that period. So your evidence is being chewed up by the family pet.

I tell you—Dogs are more loyal than cats. Cats will wait only a certain period of time and they'll start chewing on you. Dogs will wait a day or two before they just can't take the starving anymore. So, keep that in mind when choosing a pet.

You know how a cat just stares at you, maybe at the top of the TV, from across the room? That's because they're watching to see if you're gonna stop breathing.

CRIME SCENE PROCESSOR/LAB ANALYST

Tracking Down Leads

One of the guys who trained me in the detective squad always says, "You never have nothing." As a statement of fact, it's sometimes not true. It more reflects the attitude you need to have when you're really good at this. It's just the belief that, out there, somebody knows something. Somebody saw something. Somebody said something. Somebody left something. That's what you've got to work with.

Even if it's one guy who did a homicide in a robbery gone wrong, if two people know it, it's not a secret. You know what? He's probably at least going to tell his girlfriend. And then, hopefully, he's gonna treat her wrong at some point down the line. And then, instead of throwing his clothes out the window, she's gonna call us. Maybe both.

VIOLENT CRIMES DETECTIVE

Everybody's skills are different. But you have to really care to begin with. You have to go in there and say, "I want to find out who did this." The case depends on— What's your observation, what's your motivation, what's your level of commitment to try and solve what goes on? It comes down to the passion of the individual investigators that have that case.

SCENE SUPERVISOR

I think the new guys are getting spoiled. We used to spend days trying to get names, talking to people, who they're connected with. Now you get a lot of this on the computer.

Now? These guys think the computer is the end-all and be-all. The computer has only certain data entered into it. It doesn't have certain key things: Who'd the guy call from the lockup? Who bonded him out? All of those things are important.

ROBBERY/HOMICIDE DETECTIVE

Science from the crime scene stuff is great. It has to be done right. And all this DNA, computer databanks—it's the wave of the future. It's great to have those tools.

But what we're afraid of with the new detectives? They'll rely *only* on those tools and forget how to be a detective. The crime scene is your tool to use. But you've still got to get out and pound shoe leather, talk to people, make street contacts. You've got to have the ability to talk to people. If you lose that aspect of it, you're through. It's gotta be the total package.

HOMICIDE DETECTIVE

We got a body under a mattress in an Atlantic City motel room once. A couple from Germany had come to the city for a convention and stayed in this motel. All night long, the room stunk. They kept calling Housekeeping and Housekeeping would come out and they'd, you know, spray some air freshener, and they put some stuff in the carpeting and the whole nine yards.

The next day, the couple checks out. As the maid starts

making the bed, it's really, really stinking. The mattress is sitting on a box spring on top of the bed frame. The maid pulls off the mattress.

Well, here's a dead body inside the box. And all night long, the German couple was sleeping on top of it.

Our investigation started up. It turned out the guy in the room before the German couple had brought a young girl back to the room. We established who the young girl was, and we established that the guy's car was missing.

We found out that the expressway had a video camera to monitor traffic at different times. Our investigators got the videotape, they see the guy's car, and they see a girl driving the car. So now we get the Tag number from the car and put out an "Attempt to Locate."

The Pennsylvania State Police reported a motor vehicle accident on that vehicle on the expressway the night before. The victim of that accident was taken to the hospital. She discharged herself. Once we identified her, one of the guys tracked her up to Brooklyn. And the team found her and brought her back.

Here is a young lady who had been picked up by this guy the night before. She claimed that he sexually assaulted her and, in self-defense, she stabbed him to death. She was Islamic; her thing was that she had been dishonored and her family disgraced. She finally confessed.

Coincidentally, when she left, she also took his wallet. And his car keys. And his car. She took all the bloody clothing and stopped along the highway and threw them into a stream. All of which was later recovered.

Here was this girl who was about a hundred ten pounds soaking wet and this guy was about a hundred and eighty pounds. Stabs him, drags him, and throws him under the mattress. And makes the bed.

HOMICIDE DETECTIVE/COLD CASE SPECIALIST

This happens a lot. We get these kids out here in LA, especially gangbangers, they like to play Russian roulette. And what happens—one of them will spin the chamber around in a revolver, click it, and then boom!—they're dead. And their friends are sitting there, and obviously, they're shocked when this happens. And the kids will take the gun and hide it. We get there and we got a dead body, gunshot to the head, and no weapon. Obviously, it looks like a homicide. Then we have to go back, find out who was there, question them, and get them to finally admit to playing Russian roulette. Even if they tell us that, if they've taken the gun and thrown it in the ocean or something, we can never recover it. So we never actually know for sure.

HOMICIDE COMMANDER

When you're talking to people, to crooks especially, you cut the crap, you cut to the chase. The personal language isn't always the best that you have to use; you have to talk to them on their level. So you know, you might say something like, "Look, I'm tired of fucking around with you. I'm here to find out what's going on and I know you know what's going on." And look them in the eye and they *know* you know what's going on. They don't hesitate to tell you at that time.

But you have to go in different directions. You don't want to start *off* like that, but it gets to a point sometimes where you say, "Okay, I've wasted enough time with you." And you tell them what you know. "Hey, I know you did this, I know this, I know this. Now, if you want to go to prison and you want *this* guy to get away with it, that's fine with me. But if *I'm* sittin' in your position, I'm gonna think there's other people involved with this. You got one chance to tell me. I'm gonna leave here, and after I'm outta here, I've got a case, whether it's you or the other people involved. *I* can live with that. If *you* can live with that, fine." "Well, well, wait a minute. Maybe I *do* want to reconsider this." But you see what I'm saying.

HOMICIDE DETECTIVE

Figuring Out Motive

We stress the different types of motives in homicide. Too often, detectives try to concentrate on "Get the murderer" instead of on "Why did it happen?" Why it happened will lead you to who did it.

CRIME SCENE RECONSTRUCTIONIST

We spend an awful lot of time chasing down leads. All the BS. Was he killed for insurance? Was he killed because he was goofing around on his wife? Was his wife goofing around on him? A jewelry store owner: Was he buying stolen jewelry? Was he running stolen credit cards? Was he in the Russian Mob? I mean, on and on and on—until you can eliminate them. It can take weeks to get rid of that stuff.

ROBBERY/HOMICIDE DETECTIVE

The nature of homicide, statistically, has changed in the last thirty years. It used to be that offender and victim knew each other. That's changed. Now, many times, it's unknown offenders. And that affects how we investigate. If there's no prior relationship, we don't really have a starting point. You have to work to get to that starting point, and that can take a while. I refer to it as "washing the crap off the case," trying to eliminate all the other possibilities so you can get to what you think is the real motive.

For instance, take this scene: You have a dead woman in an apartment and there's some property missing and she's been sexually assaulted. Was this a burglary that went bad? Was this a sexually related homicide to begin with? You don't

know that going into the scene. That's what you gotta try to
work through. Wash the crap off.

CRIME SCENE TEAM LEADER

If you have a domestic homicide, it's probably gonna occur
within just two rooms of the house: the kitchen or the bedroom.

Most murders are either over money or sex. That's why
they're in these two rooms. People often keep a gun in the
bedroom. The kitchen, a lot of times, is where you'd be ar-
guing over money because you're doing bills at the kitchen
table. And you have all these weapons in there—you've got
forks and knives. Everybody's got a drawer with a screwdriver in it. You'd have to see somebody killed with a screwdriver to appreciate just what an effective weapon it is. So, if
you and your husband ever get in an argument, move to the
living room or the bathroom. He can't kill you with a Q-tip.
He can throw the remote at you, but you won't die.

TOOLMARK SPECIALIST

Collaborating with Crime Scene Investigators and Forensic Scientists

Some really good young officers walked into a scene a few years
back. They were the first on the scene. They walked into a
typical little Cape Cod house, where, when you walk into the
house, you walk directly into the living room. This person
had put in ceramic tile, about a three-by-three-inch ceramic
tile, in front of the door.

Both officers could see the victim in the kitchen through
the living room front door. They jumped over the tile. We
came out, got the crime lab out, and they got a partial ten-
nis shoe print. It ended up being YEWTAH, the way Nike
spells Utah.

My partner and I were sitting in the car, talking to a

young kid we thought might have been a witness to the murder. Just before we got out of the car, I said, "Do you mind if I look at the bottom of your shoes?" He said, "No, go ahead." And, my God, the bottom of his shoes said YEWTAH. And he was one of the murderers.

HOMICIDE DETECTIVE

The owner of a jewelry store was found beaten to death behind the sales counter of his store. He typically opened his store about ten in the morning and he was found by his wife in midafternoon, lying behind the counter. A number of jewelry items were missing.

The scene was processed for a number of days—all the usual fingerprint processing and trace evidence collection, and looking for footwear impressions and everything. A few suspects were developed. Ultimately, we had enough evidence to charge three suspects with the murder. Two of the three gave statements. They basically minimized their roles and blamed the other guy for the murder.

But we found that there was physical evidence that supported exactly what these guys were saying. You know, it's pretty tough to make up a story that's going to match the evidence from the scene.

What the two said in their statements was that the three of them went there with the intention of robbing this guy. One of the three had a steel pipe. While the store owner was on his side of the counter, they threatened him. And then the guy with the pipe grabs the store owner and starts hitting him with the pipe. Ultimately, the store owner drops down to the floor area behind the counter. The suspect with the pipe goes behind the counter and continues to beat this guy on the floor. At some point, he reaches into the display case where the jewelry's at and removes some of the jewelry from the case.

We had bloodstain evidence of all of that at the scene.

Typically, the area that has the least amount of blood indicates the beginning of a blood-shedding incident. In this case, some blood drops had fallen on the surface of the counter. So we know that our victim is standing at that point in time. As he goes down to the floor, we're getting this forceful impact spatter, which is the result of his already having a bleeding head injury, and now he's still being beaten. The door to the jewelry display case was open. There were bloodstains and blood spatter inside the case, along the bottom surface. This places the victim's head at about the level of the display case at this point. He's still being hit. Ultimately, he goes to the ground. And he's still being hit, because now we've got blood spatter coming *up* and hitting the *other* side of the display case. So we can position the victim at, or just about at ground level, being beaten.

And when the offender reaches inside the case to get the jewelry out, when he does that, the blood stains that are already at the bottom of that jewelry case get wiped over, so the stains got smeared in the direction of the offender reaching into the case. By the appearance of the stains, you could tell that it happened very shortly after the blood was shed.

So, we could take, in stages, the position of the victim. And then we could also show the actions of at least one offender reaching into the display case. What was nice about that was, it's always nice to have a confirmation of what you think occurred. A lot of times, that doesn't happen. The only people who can truly tell us what happened are the suspect and the victim. And one of them's not going to be talking to us.

BLOODSTAIN PATTERN EXPERT

The Bodies in the Basement Case. A guy was in the process of renovating a house. And he took his Bob-Cat and he dug a ramp so he could take it down into the basement. The basement was unfinished, so he was gonna dig it out and, you know, finish off the basement and increase the value of the home.

So he removed some of the foundation to get into this basement area and as he's scooping out everything, he picks up a load and it looks like there's some kind of clothing or something hanging out. He's with some buddies. They give it a look, and it's a leg. He goes, "Whoo! Time out here, boys!" So he goes and calls a cop he knew who was off duty. So the cop comes over and looks, and sure enough, he's got a pant leg and a boot hanging out of the front end of this loader. He calls his department. The department calls the major crimes squad.

This thing came in around three thirty in the afternoon. They call up the crime scene unit. I get sent over there. And I look, and "Yeah, it's definitely a body."

So now it's a case of what do we do now? It's like, Oh, boy. And everybody's lookin' at me, "Whadda we do now, boss?" And I say, "We're gonna hafta exhume this thing."

I end up changing clothes because, of *course,* I was in a nice suit jacket and tie. They always want us to look present-able, but they forget where they keep putting us.

We exhumed the body that night out of the Dumpster and we had a whole entire leg. Then we got part of a torso.

We sealed off the scene and we started working this thing the next day. We start doing our policy and procedures, go-ing right by the book. While we're doing the crime scene work, we have an investigative team behind us. The investi-gators go and get the guy who formerly owned the house, and they say, "Look, this guy was digging out the basement and it looks like they may have recovered a body."

Now here's a guy where this house has been in his family for like thirty years. His first question was "Well, why was he doing that? Why was he digging out the basement?" That was his first question.

I found the victim's wallet. Now, remember, this thing's

been buried for fourteen years. The wallet contains a laminated driver's license. The moisture got between the lamination and the paper material. So the Polaroid product was disintegrated. But the colors from the picture had leached into the plastic, and when they separated it, there was like a slide. There was the guy's picture. Gave us somethin' to work with!

So we're down in the basement sweating our asses off because, of course, it's July and it's like ninety degrees down in this basement, with no ventilation. You know, they only take us to the best places and we only meet the finest people.

We're down there doing this thing and we identified the one guy tentatively and that's when they identified the three bullets in the torso. Two of them were in the spine and one was kind of lying loose within the clothing. After fourteen years, there's not a whole lot left.

We're in there digging things out and we're taking our time because it's an archeological dig because you don't know what you're gonna have. There's small bones; there's teeth; there's the possibility of DNA; there might be a footprint left under the body from when the guy was digging the hole; maybe there's cigarette butts. So you're taking all these things into consideration.

Every time we take a bucketful of material, it all has to be sifted a couple of times. And everything that's left over has to be analyzed before you dump it. And if you find anything, you have to take progressive photographs, and it's all gridded out so you know where everything is and how deep everything is. You're gonna end up with a body that you've dug up lying on top of a table. And to do this, we're using paintbrushes, tongue depressors, trowels.

So, we're doing all this nonsense. The assistant medical examiner comes in, and I say, "Look, we've got a second person here." "Nah, nah, nah." "Look, I'm telling you there's a second person here." I call down to the morgue and talk to the ME and say, "Take a look through the bones. I think there's another person here." They call back and confirm. I say, "What was the clue, other than we got three legs here?" They also found a second mandible. A guy's not gonna have two jawbones.

It started on Monday night. This is Tuesday. The media is now showing up. They're trying to get pictures. And we're down at the end of the block, in this cul-de-sac. The news media is trying to send television cameras through backyards and over the fences and all sorts of stuff.

We have a new boss that day, his first day on the job with us. He came out of Narcotics. He's never had to deal with crime scene guys and the homicide team. The prosecutor's putting pressure on this guy because of the media. And, finally, in exasperation, our new boss says to the prosecutor, "I don't know *what* they're doing. All I know is they're down in the basement digging holes with Popsicle sticks."

The boss wants to know when we'll be done. I said, "When we're done, I'll tell ya. Look, it's just gonna take us a while." It's all stone and clay, so it's slow going trying to get this stuff. It's taking us forever. And there can only be two of us in the hole at a time, but we got all these other officers—everybody wants to help. You got guys on perimeter, you got guys that are sifting, you got guys that are searching. . . . We had to come out periodically for air and then we had to oversee what they were doing.

Then we get a call: "Prosecutor's coming." I said, "Good. Is he gonna help dig?" He shows up and he says, "How soon before you're done?" I'm looking at this hole: "I don't know." "Well, whaddya need? You need shovels?" "No, we don't need shovels." If we do that, we destroy everything.

Meanwhile, based on what we've given the outside investigative team, they find out that there's a missing persons report on the guy we dug up—and his fourteen-year-old girlfriend from fourteen years ago. She was fourteen; the guy was nineteen. There were some problems with the families.

The kids thought they'd run off together and then they'd call their families. But there's a missing persons report on them.

It's slow, hot, sticky. There's only two of us that can go in there at a time, my partner and myself, and one of us always made it a point to be in the hole so nobody would screw anything up. I'd been down there a whole entire morning. I finally come out for air and here I find out that two rookies had been sitting there all morning, sifting. So I tell them to take a break and I start sifting. But, stupid me, I was wearing a shirt from a forensic association and, of course, what color was it? Red. So now the media sees through the trees that here I am, and that sets them off into a frenzy: "We know you're doin' somethin'!" The cameras are going like crazy. Next thing I know, I got a news helicopter hovering over the top of the crime scene. It just got nuts.

The worst thing about it—For three days, everybody, once they hear about it, wants to drive through the neighborhood. And, of course, because there's people there, you've got that little ice cream wagon that comes around and plays "The Entertainer." The same tune. For three days. And we're doing the crime scene—We're there for about sixteen hours a day. And the same tune is playing over and over and over again.

Finally, on the second day, I said to an officer, "You either turn that guy off—get rid of the music—or I'm comin' out there. And I got a gun."

On the third day, we exhumed the bodies; we put them on a board the fire department guys gave us. We're going over and we're looking at this whole thing. We've got these two bodies intertwined and some of the clothing is still there. The forensic anthropologist is there, and she's looking at the head and the bones of one of them and she looks at the pelvis. She has to remove part of the clothing. And she says, "This is definitely going to be a young female." And I go, "No shit! You think maybe the bra and panties might have given it away?" Normally, I'm pretty careful, but this was three days of being in that hole.

The media had been standing vigil. We shut down for the night. I walked out last, as I always did, but I was carrying the remains out and just stuck them in my truck. And I went down to the morgue and met the medical examiner's staff there. So the media missed it.

We finally identified conclusively the girl through mito-chondrial DNA, which looks at the maternal line. It gave peace of mind to the families.

They interviewed the original owner of the house again. The victims had some kind of connection to him—they were selling him dope or something. He finally confessed that he killed the guy. They booked him on the murder. The next morning, before he got arraigned, I called the station up and said, "We got a second one here, guys." They went out, grabbed him, brought him back, and he said, "Oh, yeah. The other one was the girlfriend."

It turned out, in that mess also was a baseball bat. He had beaten her to death with a baseball bat after he had shot the boyfriend to death. He was also connected to a group in-volved with pedophilia.

Like they say, a cop's lot is not a happy one. You always end up with more questions than you get answers.

FORENSIC INVESTIGATOR/SCENE SUPERVISOR

Using the Scene in Interrogating Suspects

You have to look for both consistencies and inconsistencies with what people say and what the scene indicates. Is this consistent with what I see? Or is this inconsistent?

It could be as simple as somebody reporting that he found his wife dead at seven in the morning and he's completely *shocked* by this event and "She killed herself without me hearing it. I didn't hear the gun go off." But he heard his *alarm* go off. Now, is that consistent or inconsistent? Bingo! So keep talking to us.

And what you do is, "Wow! No! That's terrible! You must have been shocked." Keep them talking, because you don't want them to lawyer up or "liar up," I call it.

Or—preliminary examination of the body. I take note that I have seen the presence of lividity in a body that's only been there, according to the statement of the witness, for half an hour. Yet it's my training and my knowledge of pathology that this presence of lividity is at least four to five hours old.

Or—somebody says the man shot himself twice in the head with a .308 semiautomatic rifle. Once, yes. Twice, no.

HOMICIDE DETECTIVE

After the murder of a woman, during the interview process, the guy arrested claimed that he and his girlfriend were abducted at knifepoint by two guys, taken back to their original motel room, and forced out of their clothing, to be robbed. And the girlfriend got fresh with one of the guys and he ended up stabbing her. And there was blood everywhere. So the story was good, except for one little problem. The boyfriend's pants at the scene were turned inside out, and there isn't a drop of blood on the inside. All the blood was on the outside. I mean, something isn't reading right. We confronted him with that little discrepancy, and he confessed.

It's like the quote from Sherlock Holmes I use when I train detectives: "If you take away the impossible, what remains must be the truth."

SCENE INVESTIGATOR

I don't know *why* people talk to us. There can't be an individual in the *land* who doesn't know about Miranda. But people do. They talk.

Part of that is the personality of the interviewer. The other part is the personality of the suspect, because usually they're pretty arrogant and they think they're smarter and they're slicker and they're gonna be able to get away with it.

Just keep him talking. Because once he takes a position, he's gotta remember that position. He's gotta *remember* what he said before. And inconsistencies eventually crop up, *as long as* you can keep him talking. If you keep him talking, eventually you're gonna be able to trip him up.

HOMICIDE DETECTIVE

Police have a reputation for being rough-and-tumble, right? So everybody thinks you have to beat a confession out? That's garbage. Let me tell you something. I always use this line in front of juries. The defense attorney: "Did you beat my client? Did you beat my client? Otherwise, he wouldn't have confessed." "No. Brought him chicken, sat down, ate with him, took him to the washroom, treated him decent."

Chicken and kindness will guarantee you many, many confessions.

And even guys who've been to the joint a couple times? They tell the state's attorney—who'd asked the guys, "Why did you confess?" They tell him, "Man, I know I'm goin' back to the penitentiary, but at least he treated me like a man."

HOMICIDE DETECTIVE

Sometimes, right before somebody confesses, they sort of sway back and forth a little. And then they sit back. And they sigh. The weight's off. The weight's off your chest.

Here's what's wrong. A lot of detectives give up too quick. Ahhh, this guy's never gonna confess.

If you keep talking, after a while, out of the *blue,* they decide to make that change.

And then you see them sit back. You hear that sigh. It's

almost like a catharsis. It's a relief to get it over with, for a lot of them.

HOMICIDE DETECTIVE

Making Sense of the Senseless

I remember my first homicide scene. It was in 1986. This guy was lying on his couch. He had his screen door open. It was a second-story apartment, with a landing outside. He was just lying there, it was in June, that's when I went to Homicide.

It was a summer day in southern California. He's lying on his couch, not bothering anyone, watching television. He lived alone. He was probably twenty-two, twenty-three years old. Just a nice guy who never bothered anyone. He's off for the weekend, watching sports on TV. His screen door is closed, but his front door is open.

This lady who lived a couple doors down had some mental problems. She stopped by his door, said something to him through the screen, he replied back. We're not sure what he said, but it was probably "Hi" or something. She opened the screen door and she had a gun and she shot him to death. And then she went back down to her apartment.

As it turned out, she felt that voices were telling her that he was a bad person and she had to do something about it. He had no idea he was going to die that day.

That's one thing—I've come to a conclusion, after all my years working Homicide. I truly believe that when it's your turn to go, it's just your turn to go. I mean, no matter what you do to avoid it, when your number's up, your number's up.

I saw a guy one time shot in his leg and the bullet actually traveled up his body and took his heart. There was no way in the world you'd think this guy was going to die from it. It was a little .25 automatic that shot him, and that's not even that powerful a gun.

And then I've seen people shot in the head five, six times, even more than that, really, and they're back out on the street within a month or so. There's just no rhyme or reason to it. I've seen a lot of it.

HOMICIDE CAPTAIN

There's a real transactional thing that takes place between the murder cop and the surviving family. It's hard to describe. You have to be very careful not to be pulled down into it, because it would be very easy for you to be emotionally pulled in. You have to maintain that objectivity that's so important to the professional investigator.

Because if you're not objective, then you become subjective and now you start disregarding evidence that may go to the contrary of what you believe. It's very difficult.

HOMICIDE COMMANDER

One of the more stirring things I remember that really stands out: One time we got a call to a homicide in the park, on the borderline of the Bronx and Yonkers. A young seventeen-year-old boy had been stabbed to death in the park. His companion, after he got beat up, was able to get away and call for help.

It turns out that these two innocent kids, both Catholic high school kids, were out on spring break and they saw a bonfire in the park, and they thought maybe their friends had a fire and they wanted to go see. One of the kids is carrying his brother's radio.

Turns out to be the local hooligans from South Yonkers. And so, as they walked in, they realized they were in trouble, they couldn't get out, they get surrounded. A guy says, "Gimme that radio!" The kid says, "That's my brother's radio!" And with that, the guy slams a Bowie knife into his chest. And he goes down, the other kid gets beat up, he gets thrown down the hill, and the last words out of the kid's mouth were, "I have to get my brother's radio back."

We ended up making the arrest. We had to go into Yonkers to get these little fuckers. I got hold of the Yonkers dispatcher and said, "Listen. Get the sectors that are assigned to this unit and have them meet the New York commander at the scene." And I said, "Listen, guys, will you call your local assholes? Because this is definitely a Yonkers operation."

So they did. And who shows up but this patrol sergeant from Yonkers. And he is all bent out of shape: "You ain't takin' anybody back to the city! I got fucked on the David Berkowitz case!" I said, "Whoa. Slow down. What are you gonna lock them up for, Sergeant?" "Homicide!" Then I said, "Where's the homicide?" He looks at me. "It's in the Bronx." "See? You're all gonna get credit. Relax." So we got the hooligans in, locked them up.

That night, we went to the funeral and met the family. The father of the murdered kid had come from Ireland many, many years ago. He and his wife had struggled to save their pennies to send their kid to Catholic high school to get a better education. He was gonna be the prince, so to speak. He was gonna be the one to make the family proud.

About three years later, I got called to another body case out of the river. I'm at this college that sits on the Hudson River. I get out of my car and I'm walking over to take a look. And I see a security guard coming toward me. And he says, "Oh, Commander, you're in our prayers. All the time. We really . . . We'll never forget what you did for us."

And I'm thinking, "Who the hell is this old guy?" The guy had aged about twenty years. I looked at his name tag. Holy shit! That's the father of the young kid! And he's thanking me.

So now the father worked as a security guard at this college. He had a regular job, but he lost that job because of his grief and he took this job. You wouldn't recognize him.

That's what we all forget. For the families, the loss is for-ever.

HOMICIDE COMMANDER

When you're investigating a homicide, you never get to know the victim, obviously. You're never gonna *know* the victim.

But—you get to know people in reverse. That's the way I describe it. Because they're dead. And so you flash back, and you think, okay, what was this guy like? And sometimes you get to really know these people. And you really get to like these people. And you think, "Man, I would have liked to have known this guy, or this gal." You think, "What kind of guy was he?" Wow. He was a schoolteacher. Wow, jeez. Did he have any problems? Was he married? Had he been mar-ried? The more you ask, the more you talk to people, the bet-ter an idea you have of what kind of person this was. And sometimes you think, "Boy, he sure never did deserve it." Most of them don't.

HOMICIDE CAPTAIN

When you're in the solitude of the crime scene . . . You go in with your partner, or you may be there by yourself. You're stand-ing there and you're looking around and you're imagining what the sounds were like when this murder was taking place or, even more, you wonder what the sounds were like before the people had any idea that this murder was going to take place. And you look. And now there's just deadly silence, un-less you hear the insects that are flying around. And, you know, you look at the photographs on the wall and you see the smiles on their faces, and you just think, "Man. This is tough."

HOMICIDE DETECTIVE

Three

CRIME SCENE INTERPRETATION— OUTSIDE SCENES

We get bodies in the ocean all the time. Step one: How do you process that scene? How do you rope off the Atlantic Ocean?
—New Jersey Homicide Detective

Most of our crime scenes in southern California are out of doors. In Los Angeles County, we have mountains and deserts and rivers and oceans. You're going to document a crime scene; you're going to do a search or do your measurements. Well, if you're in the middle of a desert, what are you going to use for your points of reference?
—Los Angeles County Homicide Detective

OUTDOOR SCENES ARE RIFE WITH CHALLENGES. IF THERE'S A street gang shooting, or an outside altercation that leads to a homicide, the scene may be in a high-traffic area. Every moment, every movement of pedestrian or vehicle traffic, can obscure or eliminate evidence before the first responders can even arrive at the scene.

An outside sexual assault scene may be difficult to find, if the terrorized victim is confused as to where the attack occurred, and difficult to process because rain, snow, animal activity may obliterate fragile DNA evidence, or move trace evidence. In all these cases, crime scene processing and interpretation can be slowed down and even crippled by outside circumstances.

Bodies discovered long after the crime—victims dumped from vehicles into ditches or woods next to the highway, victims buried in clandestine graves, sometimes dug deep in a forest or a cornfield, sometimes placed right in the murderer's backyard—present investigators with a different set of challenges. The site may be stumbled upon, discovered from a scrap of information or intuition, pointed out by an informant or suspect who has confessed, or excavated like an archeological dig. However the body is found, these kinds of outdoor scenes call for intense collaboration, at the scene and after, between evidence technicians, forensic specialists like forensic archeologists and anthropologists, and homicide detectives.

Outside scenes often point to more scenes—where the body is discovered or the sexual assault has occurred may be the terminus point for other scenes, all of which must be discovered and processed. This chapter presents the experiences of cops, detectives, and forensic specialists called to outside scenes, ranging from street crimes through crimes discovered in the wild, starting with responding officers' and detectives' takes on the chaos of scenes committed on public streets.

Everybody always talks about how a crime scene *looks*. But when you're a police officer, there's also how a crime scene *sounds*.

Say a drug murder goes down in the street. Or it's a gangbanger shooting, a drive-by. There's a wailing. There's like a death wail. There'll be women wailing at the crime scene. Girlfriends and mothers. There's just like a wail. A high-pitched female wail. Waaaaaaa! Just a wailing noise.

Women are collapsing. The grandmother arrives and she's collapsing, her knees are buckling, and she's wailing. Girlfriends are just—out of control. Women's knees are buckling; they're hitting the ground. And the others are walking over them to see the body.

The whole neighborhood pours out, onto the crime scene, and word travels really fast. And before you know it, the person who was the closest to the victim knows what has happened. And probably knows who did it.

They all arrive. And then, all of a sudden, they turn all

this aggression on the police. And everybody's yelling at the *police*. *We* didn't shoot the guy . . . but everybody's mad at *us*.

Everybody is just yelling at the police because they want us to—do *something*. We *are* doing something, but they don't understand. Their perception is "Catch this guy!" We're protecting the crime scene. They don't understand.

We've had many instances where there are "Officer Needs Assistance" calls at crime scenes. People are beating up the police trying to get close to the crime scene.

PATROL OFFICER

You have scenes where you're waiting for the crime lab to arrive and the family—they're going "Ooh-la, ooh-la," they're going nuts. And they're like, "Why are you leavin' him like that? *Why?* Blah, blah." Well, we're waiting for them to come and take photographs and process the scene. The dramatics and the antics they do. And, then, granted, they may be grieving. And they're not thinking what you're thinking.

HOMICIDE DETECTIVE

Sometimes we come upon guys that *aren't* dead. They've been shot; they've been stabbed. They're not dead yet.

We don't stand around and give them their space 'cause they're dying. That's not our job. No way. You want to talk to them as quick as you can. For two reasons: one, they might die. And two, once they realize they're gonna live, they don't *want* to talk to you. You gotta get them in transition, before their birth certificate expires.

HOMICIDE DETECTIVE

I'll be in the ambulance, this gangbanger's been shot in a drive- by, and I've got him by the shoulders, and I'm shakin' him— "Who *did* this? What *car* is he driving?"—and he's screaming, the paramedics are trying to tube him, and I'm tryin' to get the words out of his mouth because then I can get the information out on the radio. And this guy's bleedin' all over, and screamin', and you know, you're like, "Who *did* this?" And he goes, "It was the gray Bonneville," or what have you, and then you can get the information out over the radio.

Most people are like, "You're crazy." But if he dies and doesn't tell me, no one's gonna know. Pumping the victim for information is very important. *If* you can get him to talk. Usually there's a woman around yelling, "Tell him! Tell him!" and he's trying to be all macho. Of course, if he's *really* in pain, I might just go, "Was it such and such a car?" You know, ease up a little.

PATROL OFFICER

A crime scene in the street—it's chaos. People try to walk through the crime scene. People are like— They'll look at you: "Can I get through here? My house is right there." And there's yellow tape all over the place and like a zillion cops around. "Can you just walk on the other side of the street? Is that asking too much?"

Certain neighborhoods, you see yellow tape all the time. They're used to people being shot. A guy's lying on the ground. Another guy walks past and goes, "Oh, that's so-and-so." And they keep walking. "Whoa! You *know* this guy?" "Yeah, that's Pooky." "How do you know him?" The guy keeps walking. Then you're trying to grab this guy; he's walking; he doesn't even care. He's like "Ahhhh, I got business to do."

PATROL OFFICER

Many times, when the first responders get to the scene, the of-fender is *in* the crowd, watching the activities, almost like entertainment. Some of these folks who have perpetrated the crime are drunk, or disorderly, or on drugs, and they end up doing something obnoxious.

And the first officer, basically, tells the guy what he's gonna do to him if he doesn't get outta there and he ends up chasing the guy away. They could be getting rid of a witness or the perp himself.

It's unbelievable how many times this happens. That's how I came up with the idea of taking photographs of the crowd. What happens, usually, the perpetrators and/or folks of interest, meaning people that you've had dealings with before, they have no problem hanging out when the cops and the ambulance crew is there, and the fire department, and everybody's running around, they think this is kinda great. When the suits arrive at the scene, these people suddenly get into the wind real quick.

I train my people: Whenever you get out of a car, you take the big picture. You don't focus on the little picture; you take the big picture. Check out the crowd. See who's there. You might see some of your former clients, okay? Just give them like a little nod of the head. That means, "I'll be talking to you. Not here in front of everybody, because I know you can't talk to me in front of everybody, but you will be getting a call."

Bad guys—drug dealers, gangbangers—tend to know shit. And they hate to be seen by the suits because that means they're gonna have a bad day. If you're a smart detective, you never try to interview these people in the street in front of their friends. You want to get them on *your* territory, by themselves, and say, "Okay, what the fuck went down over there?"

HOMICIDE COMMANDER

I had a great Homicide commander who never missed *anything*. I'd get to a scene and I'd ask where he was. Nobody knew. He'd be just walking around, checking things out. He never missed a thing.

He'd just walk around. One day, we were called to a murder in the street. And the Homicide commander walked away from the scene, about a block away. And there's an officer standing there and my commander's talking to him and he looks down and he says, "Have you checked over this area pretty good?" And the guy says, "Yeah." The commander stands there, staring at the officer's feet. The officer says, "What are you looking at?" And the commander says, "Well, there's a *gun* in that sewer right below your feet down there." And it was the murder weapon. The offender had just thrown it into the sewer.

HOMICIDE DETECTIVE

It's a much greater challenge if the victim has been shot outside. Bullets have a tendency to pass through the body. They become very difficult to find outside. If you can establish the line of flight, and precisely track along that line, you can sometimes find impact points through leaves and twigs and brush.

We use metal detectors to help locate cartridge cases and shotgun cases outdoors. We also use metal detectors to find bullets that are embedded in the ground. On every outdoor scene, you use a metal detector to see if the body was shot while lying on the ground, and the bullet passed through, into the ground.

FIREARMS SPECIALIST

This happens a lot with street crimes, like with gangbangers. You see them die. To actually see somebody die is an odd thing. I mean, I can see the moment when they die. I remember a gunshot wound, the guy's bleeding, he's curled up in a fetal position, he's puking up, and he's bleeding from the stomach. So the stomach fluid and the blood are mixing together, almost like the yin and yang of sweet-and-sour sauce, you know like the mustard and the red sauce, they put it in a dish and make that little swirl? You know? That's what it reminded me of. The pink vomit and the blood coming from the stomach. And you're thinking, this guy's in bad shape. This guy's not gonna make it.

And then you watch 'em, and after a while, that's it. They're gone.

HOMICIDE DETECTIVE

The thing that *is* for sure is the finality of it. When you're stand-ing there and looking down at some . . . what used to be a human being, and you think, "Gosh. What could he have done, or what could she have done?" Because a lot of them are really good people, obviously, that are killed.

Even the gang members. I look down at them. Their mothers are over there behind the tape, telling me, "You know, he was such a good little boy in Sunday School!" And I can look at them and say, "You know, I'm sure he was, but look what he became." I'm looking down at this guy and I think, "You know, I was looking for this guy last week for a similar murder. Now I'm looking *at* him." The violence just kind of perpetuates itself.

HOMICIDE DETECTIVE

We kid among ourselves that when we go out on call, some-where out there, someone is circling the drain that has no clue that we're going to be looking down at them in a couple hours. Homicide humor.

HOMICIDE DETECTIVE

Stranger-to-Stranger Street Crimes

You'll get a prostitute that's been killed and set on fire in an alley. Unfortunately, that's almost like a spectator sport here in Los Angeles and other big cities. You find a body in this alley, and as you do your search, you may find twenty-five condoms, be-cause this is where the girls go to trick. Okay, pick the right one. Or in your typical alley, think of how much junk is there.

How much do you have to pick up? Everything you pick up has to be analyzed, which backs up your crime lab even more.

HOMICIDE DETECTIVE

You can have several crime scenes for one crime. Some years ago, an off-duty detective was waiting in a drive-through at a bank. And he observes a guy walking into the bank lot with a ski mask on. At the same time, a uniformed police officer is driving by and observes the same thing. The guy with the ski mask sticks up an armored car delivery guy right in the lot. Takes the bag of money that the guy was delivering to the bank and starts to go down the alley, running to where the getaway car is waiting.

The off-duty detective gets out of his car, goes around to the next block, confronts the robber, announces his office, and is shot. The uniformed officer closes down the alley and he has an exchange of gun shots with the offenders in the getaway car.

During the shooting, the offender is shot in the hand. He drops the bag of money at the scene. The car now speeds away, and there's a flash message put out for the car. The car is spotted by a squad car several miles away.

The offenders now turn down a side street and they see what they think is an unmarked squad car coming toward them. The offenders were two brothers. The one brother stands up through the sunroof with a shotgun and starts shooting at what he believes is an unmarked police car. It's not. It's just some poor citizen who happens to have a Chevrolet that *looks* like a squad car. Can you imagine driving down a side street, and next thing your window's exploding with shotgun pellets?

The driver of the Chevy loses control and crashes into a building. The getaway car now backs up across the street and crashes into some more cars. At that point, police officers arrive on the scene and place them under arrest.

Everywhere there was gunfire and everywhere there was

some kind of crash was a crime scene. So we had about eight crime scenes that had to be processed stemming from just that one robbery.

POLICE CHIEF

Robberies, in a lot of ways, are harder to solve than homicides. I'm a regular detective, which means I do everything from homicides to missing persons to stupid threatening phone calls. In busier precincts like mine, you start out doing Robbery. And they're more difficult investigations because— Most homicides, there's some relationship, there's some acquaintance between the perp and the victim. Robbery is between strangers.

In a robbery, very often there's nothing for the lab. DNA evidence is very, very rarely going to be of use to you.

What you have is, Did the victim see the perp? If the victim didn't see them, and nobody else did, and there's not a camera on the street, then your options are traceable items, like credit cards and cell phones, or looking at patterns: Does it tend to happen late at night? Is the physical description of the perp similar over time to the one last Tuesday, to the one last Wednesday? Is he left-handed? Does he say something in particular each time, aside from "Run, you shit," or "Don't look at me"? Anything singular that might stand out.

Is there video? That's a new aid for us. And cell phones. We tell people not to turn off their cell phones because often the perp will flip open the stolen cell and make a few calls. you know, call home, call a friend. Sometimes they take the cell phone so their victim won't be able to call the cops. But with the younger and dumber criminal, Hey, it's a free call to make. Believe me, we've gotten people this way.

ROBBERY DETECTIVE

With robbery victims, if they make an ID through the mug shots, if somebody picks someone out and says, "I really think that's him. I'd have to see him in person, though," then you've got your probable cause to take him in for a lineup. You scoop him up and they view the lineup.

It still can be very frustrating for everyone concerned. You take people behind the one-way mirror and make them look. A lot of times they're almost like trying to jump back from the window, they're so afraid of the guy who robbed them seeing them. "Step right up. Step right up. Come on, look through the window. They can't see you, they can't hear you. Don't worry." As if the guy is going to jump through the window and rob them again.

"Look slowly at every face." They'll look at number one— look at number two—and if the guy is number three, their heads will practically spin off their necks to avoid looking at number three. You know that they know it. They'll say, "No. I don't recognize anybody." Just because they're afraid. They're reliving the crime by seeing this person.

You want to talk to them more. But you can't put words in their mouth. They're the one who has to say, "That's the guy who robbed me." If they say, "That's the guy who the detective told me to pick," well, you know, everybody's got a little problem on their hands then.

VIOLENT CRIMES DETECTIVE

We've had a number of kids killed in the LA area over the past few years by total strangers at flier parties. This is a relatively new thing.

People set up these parties for a living. They rent out houses, they hire a deejay, get some music, get booze, and they put fliers out in the neighborhood, or in schools. They charge kids ten bucks, twenty bucks to get in.

Kids find these fliers. They go to the door— It's not like you go to a party and it's like, Oh, yeah, I know who's going to be there, because you *don't* know. It's like going to a stadium or to a concert: you don't know *who's* gonna show up.

So you go to this party. You're there with your friends, maybe. But then all these other people are in there, and you may or may not know them. You're not gonna be disturbed if you see people you don't know because of how everyone was invited. The *world* was invited, basically.

These parties do attract gang members. They attract good kids *and* gang members. That's the problem. The gang members are typically bullies. And they carry guns, unfortunately. And these other kids that are there—it's like they're totally unequipped to deal with this type of person.

And then, all of a sudden, the wrong thing is said and the gang members pull their guns. Maybe they're shooting at someone from a rival gang that showed up, or they see somebody there that they think is an acquaintance of somebody from a rival gang, and they'll pull a gun out and shoot them. And then, of course, when the random gunfire goes off, anyone is likely to be hit, and it's usually some innocent kid that has no ties with gangs, who just happened to be there, and forevermore, his family's devastated and wondering, "Why did we let him go to that stupid party?"

The whole thing is, we get called in. You've got a house full of people, so a lot of times, it's spilled out into the backyard. You've got a backyard full of empty beer cans, there's booze laying around, there's a disc jockey's equipment sitting there, there may be two or three people still there, the rest of them have fled, they don't want to be there, they don't want to be part of it, they don't want their parents to know they were there.

So all the witnesses who were there are no longer available to you. You ask the people running the party to give you a list of the people who were there. Good luck! They don't know who they were, and if they do, quite frankly, they're not going to cooperate with you a lot of times.

And the two or three people who are left will say, "Hey, these guys came in and everything was going great and all of a sudden, they started asking what gang we're from and we're not from any gang and one guy pulled a gun and just started firing into the crowd and I thought everybody was fine and then I looked over and my best friend was lying there. And he's dead." Or she's dead.

You're as likely to have a female victim as a male victim here. Bullets don't know the difference. They go wherever they're shot. Somebody's diving to get out of the way and they may dive right into where that bullet's being shot. May not have been intended for that person, but that's the way it goes.

We get there and there's a body, maybe there's a couple of bodies, lying around, and there's blood throughout the place. Everybody's gone and we're there an hour or so after the event has occurred. The patrol guys got there right away, and they tell you they were able to scoop up a couple people, but everybody else has fled. So you talk to them, you get a description if you can, if they want to cooperate; some of them are afraid to. You may not get anything.

Basically, what you're left with is whatever physical evidence is there. And I'm talking about the round that is taken from the body of the victim. You take that, and you hold onto that precious evidence, because that's all you have, and then down the line, you know, you arrest a gangster for another shooting and you take his gun. You check it through Firearms and it's the same gun. And that may be the way you're going to solve that crime. Short of that, you may never solve that crime.

A drive-by shooting can be a lot easier to solve than a flier party.

HOMICIDE COMMANDER

Advice on Catching Burglars on the Street

One thing I tell police frequently is this: If you get a call of somebody breaking into a house, and you see somebody walking down the street as you pull up, as you question him, ask to see the cuffs on his pants. If he's climbed through a hedge or walked through a yard—most people have weeds around. Weeds get around in lots of clever ways; they often have little sticky parts that stick to your shoes, or your shoelaces, or your pants cuffs, or they land *in* a pants cuff. If the suspects says, "Oh, I got those in my grandmother's yard," those particular weeds may not be there. So we've hooked people to certain sites through what kind of weeds have gotten stuck to them.

Almost no one can lie about plant evidence.

FORENSIC BOTANIST

Mobile Crime Scenes

Everybody thinks a crime scene is the old chalk outline of a body. You may have several scenes: primary, secondary. Rape victims are crime scenes. If a woman is raped in an apartment, the apartment is a crime scene. So is the victim. Say the rape victim gets in a car to drive to the hospital. *That* is a scene.

So, you've got to define "crime scene." A crime scene can be any location that *may,* and the operative word is "may," contain evidence of a crime. Sounds stupid, but it is.

So, if a woman is raped in her bedroom, then she gets up. She goes to the bathroom and she brushes her teeth and takes a shower. Then she gets in the car and drives herself to the Rape Crisis Center. And they take her to the hospital.

You've got the bedroom, you've got the bathroom, you've got the bathtub, you've got the drain in the sink, you've got her car, her car seat, and then, perhaps, even the bathroom or chair at the Crisis Center. And then, of course, at the hospital— You know, when they do the internal exam and things like that.

The woman's body is a scene. When I teach that, it's with all respect to the victim. I'm not saying you have to be less delicate or anything, but you need to get what you need to get. And the victim's a scene.

You've gotta learn to think that way.

POLICE CHIEF

Scenes can be mobile. Say you've got somebody murdered in one place and then transported in the trunk of a car and then dumped someplace else. Wherever evidence is left— that's a crime scene.

HOMICIDE SCENE SUPERVISOR

I used to work in the bloodhound tracking unit. Say there was a robbery or a burglary, they'd call us out and we'd track the suspect. You know, as people walk around, skin cells and hairs and fibers, all kind of junk, are falling off our bodies. The dog's nose is sensitive enough so that he can pick up the scent of a person and follow it. It's not like you find a stocking mask at the scene, you stick it in the dog's nose and the dog will go right to the guy.

But if you can get tracks at a scene—I'll give the dog a command as he's smelling the tracks and he knows that the smell he's smelling at that moment is the one he's supposed to be tracking. So he follows that scent as far as he can. The dog is a tool.

There's different types of tracks. A person moving through a wooded area will actually take the vegetation and flip it over. So if you shine a flashlight at night, you'll actually see where he went. I've had cases where a guy will jump out of a stolen car, say, and we'll follow him into the woods.

A man broke in on a lady and he stabbed her to death, robbed her. Very bloody scene. They called the bloodhounds out. There were a lot of trees and vegetation around the house. We picked up on a scent and found where the man dropped the knife that he used to kill the woman with, along with some money and other evidence. These probably would not have been found without the bloodhounds because police officers being police officers, they're in their nice, neat uniforms, and don't like to go crawl around in the briar patches and stuff like that.

CRIME SCENE TEAM MEMBER

On the average, in a metropolitan area, people are on video about eight times a day. Banks. ATM machines. Freeways. Security cameras outside and inside buildings. Mass transit. So now, when we go to a scene, we're looking for video—not only at the scene of the crime, but from where the suspect may have departed and fled, and also to see how he approached.

Vancouver PD had a case where a guy was being followed and murdered. They pulled video of all his activities for several days and they'd see the same suspect following this guy.

My partner and I had a case recently—it was a young couple, just started dating. They went to the beach, Venice Beach. He told her, "Hey, I went to a casino last night and won some money. Want to go?" "I've never been to one. Sure." They went to a casino in Englewood, near LAX.

They were followed home, some forty miles away. When they stopped to get gas in their truck, these guys robbed them. Our male victim resisted and was shot to death.

We were able to pull video from the casino, where you actually see the two suspects following them around the casino, standing at the same table they were standing at, following them out to the parking lot. And then by pulling video where they got off the freeway going toward home, we got two different videos: a Burger King had video of the victim's truck going by, followed by the suspects' car. A few minutes later, suspects' car is seen going in the opposite direction. At the service station where the victim was shot, we had video of him and the suspects in the store together. So that's what we're looking for all the time now.

HOMICIDE DETECTIVE

Our task force had a case where we had to find a burial site in another state based on some photographs of the victim and the suspect.

The Russian to Judgment Case. The murderer was a guy named Igor, from Kiev. The victim was a Polish immigrant called Tomas, a roofing contractor. His brother reported him missing. The previous Friday, some employees overheard an argument Tomas was having over his cell phone about a loan with a guy named Igor. He told the guy he'd never do work with him again and he'd need his money back right away. Then, according to the employees, he left to get the money. Friday he disappears and leaves two crews out on the streets working. A friend of his who had just come over from Poland was staying with him. When Tomas didn't come back, he had no way to get home. And the crews didn't get paid; they always got paid on Friday.

That weekend, Tomas's truck was found in a Builders Square parking lot about three blocks away from this body shop where he went to see Igor. A ticket was on the windshield. The cab was locked. The side boxes, with all his tools, were unlocked. His checkbook, his stock quotation machine, and a bag of toiletries were all inside.

On Tuesday, I listened to the brother of the friend—the friend didn't speak any English—tell the story, and we started investigating. I just knew that this guy didn't go to Vegas in his work clothes Friday night. Something happened to him.

I took five of my detectives to the body shop that Igor ran. Walked in, introduced myself, you know, "Hi. How are you?" There was the owner, Igor, a Russian from the Ukraine, from Kiev. I didn't like him immediately, just something about him. I asked him if he'd heard from Tomas. He said, "No, I don't even know who this guy is."

Well, on the bulletin board he's got a picture of our victim and himself when they were on a diving trip to the Caribbean the previous October. Then he plays it—"Oh, yeah, I know who he is. Yeah, he was here Friday. He stopped in. We talked a little bit about diving. We talked a little bit about a car I have that's for sale; he wanted to buy it."

So I said, "Is it okay if I look around?" I was with five detectives. He says, "Sure, go look around." So, I go back to my old dope days and I go right to the garbage can they have at the back. I start pulling the garbage out, and about half way down, I find a Thursday, May 14, 1988, *Chicago Tribune* Sports Section. I pull it out and open it up and here are two shop towels with what appears to be blood on them. It looked like somebody wiped their hands on them.

I put it down. I went and found Igor and said, "Anybody get hurt here? Any reason there would be blood?" He said, "No. No reason."

So we called some of our ETs to come out. While we were waiting, I went out behind the place. There was a gravel apron between the back door and the alley. I start looking around and I find a small-caliber shell case in the gravel. One of my other detectives came out; he found two more. So what have we got? The town the body shop was in wanted nothing to do with it. Four days before we ended up finding the body, the chief said, "This is BS. There's been no murder. The guy's missing."

So we got the task force for the region activated. The first thing we did was request everybody's phone records. We brought Igor and all his employees into the police department that first night, but they lawyered up. They didn't say a whole hell of a lot.

Our forensic guy took about thirty photos he found in the body shop. Those turned out to be key. They depicted some kind of trip up north with Igor, his wife, Tomas and his girlfriend, the friend from Kiev who was visiting Tomas, and the friend's girlfriend. And they're sitting next to some kind of a river in the North Woods. In the initial interview, Igor said it was Iron River, Wisconsin, which doesn't exist. And then Igor stopped talking.

So we do a quick victimology. We find out that in 1996, Tomas was sued for paternity. He got his girlfriend pregnant, she had a baby; she wanted child support. They did DNA for a paternity test. The DNA lab still had Tomas's DNA on file. We took the shop towels, with the DNA, and compared it, and lo and behold, it's Tomas.

When we got the phone records back, we checked Igor's alibi. He said on Saturday, May 16, he was in Buffalo Grove, Arlington Heights; he went into Chicago, then went back to Buffalo Grove. But in actuality— We followed the cell phone records by towers, and he's gone about eleven hours for the day, and the area code showed he was up in the Upper Peninsula of Michigan. There was about a two-and-a-half-hour dead period, and I mean *dead,* where we believe he was burying the body. And then he came back to Buffalo Grove.

We charted the phone records all out, from when he got on the highway all the way up. If you do the math, if you deduce from the time it would take to drive a certain distance, he appeared to be driving at or near the speed limit going up. You know, those towers, they fix you within a two-mile radius. Going up, he's doing the speed limit. Coming back, he's *haulin' ass;* he's goin' *way* over the speed limit. What does that tell you? He doesn't want to get stopped by the police going up. Because he's got the body in the back of the truck.

So I take eight detectives with the photographs; I take an FBI agent I know in Green Bay, and we go up to try to find the site. In one of the pictures, there's a bunch of them on a river; it turns out to be the Menominee River. On the west side is Wisconsin; on the east is the Upper Peninsula. They're standing on a rock outcropping and you can see a bridge to the north. So we showed the pictures to a detective sergeant from the Marinette, Wisconsin, Sheriff's Department. This guy's a deer hunter. He says, "Gee, that looks like the bridge running over County Road Z, about sixty miles from here."

We went up there and got out of the cars on the bridge. We looked to the south and we could see the rock outcropping where they were standing when they took the picture.

We spent four days there looking for the body. We had eight cadaver dogs, six horses. It was state forest right along the river. It was about ninety-three degrees out, hot, humid—it rained just enough every day to get you soaked through. They had Lyme disease ticks all over. We had bought flea collars for dogs and put them around our ankles, which the locals got a big yuck out of.

The search was four days. Based on the photos, we found all of their garbage—a Coke can, a vodka bottle, it was all there. But no body. The scariest thing was, one of my detectives on the first night said, "Lieutenant, I was out walking on this dirt track and I felt the hairs on the back of my neck stand up." It turned out later he had walked over Tomas's grave.

Five months to the day of the disappearance, I'm sitting in my office and I get a call from a detective sergeant with the Michigan State Police. He said, "I think we found your guy." What happened was a state trooper and the post janitor were out and the trooper said, "Do you wanna go look where those Chicago guys were lookin' for the body?" And the janitor said sure. It was about eighty degrees. They didn't want to go back to work, I'm certain.

They ride over to the spot. Keep in mind the photos that we had—there was no foliage growing up. When we were there, it was all up to our hips. These guys are out in October; the foliage is all down again. The janitor's a deer hunter and he sees some fresh animal digging. They get two shovels, they drive back, they start digging, and they expose his head. Right exactly where the photo showed they'd been picnicking. The rest of Tomas followed. That, and all the evidence we found around the body shop, were enough to convict Igor of first-degree murder.

CRIME SCENE COORDINATOR

Crimes of Passion Discovered Outside

We got a call that a construction worker was just found, with his head half cut off. They send us evidence techs out. So we get there—and the paramedics come running in. This guy almost got his *head* cut off and they're gonna try to do CPR on him. They're gonna save *another* one. They put a tourniquet around his neck and they all start doin' CPR. Then they start to throw *their* debris all over and they've moved things around the crime scene. So, then, when the paramedics realize there's nothin' going on, they get out.

Anyway, we start documenting the scene. Here's this white male lying in a prone position and he's got some severe incised wounds on top of his shoulders and on part of his neck. And there is a seven-and-a-half-inch circular saw setting off to the side and it's in a little bit of blood. And there is a drill with a one-inch paddle bit lying nearby. There's also miscellaneous tools around. This is on a construction site. The murdered guy had been working pretty much by himself and he had an apprentice.

You have to start somewhere in the investigation. So I go in there, I start looking: "Wait a minute. These tools have definitely been used on this body." I can see where there's a couple of holes in the guy's neck and back from the paddle bit, and I can see where the circular saw had been used on the neck and across the back. And what had happened was, the circular saw had gotten bound up in the guy's shirt and sweatshirt. I can see there's some kind of mark in the middle of this guy's back, so you gotta photograph this thing all round.

On this particular case, the investigators are talking to the murdered guy's foreman. And the foreman said this guy worked with somebody, an apprentice. The investigative team goes over to talk to this guy. They start talking to him and things aren't looking right. They look down, and here his work boots, over in the corner, have got red stains across the toes of them.

You go into a crime scene, after a period of time, you have to back out and take a breather. If you're gonna keep your thoughts together and see what's going on—your attention is only so long. My partner and I backed out and were talking it over. We got back to headquarters—"Have the investigators found anything?" "Guess what? We need you to go over to this guy. His boots have got red stains on them." Okayyyy.

So we go over to the apprentice guy's apartment after we got a "consent to search" from the guy and his girlfriend, who was also living there. I start going through the place. I open up a drawer, and here's a pair of jeans he was wearing the day before. And across the right thigh of the jeans there's like a pour pattern of blood. I said, "Now this is real interesting. What is this?" So, it's a call back to the boys: "Hey, guys, does this guy have any cuts on him? I got these jeans and it looks like a pour pattern." "Nah, this guy's as healthy as an ox."

So we go back to the scene. We start to talk to this guy and he's not goin' for anything. I told the captain we needed a blood spatter expert here because the apprentice had legitimate access to the crime scene. He could say he came upon the body and panicked or he checked the guy for signs, moved him or whatever, and got blood on himself that way. So we had to establish whose blood it was. We had to use DNA.

All these different disciplines are starting to come into play. We finally moved the body. We ended up bringing in a blood spatter guy the next day. He has a vanity plate that says BLOODY 1. Kind of a warped sense of humor.

When they did the autopsy, we saw how things were. The victim had some deep cuts with a circular saw. There were two holes—one in his neck and one in his back. Apparently, what happened was the guy was trying to cut and dismember the body. But in doing so with the power saw, when he went to cut too low, the shirt and sweatshirt got all bound up on the blade and he couldn't do it. So he broke it free. He went over and got the next power tool he could find, which was a drill with a one-inch power bit. He drills once into the neck. It goes in, about halfway through. He reverses the drill, pulls it back out and then forgetting it's in reverse, he tries to drill a second hole, except it wasn't taking.

And the victim's got a mark in the middle of his back. We find out that this guy's vertebrae had also been injured from a heavy blow. Sure enough, you go back to the crime scene photos and lying right near by was this big twenty-pound sledgehammer. Oh, yeah.

The problem we're facing, though, is, you figure with a circular saw going at high speed, where's all the blood going? Why don't we have more blood all over our suspect? Why don't we have more blood all over the scene?

The blood spatter guy starts talking to some of the guys he knows in building trades. He finds out, what a lotta guys do is they remove the spring off the blade guard. It's like a shield that goes across the blade so that when you're cutting, it lifts up and allows the cut and as soon as you take it out of the material, the guard comes over and covers the blade so you don't inadvertently cut yourself. What ended up happening—This blade guard also serves to direct the material that's being cut and it's throwing it away from the saw. So there's no blood spatter when it comes back on him. The bad thing is it's going through the blade guard.

I took fifteen, sixteen rolls of thirty-six-exposure film, between the crime scene and the boots and the spatter marks and the tools. I transported everything back to our office where the guy was in the interview rooms. The investigators are talking to the guy. He's not goin' for anything. Finally, they say to me, "Bring those pants in here, will ya?" They said to him, "What is this? How did this get here?" And his answer was his girlfriend was having her period. That was his comment.

As we got into the investigation, it turned out the incident occurred on payday. The suspect had been docked for hours where he had quit early. The guy thought he should be paid more.

He went back to the site. While he was talking to the guy who was training him, he took the sledgehammer, hit him in the middle of the back, making the guy sink to his knees. He hit him a second time, putting him down and rendering him semiconscious. And as he was going through the victim's pockets and turning them inside out and taking his paycheck which had just been cashed—the guy started coming to. And he hit him again, and while he was still alive, he used the saw on him.

The DNA report came back and said the blood on the pants, the blood on the shoes, were all from our victim. The apprentice called us a couple times while we were waiting for the results to come back from the laboratory. He wanted to know when he could have his boots back.

So the night the results came in, the investigators found him on an outdoor basketball court and said, "Hey! Your boots are over here!" And then they arrested him.

We made notification to the victim's family. This guy left a wife and two young kids. We explained that we had made an arrest. When the wife asked who did it, we told her it was the apprentice. You know what she told us? That we made a mistake, there's no way he would have done this because he'd been to the house for dinner on several occasions. And it wasn't till the end of the trial she finally believed it.

You know how cops give their cases nicknames? First thing one of our dicks said when he got to the scene was,

"You know who did this? Tim Allen." We called this one the "Tool Time Case," after the TV show.

EVIDENCE TECHNICIAN

We had one we called the "Ice Man." We also called it Brown, Brown, and Brown on Brown Street. Mr. Brown was separated from his estranged wife. He was seeing another woman. Mrs. Brown still lived in the house on Brown Street—really— and was extremely ticked off about the whole situation. Mr. Brown had an old Cadillac and he had had some repairs done by a young man, also by the name of Brown.

We get a call to go out by an old country club. A guy was out walking his dog and the dog came across the body.

It's all dirt roads out there. We had snow the week before and it's February. So, not only was the ice and snow melting, but this road, which was gravel, is all mud. Oh, yeah.

And, of course, we're in our detective getups, jacket and tie. We get out and we're stuck up to our ankles in the mud.

We start taking pictures and start looking at it. Here is a black male, elderly black male, lying off the side of the road in this rural area. And he is frozen stiff. I mean, he is rock solid. And he's naked, except for a pair of jockey shorts. We're thinking it might be hypothermia. One of the things with hypothermia—at some point in time, victims may take off their clothes and throw them away. They think they're warm.

We try to recover the body. We can't. The body's frozen to the ground. And the substrate that he's stuck to is frozen down about a good ten inches.

We're trying to figure how we're gonna get this guy outta there. We go over, we have like a small hatchet, we figure we'll break the ground down around him and we'll bring him up. Unh-unh. It ain't breakin'. It's frozen solid.

Okay. What else have we got? Maybe we can take an ice pick—we use it for different things—and break around it. We start trying to break around; we're breakin' the ground a little bit here and a little bit there. I've been going at it for a while. My partner comes over. He's new; he's been training with us for about a week.

He takes the ice pick and he starts going. All of a sudden I hear, "Oh, shit!"

Well, that's a *clue.* Anytime you hear that, that's a clue.

I turn around and look. And here the ice pick is sticking out of the shoulder of our stiff.

He had missed on a swing with the ice pick, or somebody had said something to him or something, and he hit this guy square in the shoulder. And it's like, "What do I do?" I said, "Pull the damn thing out!" So we put it in the notes and moved on.

We're still stuck with the situation: How do we get this guy up off the ground? And we have an interim medical examiner who's about a two-hour drive away. And there's no way they're coming down. The brass comes over and says, "Well, what do you think we oughta do?" I said, "Wait for a spring thaw."

Okay. I go back to the crime scene van we got. I go in there, I pull out a crowbar. And I bring out a big mallet. I figure I'll drive this thing in, I'll break the ground around him. I do this once, twice, and I figure, okay, it's broken around him a little bit. Let's see if I can pry and break it loose. I bent the crowbar. The guy's frozen big time.

The stuff we gotta do—it gets nuts. And, of course, all the guys are breaking up, laughing like crazy. Cops. And we've got a team going off. Another couple guys are coming on. And my partner and I have each put out about forty bucks for a retirement dinner that evening that we're obviously not going to go to. And now it's getting dark. So now we're working in the dark. But then, again, we're used to working in the dark.

We finally ended up getting things broken enough so we could get him up. We took up about six inches worth of ground underneath of him—with him. This is Friday. This guy wasn't thawed enough for autopsy till Monday.

We still don't know who he is. We run his prints and we come up with the fact that this is Mr. Brown. What's that mean? It's time for us to go back out and do more field searches.

So we get a day of sunshine and fresh air, you know, going through all the scrub brush and everything else. We can't find this guy's clothes. That doesn't add up. How did he get here? He was wearing a pair of jockey shorts, so obviously he wasn't out here jogging and just sort of keeled over. So we got more questions to answer.

We bring in the family. Maybe they have something to give us. This was Tuesday afternoon. It turned out that Mr. and Mrs. Brown had a developmentally disabled daughter in her late teens. And a lotta times the victim is known by the suspect. So the mother is in being interviewed by a couple guys.

We're getting nowhere with her. Then, while we're out there, this daughter says, "I saw the man beat Daddy up." Hello? "Well, how did you see that? Where did that happen?"

And she says, "I was out in front of the house. The man beat Daddy up. Mommy was watching."

We start looking around. Across the street from the house, where the girl said the man had parked the car, we find the victim's wallet. Where the fight took place, in the front yard of the house, we find the victim's glasses. Now we're looking for the car.

What ends up happening is, the guy comes forward who had the fight with the victim. He finally rolls over, you know, flips, and gives up the victim's wife. He explained that the wife was angry. And this guy was *also* mad because the husband owed him money for car repairs and had been jerking him around. The wife knew this. She called him up and said, "Would you come over when I tell you to? I'll tell him to come over here and you can come over and you can kick his ass."

He did. He came over with a friend. She said, "Look. We're gonna teach him a lesson. We're gonna make him walk home. Drive him in his car over there and I'll follow you in my car and bring you home."

They beat him up, drove him out there in his own car. The wife's told them, "Take the car and you can sell the parts." They then beat him unconscious. She drives them back. Then she goes back out to where the guy is lying unconscious and she takes off his clothes. And she *leaves* him out there. He died from exposure.

About a year later, this comes to trial. The wife still ain't goin' for nothin'. She figures that with the retarded daughter, nobody's gonna do anything to her. Well, she got slam-dunked. She got thirty years.

Cops being cops—we go in to testify. Everybody's outside the courtroom, waiting their turn to go in. They called in one of the investigators. He came out. He looks at our guy Tommy—the one who had hit the body with the ice pick— he looks at Tom and says, "Tom, I tried to protect you, but I couldn't do it." Tom says, "What do you mean?" He says, "That ice pick. I had to tell them." We'd been bustin' Tommy's chops for almost a year. We called him. "Tommy the Ice Pick."

So Tommy's gotta go in the courtroom now. He goes in there and he is waiting the whole time—he's trying to figure out how he's gonna answer this question if he's asked it, especially under cross-examination. What are you gonna say? The defense attorney might end up saying that ice pick blow was the cause of death. So he's sweatin' it out.

He gets off the stand. He comes out to the corridor and he says, "Thank God!" And all of us are laughin'. We're dyin'. He's been set up. There's no way his goof with the ice pick was ever gonna come out, but we got him. Cop humor.

EVIDENCE TECHNICIAN

Finding Bodies and Evidence

Outside crime scenes can be more difficult than inside scenes.
They're so subject to environmental changes. You know, all
of a sudden, you've got a thunderstorm and your body's
floating down the street. You have a guy killed and dumped
on a golf course and you're out there investigating, and at
four in the morning, the sprinklers come on. If you have a
scene on a freeway, you've got to close the freeway down.
The entire city is now a victim of that crime.

We've had crime scenes in the desert. There was one victim that was dumped in a locker. And, as we made the approach, we found out that this locker had been taken over by
a nest of Mojave green rattlesnakes, which are among the
more aggressive rattlesnakes in the West. We had to deal with
them first.

HOMICIDE DETECTIVE

Sometimes you can't find the body. You know there was a crime,
but where's the body?

So you *train* for finding bodies. How do you get the
money and the time to learn this stuff? Sometimes, you have
to do it on your own.

I mean, there were a bunch of us evidence techs. We did our
own Clandestine Grave course. We had one guy that had some
training, he had been a medical examiner's investigator. What
we did was take road-kill deer— You put out an order to the
Road Department. "Hey, guys, got anything, give us a call."

So the road guys would pick the body of the deer up and
drop it off. Then we'd get some old clothes and things and
dress the deer up. It was tough explaining to the cops how to
dress these things up, especially when rigor had started. In a
few cases, we shot the corpses. And we buried them in graves
out in the woods. Covered them back over and two years
later, we'd go back out and find those deer. We had to find

the graves. Then we'd exhume the bodies and work the scene like an archeological dig.

CRIME SCENE INVESTIGATOR

In mountain scenes, you'll get an awful lot of animal interven-tion. The body might be scattered over a three-hundred-yard area, because the animals have taken it.

HOMICIDE DETECTIVE

Finding Evidence Aided by Forensic Anthropology

One of the things forensic anthropologists have learned is that many of the animals that come in, like birds and rodents, will actually take some of the small bones of the hands, they'll take teeth, they'll take jewelry items, and they'll also remove hair from the cadaver. And they'll take this back to line their nest. Many times, in looking for hair evidence, or a piece of paper, say, that a number may be written on, we will look for birds' nests and rodents' nests, and many times, we find evidence in their nests. We've found bullets in nests, hair, jewelry, teeth that led to identification of the victim. We refer to this kind of evidence as "bioenvironmental evidence." And these animals are referred to as "nature's evidence technicians."

FORENSIC ANTHROPOLOGIST

A body that has begun to decompose or skeletonize presents the most challenges. When we see this, they're typically high-profile cases, like the rash in California in the past few years of kidnappings of very young children. Those bodies are typically not found till later in time, when the body has undergone significant decomposition.

In the past, when investigators have come across this kind of case, they've thrown their hands up, thinking there's very little they can do because here you have a body; it may have been scattered by animals.

How do you work a scene that is basically in an open, un-controlled environment? If you go into a scene in a house, you can fingerprint the walls and surfaces, and there are all kinds of evidence you can traditionally collect. But if you have an outdoor scene, what is there to collect?

What we're trying to do is get law enforcement into a different thought mode for these cases and look at it like this: Nature leaves all these clues for you. And we have all these different sciences now that can interpret what Nature is telling us.

FORENSIC ANTHROPOLOGIST

You find a body in the woods. Where was it brought into the woods? We want to see what the path was that the killer took to move that body into the woods. Well, as that body is being dragged, it's gonna pick up various types of plants. Leaves are going to get caught in the clothing and such, and they either stay with the body, or, for example, if that body is buried, if we exhume it correctly, we're going to find evidence of these leaves, or plant pollens, or seeds. And basically we can track them to where that person entered the woods because of the difference in vegetation. So, you can say, for example, the killer came from this side of the road because we have these two poplars here alongside the road area—poplar trees are not found deep inside the woods—and we found poplar leaves with the body.

FORENSIC BOTANIST

You can locate remains by knowing something of the animals' behavior in the area you're searching. We know that wolves and coyotes will remove remains, but they don't move them very far out of the area. Whereas, if domestic dogs are involved, they will carry human remains for a very long haul, up to a mile away. We can look for areas where there is some type of back cover, because within the canines—dogs, wolves, and coyotes—when they take remains, they will look for areas where they have a protective back cover. When you look at these spots, it increases our chances of finding remains.

If there are domestic dogs nearby the scene, we'll canvass neighborhoods and we'll go into backyards and do searches around the dog pens. Many times, dogs will take the bones to their doghouse. We've found bones in yards a number of times. The owner may think it's just some kind of animal bone.

FORENSIC ANTHROPOLOGIST

One of the key questions with an outdoor scene is where was the body initially placed after death? We want to concentrate on that area for various types of trace evidence: hairs and fibers, for example, something the killer may have dropped, or a print. We want to key in on that area where the body was initially placed.

With animal scatter, how do you reconstruct where that body was? As a result of decomposition, the leaching of various bodily fluids actually enriches the soil, much like a fertilizer. You will see changes in the color and texture of the soil; many times you'll even see changes in the plants growing in that area. The vegetation may turn yellow and take on a waxy-looking appearance. We can look for these environmental changes, plant changes, and the presence of insects can tell us that a body was decomposing right here.

Then, many times, we'll find things, like the bullet that's dropped into the soil, hairs and fibers, all this material right there in the site. Even though that body has been scattered by animals, Nature, basically, has told us, "Here is where you need to look."

It gives you all kinds of information about what happened to this body. But you've got to be able to decipher it. We tell police, "Take off your regular police cap off and put on your

Daniel Boone cap and start thinking like a woodsman or hunter."

FORENSIC ANTHROPOLOGIST

A young woman, Katie Poirier, was abducted from a convenience store in Moose Lake, Minnesota, in the early summer of 1998. She was working alone at the store at about eleven P.M. She was captured on videotape being escorted from the store by a man. This was a big case in Minnesota.

The killer, Donald Blom, was not known at the time to be a convicted felon or a registered sex offender because he went by about eight different names. But he *was* a sex offender. He had a couple of previous convictions of sexual assault where he just grabbed young females, and took them off, and sexually assaulted them. He was married, had some kids. He lived in the Twin Cities area and had a lake property up north.

Information finally led us [the Crime Scene Team] to a thirty-acre lake property that the suspect owned about eight to ten miles away from the Moose Lake convenience store. We're searching the entire area.

There were about five or six buildings there. We spent most of the day looking in those buildings for any traces of the girl, looking for fingerprints, hairs, fibers, you name it. I mean, this was a big case. They wanted *everything* done.

They brought in cadaver dogs to search the property. The dogs hit on a couple areas where they thought decomposing flesh was buried. Of course, that stops everything. Everybody in the world comes over to you at that point and is just standing around.

We did our typical excavation of those sites, where we use a cemetery probe to figure out the size of the hole. I found about four or five holes right in front of a shed. But, of course, when you start excavating and digging away—in the old days, we just took a shovel and dug straight down; now we do the excavating like the archeologists do so they can't make as much fun of us when we do something wrong—it's a fairly long and tedious process.

Three or four hours into it, we finally get to these five individual flesh pieces that we're looking at. I recognize fawn fur. The suspect was a poacher, as well, and what he had done was shoot a doe with a couple fawns in utero. He buried those, and cut up Mom, took the good things off, and buried the remnants in the other holes. He had buried those deer pieces everywhere.

Big disappointment. I've got a crowd of about fifty people behind me and I say, "It's a deer." Next time I turn around, everybody was gone. I was the only one there. That's the way it is. People think, "This is gonna be really exciting," and all of a sudden, something's really disappointing, and you can hear the whole crowd go, "Ohhhhh." And they walk away. It's like, "Hey, guys! We're not done processing the rest of the scene yet!"

To this day, I don't know what drew me to a fire pit that was outside. Maybe it was my old training as an arson investigator. I've never done this before—or since—at a crime scene.

I looked in the pit and I recognized fresh ash. It was early summer, so I could recognize the difference between fresh ash and something that had gone through the wintering process. A fire pit, when it goes through the winter, it kind of turns into a cement crust. But there was fresh ash on the top and a fair amount of it.

And I could also see man-made, or nonwood, products in there. And I thought, "Well, here's a person that likes to get rid of things by burning."

I got the rest of the team over and I said, "You know, let's sift the fire pit for anything that might be in there." This was about an eight-feet-in-diameter pit. We sifted the top part. I told everybody, "Unless it's a twig or a rock, I want to see it."

And we started finding a significant amount of bone in there. Of course, I'm no bone expert, and I'd just finished excavating some deer, so I'm wondering if these might be deer bones. But as we're digging along, a tooth is found. I take a look at it. And, again, I'm not an expert, but I've never seen anything that looked like a human tooth except a human tooth. The forensic odontologist later said it had an abnormality; one of the roots was hooked. I grabbed what I thought was a good representative sample of bones, and the tooth, out of the fire pit.

We got back to the crime lab. We have a forensic anthropologist we work with fairly closely. I asked her if she'd come over and evaluate this set of bones. She evaluated them and said, "Well, these are definitely human bones." We couldn't tell how many human bones we had at that point. Almost none of them was bigger than a pencil. The bottom of a coffee cup would be about as big as they were. They were all incredibly small, with the exception of one vertebra. And the victim was not a large woman, so she didn't have large bone structure. All the bone pieces had been burned to such an extent that they couldn't extract any DNA from them, either in our laboratory or the FBI laboratory.

Once we did that, I thought, 'Well, there's more fire pit." We went back to the scene, and I brought the anthropologist back, too. We recovered as many bones as we possibly could by sifting down again.

The bones indicated that this was a young woman between the ages of fifteen and twenty-five. Our victim was eighteen. The one tooth we recovered had recent dental work on it. They matched it up to a dental x-ray that she had, showing that this was the right tooth. This was *after* they misidentified it as being from the other side of the mouth, but somehow nobody bothers to remember that whole part of the process. There was a unique cement that the dentist had used for that filling. It was a free sample the dentist had gotten at some dental show. It had a high level of zirconium in it.

And it was this one tooth in that fire pit that positively identified Katie Poirier. This tooth, and all the circumstantial material from the pit, really led the jury to believe that indeed, these *were* the remains of the victim. Blom was convicted of killing Katie Poirier, based on the fact that her remains were found in his fire pit.

This was another one of those—You find something at the scene. You don't have anything, necessarily. But you collect all the best evidence you can and then it all falls together.

CRIME SCENE SUPERVISOR

I was always very strong-stomached and never had any problem with any dead body. I've even been at scenes where the forensic entomologist, who's supposed to be collecting bugs and stuff, will clear out, and they're asking me to collect it because they can't stand it. These entomologists are all kind of pasty white anyway, like they live in a basement or something. I've even seen medical examiners disappear.

But I found myself at one scene—I've never thrown up, but I did get the gag reflex. It wasn't the scene; it was the circumstance. There was a young woman who had been lying out for a month, outside. Pretty odiferous at this point. And we're scraping there, after the body's been removed, and there's this layer of fatty tissue there. This was more my own mind than anything else, because the smell didn't get any worse. And I'm used to—When you're working a scene outside, you're continually getting flies and things, hitting you in the face, that are jumping off the dead body.

One of my counterparts was shoveling and scraping in one direction. I was doing it in the other. And she ended up throwing her stuff on me. I finally realized what it was. And I started to gag. Nothing had changed, except my thought process.

EVIDENCE TECHNICIAN

The Looting of Archeological Sites

We use archeological techniques and the analysis of soil to solve crimes involving the long dead and their artifacts. There is a whole band of people out West who make most of their money by the illicit looting of antiquities from archeological sites on federal property. This looting is a major felony, with a huge amount of money to be gotten, equal to even the most successful bank robberies.

These guys go through these archeological sites, *rip* these objects from their context, and then sell them. In any of the desert states, more than ninety percent of the sites have been vandalized for the sale of these antiquities. It's no small business.

In the mid-eighties I received a phone call from the Utah state archeologist. He said, "Do you suppose methods of understanding sediment could be used in a forensic setting to try to determine if the dirt adhering to an object could be traced back to its original source?"

I didn't have a clue at the time, but I was willing to try. At that time, a notorious pot hunter and vandal of archeological sites on federal property in Utah, one Earl Shumway, had been apprehended with a spectacular collection of aboriginal basketry in his keeping which he had purloined, according to the government, from an archeological site on federal land.

The baskets were among the most extraordinary that anyone had seen in half a century. Each one of the baskets that he had obtained was worth, on the legitimate market, four or five hundred thousand dollars apiece. One of my other avenues of inquiry is the study of prehistoric perishable material: baskets, sandals, cords, nets, and so on. I've probably seen more of this kind of thing than anyone who has ever lived.

The bottom line was, the Utah archeologist wanted to know if there was enough dirt adhering to these baskets to be able to say with some degree of certitude whether or not they came from federal property or from private land sites, which were not protected. If they were from private land, Earl Shumway could walk free, basically. Stupidly, he had sold his collection of baskets to a dealer for a used pickup truck, a Winchester rifle, and a pound of cocaine.

What we did was to run a series of analyses on minute amounts of dirt stuck under the stitches of the coral baskets. Although forensic scientists have been working with sediment for over a hundred years, it's never been at this level. Usually, if you're dealing with somebody that may be involved in a murder and they've got some yellow clay on their knees, and there's some yellow clay down on the levee, you say, "Looks like he did it." But nobody's every looked at this stuff from the standpoint of its molecular composition. And we've been doing this routinely, from an archeological perspective.

We told the Park Service, "What you guys are gonna need to do is go to the alibi locations, where Earl said he obtained these, collect us some sediment, collect us some rock from the overhangs, because these are all sort of rock-shelter situations. Then go to where you guys think the vandalism occurred, and do the same thing. We will, in turn, process the samples, and tell you what we think."

It turned out that the compositional match of the sediment from the baskets and the federal location in Utah, a place called Jack's Pasture, was so statistically high that the chances that it wouldn't be from that place were less than ten percent. And the difference between his alibi locations and that basketry and the dirt on it was so great that it could not possibly come from them.

This was introduced in court and, ultimately, Earl pleaded guilty.

FORENSIC GEO-ARCHEOLOGIST

The illegal antiquities business is huge. It involves millions of dollars annually of objects that are collected by pot hunters, and these objects pass through unsavory middlemen to even more unsavory dealers. The antiquities frequently end up in museums, in private collections. The end result of the activities of these folks is the destruction of the archeological history of the United States.

This has gone on for decades, but unbeknownst to the average law enforcement person who is working with crimes of the present. It used to be thought of as not serious, just "dead Indian" stuff. Now it's seen as truly reprehensible and is prosecuted to the fullest extent.

This is a forensic application of and for the long dead. The crimes of looting and vandalism of these sites, though, are recent. And we can easily do this same application with any modern crime where dirt from a location would be important.

FORENSIC GEO-ARCHEOLOGIST

Reenacting Outside Crime Scenes

We've started doing something new. We take suspects back to the crime scene. After we interview them, and they do the video for the state's attorney, we return to the murder scene with the suspect and reenact everything. This is part of the interview process; it's all legal and everything.

We take him out ourselves. We have a video guy with us. We have to have security when we do this. I mean—You're with a killer. You talk with him like he's your best friend, but I wouldn't trust him as far as I could throw him.

This one guy we had out at the murder scene, on a train embankment. There's trains going by there on top of this embankment. I have to stop the guy a couple of times because there are all these *trains* going by, constantly. We had to do the videotaping during the day, even though our information from the scene told us the murder happened about midnight. So about the third time I stop him, I'm telling him, "We've got to video it all over because of these trains! There's just so much noise up here!" And he just nonchalantly says, "Not at night!" Yeah. Not at night.

Then he goes on to tell how he raped and strangled the woman after that.

COLD CASE SPECIALIST

We had this guy who raped and murdered four women in thirty days. He did them all over the city. I'd take him to the local district stations, give him his rights and everything, and just to lock him in, I'd say, "Remember, you talked to us earlier and you said you did ABCD." He said, "Yeah." "Okay. You agreed to go out with us and show us the scenes where it happened, right?" "Sure, yeah." So you go out there.

So we did one, right off Division Street on the North Side of Chicago. We're walking with him, he's saying how he followed the girl, she ducks down the alley, he goes down the alley, and grabs her. He said he raped her, you know, and this and that. Then he said he strangled her. Then he said, "Now she's laying here in the alley and then I left." Like he didn't kill her.

And I'm thinking to myself, "Oh, Jesus, the guy's gonna flip me out on something. It's gonna hurt the case." Then he says, "I started walking away. I'm about here, about a hundred feet away. But, you know, I couldn't just let her *lie* like that in the alley. So I went back over there." And I said, "Well, what did you do then?" He says, "Well, I put her in the garbage can then. I couldn't leave her layin' out like that. That wasn't right."

VIOLENT CRIMES DETECTIVE

Finding Evidence and Victims in Water

We have a lot of scenes in New Jersey where dead people wind up in the water. Water scenes pose a whole other environmental challenge to modern crime scene processing and you need to be equipped to deal with that. Being surrounded by water, we have some diving teams and things like that. But water poses its own set of problems.

I've had a Mafia contract murderer, a guy who actually raised a contract to have a guy killed with a twelve-gauge shotgun, show me where he threw the shotgun off a bridge into Bass Harbor. It's saltwater, it's tidal water, the water runs under a bridge.

He showed us this thing and it's, like, January. There's like three inches of ice on it. How do you search for that? Well, you put guys down in the boat. You put magnets down. And we had one guy who said, "I know there's somethin' here, but I can't get it up with the magnet."

We got two divers from the town where I live, municipal cops, who had an extra reputation as being good police divers. Went up and went under that ice, down into that water, and found the damn gun. Unbelievable.

This diver came up, tough son of bitch, he busted through that ice, he came up holding the gun, I was like, I don't believe this. It was a sawed-off shotgun. It had the numbers intact. The shotgun worked. Getting that, it was incredible. It just put everything together for us.

HOMICIDE DETECTIVE

When you work water, you can never look at it the same again. The Chicago River. It's pretty murky. But when you've spent years recovering bodies from it, you're glad it's murky. You don't want to know what's in there.

MARINE UNIT SPECIALIST/DIVER

A Water Retrieval

We get a call one day. They got a body floating two miles off the Golden Nugget Casino in Atlantic City. There's a body float- ing out in the Atlantic Ocean and it's all tied up. Well, that's not natural. People generally don't do that.

The New Jersey Police Department has a Marine Bureau and they have a little boat out there, a Boston whaler. And he's circling around this dead guy in the water.

Homicide gets called. We go out there. I took the new kid in our unit; it was his first job. And we have two experienced ID guys with us.

We're getting ready to go out. We're at the dock. We met the police and the Coast Guard and we're going out. We're in a big police boat and there's the little police boat circling the dead guy. Everybody's torturing the new guy about get- ting sick. The kid comes to me and says, "I don't want to get sick." "Ah, the hell with it. If you get sick, you get sick. Just—the hell with it."

We get out there and the ocean— It was pretty nice, I thought. We get there. There's the guy. He's dead. He's in the water. And the cop keeps circling him with the Boston whaler so he doesn't lose track of him.

Step one: How do you process *that* scene? How do you rope off the Atlantic Ocean?

What you do is the best you can do. The body's moving. It's moving in the ocean. First off, you have to recover the evidence; you need to recover the body.

We took a Stokes stretcher—it's like a metal stretcher—to get it under the body. The guy was a pretty good size, but there wasn't much left of him. He was skeletal from the waist up. No head. All gone.

We couldn't get him aboard. One of the reasons we couldn't get him aboard was the two ID guys, the two veterans, were getting sick. *They* were throwin' up. And the new guy wasn't. He was laughin' at them getting sick.

So we couldn't get the thing. I said, "To hell with this. We'll get it in the little boat. Be easier to get it up over the side of the Boston whaler than get it up over this monster here."

So I get in the boat with a Marine police officer. You know how we got him? Cops were yelling, "He's gonna get away!" I grabbed the dead guy by his jock strap. I didn't have any gloves, grabbed the jock strap—and it's like a cartoon. Every time the water goes, the elastic goes bloop!, the guy goes under, and we have to snap him back up. So we finally muscle this guy in, and we plop him on the deck. He's loaded with crabs. And they're skittering around the boat. I say, "Don't let the crabs get away! We can have them for dinner!" The Marine officer throws up, all over the damn boat.

So I got the two sick ID guys. I got the Marine officer on the boat with me getting sick. And the dead guy is up in front of the center console of the boat. It's just the way it had to be. So, all the way in, we smelled it. The Marine guy: "I'm gonna get sick." "If you're gonna get sick, be sick. There's nothin' to be ashamed of. But the important thing is, Bruce, we got these *crabs* to eat when we get back." And he got sick all over again.

When we get back to the dock, there's a detective sergeant from the state police there. This guy was a bright, tough state trooper. He said, "Listen, what you might want to do is, talk to the doctor tomorrow, to take a section of the femur bone. And we'll do a diatom test." "What's that?" "They're single-celled algae. If they're in the body and they match with algae in the water, they can tell you whether he went into the water alive or not, whether he was drowned or not." So there was another learning experience. So you put that in your memory bank.

We get down to the morgue for the autopsy of this poor

guy. We see the pathologist. I said I need a section of the femur bone for this particular test. He said he wasn't familiar with the test. He said, "How much do you need?" Oh, shit, I don't know. I'm like, what the hell, how much do we take? I'm scared if we take too much, if we take too little. He said, "I'll tell you what. Because there wasn't much *to* the guy, I'll give you both femurs. Intact. And you can take what you need." "Thanks. That's great."

So we double-wrapped the femurs in some trash bags. We didn't double-wrap them to protect DNA. We just didn't want the damn things falling all over the floor.

We've got the bones in the bags. Now we're waiting to leave. While we're there, the hospital security guard, we knew him, young guy, he says, "Hey, man, what's in the bag?" to the cop carrying it. The guy looks at me, winks, and goes, "Whaddya think? Jeez, he's one of us, this guy." And I go, "Oh yeah, oh yeah. We can show him—sure."

We walked him into a patient examination room. I said, "Close the door." And this guy's like, Oh man, this is great. These two homicide detectives are gonna show me what's in the bag.

We open the bag; he sees these two damn bones in there. He runs screaming out of the room. Poor bugger. He wasn't right after that.

Never, *ever* ask to see what's in a bag from the morgue. Never, ever. Somebody just might show you.

HOMICIDE DETECTIVE

Four

TRACE EVIDENCE

Have you ever seen the comic strip *Peanuts*? You know the little guy, Pigpen, who walks around with a little cloud coming off him? Well, we all have that cloud. We all carry around a little cloud of our environment, of where we go, what we touch, what we work at. Everybody's cloud is different. If you're a teacher, you're going to have bits of chalk dust coming off you; if you're a welder, you're going to have tiny bits of metals coming off. But *everybody* has that little cloud.
　　　—Terry McAdam, Trace Evidence Analyst, Criminalistics Division, Washington State Police

We had a guy in the lab at the FBI who'd always send his teenage daughter out on dates wearing a big fuzzy acrylic sweater. He knew the sweater would transfer like crazy, and if her date brought her home later with a bunch of sweater fibers on him, he and the date were going to have a serious talk.
　　　—Max Houck, Former FBI Trace Analyst, Director of Forensic Science Initiative at West Virginia University, Author of *Mute Witnesses*

IF YOU WERE TO PUT DOWN THIS BOOK AND GO OUT AND commit a crime, you would bring microscopic bits of wood pulp and ink with you, maybe particles of fiber or wood slivers from the chair you're sitting in. You'd also bring whatever you walked through on your way to the crime, or whatever you sat on in your car. Every object you handled at the scene would get some of your particular aura of microscopic debris on it. And you would carry tiny pieces of the scene back with you, depositing them everywhere you go. Even if you left no DNA, no prints, no bodily fluids, there's a good chance that trace evidence could link you irrevocably to your crime.

A lot of what gets collected at crime scenes is trace evidence. It might be hairs, fibers, footwear impressions, tire tracks, particles of glass, metals, or paint, wood, soil, vegetation, sawdust, duct tape. Trace includes everything that the criminal may bring to a scene, or take from the scene.

The basic premise of trace evidence, that "every contact leaves a trace," comes from the early-twentieth-century criminologist Dr. Edmond Locard, who pioneered the science of collecting and examining microscopic evidence from crime scenes. Locard's most famous article, "The Analysis of Dust Traces," contains this sentence, which most trace analysts can recite by heart: "For the microscopic debris that cover our clothes and bodies are the mute witnesses, sure and faithful, of all our movements and of all our encounters." This pronouncement is the foundation of forensic science.

The other criminologist of whom trace analysts speak with reverence is Sherlock Holmes. Years before the actual criminologist Locard was exhorting investigators to look deeply into tiny things, the fictional Sherlock Holmes was examining footprints in mud, bits of tobacco ash, remnants of fabric, fragments of soil. Just about all trace analysts (and crime scene investigators) quote readily from the Sherlock Holmes canon. Some of them have Holmes's name or the title of one of the Sherlock Holmes stories as part of their e-mail addresses.

The implications of trace evidence are vast. Find trace at a scene and you may establish who was at the scene, what the sequence and timing of events were, and what contact was made between offender and victim. This chapter begins with cases highlighting two very different applications of trace evidence, the first case from a forensic chemist and the second case from a forensic botanist.

When I was with the LAPD Forensic Response Team, we han-dled a case where a vehicle hit and struck a boy in the street. The driver fled the scene. In this particular situation, the kid turned, facing the vehicle head-on. When he hit, his face went forward onto the hood of the car and actually hit the metal with his teeth. Police eventually found what they thought was the vehicle. I was sent out to examine it. In the front, were these two little dents and buried down in the dents were, basically, calcium deposits from the boy's front teeth. Even though we didn't get a full tooth, by doing an elemental chemical analysis, we could show that it was consistent with the material that would have been left behind by a tooth.

TRACE ANALYST/CRIME LAB DIRECTOR

A woman in Fort Lauderdale had been sexually assaulted and strangled. Police found some fingerprints and some tree bark fragments in her room. The prints didn't match anybody they had in any system.

Six months later, they caught a burglar whose fingerprints matched. And, looking in his closet, they found bark fragments still in a pants cuff of one set of pants. They had vacuumed bark off the floor of the lady's apartment. They sent me the bark, and I identified it as coming from a gumbo-limbo tree, which is tropical.

They questioned the guy. He said, "Yeah, sure, I can tell you what I was doing there. We were both shopping. We met in a store and started talking. We hit it off and went back to her place and we had sex and I left and what's the problem?" This was a good story, because there were shopping bags in the room where they found her.

But they didn't tell him, one, that the fingerprints were on the window ledge, pointing *in.* And, two, that we'd found gumbo-limbo bark on the floor of the bedroom. They didn't tell him the trace folks had found some gumbo-limbo bark in his clothes. And there was a gumbo-limbo tree right outside her window.

FORENSIC BOTANIST

What Trace Evidence Reveals

Trace involves everything. And every case is different. Even if it's two shoe print cases, they're different. One might be in snow. The next case might be in mud. The next one might be on a piece of paper. One might be in blood. Every case is different.

TRACE ANALYST

We're dealing with chemistry, materials science, manufacturing plus—all the environmental effects. That's . . . a lot to know about.

A lot of emphasis is placed on DNA now. The trace folks get a little weary of that. A guy I know at the RCMP [Royal Canadian Mounted Police]—he's their chief scientist—said it best. We were at lunch with a bunch of DNA analysts. He said, "I don't know what you DNA people go on and on about. How hard your science is. You only have one molecule to worry about. We trace people have to worry about *all* of them."

TRACE ANALYST

Trace isn't *competing* with DNA. It *complements* DNA. There *are* times when DNA is not available, like when you have skeletal remains. Trace evidence can answer some of those questions.

CRIME LAB DIRECTOR

DNA and trace can often work together. They're very good com-plementary techniques.

The way I look at it, trace evidence can sometimes answer questions which DNA cannot. For example, rape cases. Trace evidence also is important in rape cases. What we've noticed, that the standard line from a male suspect before DNA was available was "I didn't touch her." Then DNA came along, and we could say, "Yes, you did." And then the next thing is, "Oh, it was consensual." And then trace evidence, things like looking at clothing, to interpret if the clothing was torn or ripped. DNA can answer the important question, "Was the guy here?" Trace can answer the question, "What was his intent? What did he do?"

TRACE ANALYST

At crimes scenes, but especially with trace, you have to look for the not-obvious things. You have to keep an open mind when you're looking at evidence. What am I seeing? What else might be there?"

CRIME SCENE SUPERVISOR

The key with trace evidence is, people aren't aware of it. A lot of times, it's not found. People at the scene might focus in on other things. I've seen this at crime scenes. You know, I'm trained to collect at a crime scene, not just trace evidence, but I'm trained to collect latent print evidence; I'm trained to collect blood evidence; all these different types of evidence.

We do look for it all. But I notice— Right off the bat, when we get to a crime scene, I'm thinking trace evidence, a blood person is thinking blood, a latent prints person is thinking latent prints. But it's not that we go in and we touch all this stuff and I'm going to ruin the latent prints. . . .

CRIME SCENE PROCESSOR

At the scene, a lot of things, if we can see them, we'll pick them up with gloved hands or forceps. If it's a fiber and we can see it—or a hair—we'll pick it up with forceps. Often, we'll put it in a piece of paper and fold it. It's called a druggist's fold. Then we put it in an envelope and make sure all the corners are sealed, to make sure that it doesn't get out. If it's glass, we'll pick it up with forceps and put it in a sturdy container.

Sometimes we use tape lifts to collect fibers or hairs. Clothing is packaged in brown paper bags.

We don't use plastic bags, Ziploc bags; there could be a

problem with getting it out, with static electricity. Say with paint in a Ziploc bag, it's difficult to get the paint out. If anything is wet, we don't want it in plastic, because then mold could start growing.

Sometimes we vacuum a scene to pick up trace.

CRIME SCENE PROCESSOR

When we get back to the lab, we have two search rooms in trace. If it's clothes, we'll hang the clothes up and then we'll scrape them. Like with a victim that was hit by a vehicle, we'll take his or her clothing and scrape it and look for paint. We have a database that's called PDQ, Paint Data Query. It's associated with the RCMP in Canada and the FBI. If we find paint on a victim, we can run it through this database and possibly get a make and model of the vehicle.

TRACE ANALYST

Footprints

There are three things we can identify people from, routinely. One is DNA. The other is fingerprints. And the third is footwear.

CRIME LAB DIRECTOR

People don't realize, footwear impressions are as important as fingerprints. And in many cases, they've become much *more* important. The reason is, so many people watch the crime shows now that we're running into more and more cases where there are no fingerprints that match the perpetrator because—they all wear gloves to the scene.

FOOTWEAR IMPRESSIONS SPECIALIST

Take your shoes off and look at the bottoms of your shoes. What you'll see, in addition to the general wear patterns, are a whole bunch of unique, random marks, scratches, gouges. You'll see them on the bottoms of your shoes.

Those marks start to form when you start wearing your shoes. And those unique, random marks that you get are what we refer to as individual characteristics. I can take a police department with five hundred police officers that all wear the same boot, and we can differentiate each pair from all the others. Ultimately, all shoe soles develop their own random characteristics.

FOOTWEAR IMPRESSIONS SPECIALIST

Not just the wear and tear on the soles of shoes is important. It's everything that travels along with the shoes. The best way to think about it, with footwear, is to realize— We're constantly picking up, and leaving, bits of trace: gravel, dirt, sand, moisture, soil, grass, or plant material on our shoes. And we transfer that for a number of steps, even after twenty or twenty-five feet.

FOOTWEAR IMPRESSIONS SPECIALIST

There's a common misconception that footwear is all the same. We even run into problems from a prosecution standpoint, because a lot of your prosecutors think "a gym shoe is a gym shoe is a gym shoe. Big deal. It's just another gym shoe." But it's not necessarily just another gym shoe.

I don't think footwear is overrated at all. I think footwear is *overlooked.*

CRIME SCENE TEAM LEADER

I didn't start reading Sherlock Holmes until I became an evi-dence technician. It's amazing how far ahead of his time Conan Doyle was, and how so much of what Doyle wrote applies to what we do, especially trace. It's incredible. There's a quote in one of the Sherlock Holmes mysteries, in "A Study in Scarlet," where he says, and I can quote this by heart, "There is no branch of detective science which is so important and so much neglected as the art of tracing footsteps." This is *still* true.

And it's very easy to destroy, because footwear impressions are going to exist usually on the floor. You come into the scene; you walk on it.

EVIDENCE TECHNICIAN

You have to know an awful lot about how shoes are made to do shoe prints. Oh, yeah. And they're very complicated. You have to consider manufacture, and also time and wear.

And a lot depends on the context. You might have a pair of leather dress shoes. They may not leave a very good print, for individualization purposes. But you may get an old pair of work boots that are all nicked and dinged up and, for our purposes, they're just great! They leave a terrific pattern.

FOOTWEAR IMPRESSIONS SPECIALIST

Three robberies. All at the same Little Caesar's pizza place. The first robbery occurs. The responding officer is training a new officer and he calls for the evidence guy to come to the scene. The guy working there, by himself, said he was the victim of a robbery.

You always want to use evidence to corroborate statements. And something you have to take into account when you get somebody who's working by themselves in a place and they claim to have been the victim of a robbery is— maybe they *weren't* the victim of a robbery. Maybe they needed the extra money, and just *decided* to become the victim of a robbery.

I was sent to oversee the case. First thing I asked the officer, "What was the victim's story?" The restaurant is a little walk-in area, you got the counter, you get the pizzas. The victim's story was, a guy comes in, he's got gloves on, a ski mask covering half his face, that he jumped over the counter, came after the victim with a knife, and demanded money.

So, you identify areas where contact was made. If my suspect has come over the counter, there should be something there to tell me that he had. And there *were,* in this case. There were footprints on the counter. That's unusual to begin with. Plus, the footprints are in an area where there's a lot of activity going on, pizza boxes being slid over. Even if they were there from before, they wouldn't last that long.

But here are two nice footwear impressions. You could read the word "Nike" on the bottom. So we processed the scene, documented it, collected the footwear impressions, photographed it for analysis. We distributed a sketch of the impressions to officers on the street, so they would have it if they came across somebody wearing Nikes, especially if they were hanging around the place.

A couple of weeks later, that same Little Caesar's is robbed again. Another evidence technician processed that scene. And he's got footwear impressions.

A few weeks later, the same Little Caesar's gets robbed again. This time, unfortunately for the bad guy, it was snowing outside. It was good packing snow. One of the officers responded to the scene, saw these footwear impressions outside in the snow, and he had the sketch, and he was like, "Hey! This looks a lot like the sketch!"

He starts following the footprints. This is people stuff, not high-technology stuff. He follows the footprints, and they go down, about a block down the street. And they lead right up the front steps of a house. And they go right *in* the house.

He calls me and a few other police officers over to the house. We ring the bell, a woman answers, and we tell her what happened and that we're following these footprints, they come right up to her front porch. She lives there with her son. She doesn't know if he's home. "But if you want to come in and look around, go ahead."

So she lets us in the house. And this is like—you know the old saying?—"The homicide detective will step over a kilo of coke to get to the body and the narcotics guy will step over the body to get to the kilo"—well, I couldn't have cared less about the bad guy hiding in the house. I wanted those *shoes.*

Right inside the front door, here's a soaking-wet pair of Nike gym shoes. I can see the bottom of the shoes has the same pattern as what was from the scene. Ultimately, the other guys found the suspect hiding in a closet.

He gets arrested. He's got some proceeds, he's got a Little Caesar's plastic carryout bag, he's got some rolled-up coins and things like that. As it turns out, he was a former employee. We took the footwear—the photographs, and the impressions from the scene, along with his shoes—and we submitted them to the crime lab. They were able to make a specific match, based on the individual characteristics. So we had him linked in to all three robberies. He knew the routine of the place. And it was close to home.

CRIME SCENE SUPERVISOR

We get a fair amount of outdoor crime scenes in the winter in Minnesota. Usually, as with most crime scenes, they're alcohol-fueled. There's an argument that leads to a shooting, for example. People run outside. Sometimes they die from exposure from running out with no clothes on, like idiots. But, most of the time, they're clothed, and they just tear off into the snow.

How do you process a footprint in the snow? I talk to all my crime lab counterparts throughout the United States, and the idea of taking a footprint in snow is something that they've never even thought of or considered. They wouldn't know what to do.

With snow—we've analyzed everything over the years. We've found there's a couple of different techniques you can use. One is making a plaster cast of the footprint. There's a product out there called Snowprint Wax. You just spray it in the bottom of the snow to make it nice, and then you can go ahead and pour your plaster in.

Recognize that when you're making a plaster cast, there's some heat generated when you're doing it. Back in the old days, you'd make the plaster up by throwing snow in the water, so you could make it as cool as possible before you poured it into the plaster.

Actually, the most effective way, and the best casts I've ever made in my life are from sulfur. You actually melt sulfur and make it liquid. And then you pour it into the footprint itself, and it cools immediately when it hits the snow. Makes an almost perfect cast of that print. If you ever see a set of footprints done with a plaster cast and a sulfur cast, it's amazing the differences you can capture.

You know, you always have the new people do it in the crime scene van, and of course they always heat the sulfur up just a little too hot. Then you get to spend the next day or two riding around in the crime scene van with that great rotten egg smell.

CRIME SCENE SUPERVISOR

Tire Tracks

If you want to get into something *really* complicated, try tires.

I once sat through a weeklong course called "Shoe and Tire Prints." Tires are some of the most complicated things I've ever seen in my life. Just amazing. You've got to know how they go together, and how they wear, and all this stuff, to be able to just look at this tire print and make sense of it.

TRACE ANALYST

Tire tracks can have the same value as footwear. Just like shoes have individual characteristics, so do tires. They're the same type of thing.

Additional things can be done with tire tracks, because we may be able to identify the type of vehicle that made the track. It might be a passenger-type car, light-truck tire, heavy-truck tire. Right there, that can give us a lot of information.

Some tires might be particular to a certain type of vehicle. Some tires might be original equipment tires. With tires, you can trace them right back to the manufacturer and go from there.

TRACE ANALYST

There was a boyfriend, girlfriend, ex-boyfriend situation. Old boyfriend took the three of them out in a car to a park. He ended up shooting and killing new boyfriend, driving the girlfriend back, and he was coercing her to stay in the relationship and not tell about the murder. This guy knew something about tire tracks. The car belonged to the girlfriend. He was worried about the police, when they found the body, that they'd find the tire tracks of her car, which would tie it back into him.

What he did was, he took a jackknife and punctured all four tires and then went to her and said, "Honey, the tires are leaking. We should get some more tires." He went to Kmart with her credit card and bought four new tires. But then he was so cheap, he did not want to pay the tire recycling fee. He took all four old tires, left the tires near the back porch. Couple days later, we caught up with him. We looked at the car and saw that the tire pattern did not match the impressions from the scene. But then we found the four tires, all punctured. And one of the tire impressions matched the impressions from the scene.

He saved eight bucks, but he went to prison for life.

HOMICIDE DETECTIVE

Cars

Cars are a great source of trace evidence. If you're going to commit a crime, you either walk or you drive a car, in our society. That's how you get there. You also leave in a car. And, of course, it's the classic: Every time you go into something, you take evidence in, and when you leave, you take evidence away with you. So, in a car, you're leaving evidence behind.

There are layers of trace in a car. The inside of it is like a bucket. You come into it, you move around. You're depositing trace evidence. You leave, you come back the next day, you add more, you add more. There's a *wealth* of trace on the inside of the vehicle.

TRACE ANALYST

We swab everything that could get touched for blood evidence, or prints, and pick up everything that could have been deposited for trace.

CRIME SCENE PROCESSOR

We get a lot of cases where two people are in a car, there's an accident, and one person dies. And the person that lives— not always, but often—this survivor says that person that died was driving.

But investigators want to find out for *sure* who was driving. Sometimes they'll look for blood or prints on the steering column. But if it's a rollover, things are getting thrown all over the place, so if you have fibers imbedded in a seat belt, that is really good evidence to indicate who was driving.

I handled trace in a vehicular homicide case one time. Again, the survivor said he was in the passenger seat. But what happens in a car accident, due to the impact, the friction causes the plastic on the seat belt to heat up, causing the fibers from the seat belt to imbed into the plastic. And I found red fibers in the seat belt. The suspect was wearing red. That's how we placed him behind the wheel in that accident.

TRACE ANALYST

With cars, you've got tires, of course. But you also have glass and paint. We'll get entire bumpers of vehicles in. We'll look for fabric impressions on it or look for a physical match if the car was involved in a hit-and-run. Maybe there are pieces from the vehicle left at the scene.

CRIME LAB DIRECTOR

If you flex metal, that paint just flies off and chips. Every once in a while you can take a chip of paint that's a half inch, three-quarters of an inch long, and if you get the car right away, you can physically put it on to the car. In addition to that, when the paint flexes off, it doesn't always come off clean. One photograph I have shows a case where the area where the paint is missing off the car's metal looks like a child's puzzle, where the outline of the pieces is scored into it. In this case, as the pieces flipped off, the lines between the pieces left a little bit of paint on the car. So there was an outline of the various pieces on the car itself. The officer was smart enough to find this piece of paint at the crime scene. He recovered it, packaged it, brought it to our attention. And then, when they found the car, we were smart enough to say, "Let's spend some time seeing if we can find this piece." Because as soon as we saw the car, we could see these little outlines from the paint that had flown off in the accident.

TRACE ANALYST

You can get imprints from clothing. Sometimes people wearing coats get hit and you'll be able to see the imprint of the headlight grill on their coat. It's the dust. Sometimes it's transferred to the coat. Other times you get fabric impressions which are transferred to the vehicle.

Bike riders and other people who go across the paint of the car—the pressure of the body sliding across the paint softens the paint, and then it hardens right away. And when it hardens, it grabs the fibers. We have photographs where it looks like a smear, it looks like the paint's curled up. But when you go in on a magnifying photograph of it, you see that it's actually fibers off of whatever piece of cloth slid across the paint. Then you pick those fibers up, analyze color and composition, and you have some idea of what the article of clothing looked like. And, of course, you've got a victim. It's a matter of seeing whether that shirt, coat, jacket, pants, or whatever, match. Then you can tie it in to the hit-and-run driver's vehicle.

TRACE ANALYST

Henry Lee [internationally known forensic scientist] has a story about a hit-and-run accident in Connecticut. A state trooper was assisting a motorist and got hit by a truck and killed. When they finally found the truck—Lee has a photograph of this—the front edge of the trailer has an imprint of the Connecticut State Police patch that was on the guy's right shoulder.

CRIME LAB DIRECTOR

Fibers

A burglar who wears corduroy is making a big mistake. Cor-duroy is the worst to wear if you're a burglar. If I went into someone's house to commit a crime, and I sat down, the fibers from that fabric seat would transfer on to my clothes because of corduroy's grabbing aspect. Corduroy is a napped fabric. That means all these fibers stick out of the fabric, sort of like hairs on your head. But manufacturers trim it off, so the fibers are all of equal length. And then they gouge out the little ridges. So you've got a lot of loose fibers, you've got a lot of fibers sticking up, a lot of surface area for stuff to stick to. You bring corduroy into a crime scene—it's both a big source of evidence and a big collector of evidence.

CRIME SCENE PROCESSOR/TRACE ANALYST

In general, fibers are probably some of the best evidence out there. Now, I'm biased because I'm a fabric examiner, but I think, more often than not, you can probably be more specific with fibers than you can with a lot of other kinds of evidence.

Think about it. Every year, worldwide, there's somewhere around one hundred *billion* pounds of fiber produced. *Every year.*

And think about this: When you're in a large department store, or on public transit, or in an airport—any place where there's a lot of people—how often do you find two people wearing exactly the same garment? Try this: Go into a clothing store and pick up something. Now walk around and try to find another textile that has the same composition and color. You're not gonna find it.

So, the variety in textiles is *enormous.* Variety is our friend in forensic science. We *like* variety.

FIBER SPECIALIST

There was a guy who was renting out a room in his condo to this Middle Eastern woman who was a medical student. And she went missing. This was about 1998.

Police questioned this man, and as they're doing that, another woman walks in. Police asked her who she was and she said, "I'm his new roommate." So, they take her aside and start chatting with her. They asked if she had seen anything unusual when she moved in. She said, "Well, yeah, there was a refrigerator in the living room. And I asked him about it and he said his former roommate was using the refrigerator."

The former roommate's body was found in a refrigerator behind a hardware store. The guy was not particularly bright, because there was a shipping label, in with the refrigerator, that gave his address. Even so, that by itself wouldn't be enough to prove his guilt.

The neat thing about the case was, he had tied her up and then tied up the fridge so it wouldn't pop open. He used rope that he found in the apartment complex and got a big furniture dolly that was down in the garage.

Many rope manufacturers will put a tracer in the ropes so they can track their own products and defend themselves against product liability cases. The idea is if someone is tied to a rope on a roof, say, and the rope breaks, the rope manufacturer can prove whether it was theirs in the case of a lawsuit.

This particular rope had a tracer in it. This was a tiny strip of clear polyester with the company's name on it in black letters. I called the company and described the composition and construction of the rope, along with the tracer information, and they said, "We haven't made that rope since 1984." That's one of those little geeky things that you tell another trace person and they go, "Wow! That's great!"

And it was excellent evidence. It gave a time line to the rope. In archeology, there's a phrase called *"terminus post quem,"* which means "time after which." It establishes a milestone in a time line, and after that point, something can't have happened. So, once they stopped making it in 1984, the number starts to decline, until that item disappears.

That made the evidence very specific. No one could have gone to Home Depot in 1998 and bought that rope. The rope belonged to the batch in the apartment complex, the batch he had access to, linking him directly to the murder.

FIBER SPECIALIST

Fiber evidence can be horrendously confusing. There's probably about seven thousand dyes and pigments that are used in textiles. Any one of those requires about eight to ten unit processes to turn it into a usable chemical for dyeing. There's about twelve different ways to get dyes into textiles. There's about twenty-nine different dye categories. Any one color that you see in a garment *rarely* is the result of one dye. And there's all types of finishes, both chemical and physical, that change the final properties of the dye.

And that's just color. That's not talking about the categories of polymer. . . .

FIBER SPECIALIST

The variation that's out there is almost staggering. It can make it very difficult for forensic scientists to be up on what they need to be up on. At the FBI, I had the luxury of specializing. I did four things: hairs, fibers, fabric, and rope. If you go to a state crime lab, they may have to do fibers and glass and paint and soil—with all the manufacturing information you have to know about: paint chemistry, paint application, automotive interior, all that stuff.

That's overwhelming. It can be dizzying. The hazard is that you may be missing important information, through no fault of your own.

TRACE ANALYST

We analyze knife cuts in fabric, to determine if the fabric was cut or if it was ripped, for example, during a sexual assault or a homicide. We also analyze to determine, possibly, if the cuts match a knife recovered at the scene.

There's one case, from about 2001, that stands out. A woman was missing for a while and her husband was suspected. They thought one of the children might have witnessed it, but the boy wouldn't say anything.

The woman's body was found in a shallow grave. I got the clothes because the investigators could not determine how she had died, since she was very decomposed. Wounds wouldn't show on the skin or the internal organs. The clothes stank very badly.

I looked at them under a microscope to see if they were cut or torn. I determined that a couple of knife cuts went through the clothes into her abdomen and her upper chest area.

I called the medical examiner and she said that those two knife cuts would not have left marks on any bones and that they were in areas that could have caused her to die.

Right around the same time, the child told police that the father had stabbed the mother. The clothing corroborated the little boy's story. The defendant ended up pleading guilty.

TRACE ANALYST

One of the more interesting cases we did involved a single fiber, probably as long as your pinkie nail is wide. And that was it. That was all the physical evidence police had. This was a homicide. The fiber was found in the vaginal area of a nude woman, who was found at the side of the road.

By fiber standards, this was pretty big. Here was this big, fat, ugly, baby-shit olive-colored rayon fiber. Really unattractive. In looking at it, I realized that it was a carpet fiber. I knew that because the diameter was more than forty-five microns and that generally is considered one of the definitions of a carpet fiber. The other thing was rayon. There aren't too many rayon carpets out there.

I started doing some digging, talking to people. It turns out that until 1973, General Motors used a mixture of rayon and nylon fibers in certain vehicle carpeting. Some more calls to General Motors, and it turns out that the carpeting was only in a certain make and model, up until 1972.

So, I called the investigator. "Do you guys have a suspect?" "Well, we've got a couple of people we're looking at." "Does one of them own an old car?" "Car's kind of old, whaddya mean?" "Was it made before 1972?" He said, "It was made in '72." I said, "Is the interior kind of a pukey green?" And he said, "Yeahhhh." "Is the car a Monte Carlo?" "How do you *know* all this?"

They got me a sample from the car, and it matched. I did a search of Department of Motor Vehicle records in a five-state area around the state it occurred in. There were only eight vehicles that matched the make, the model, and the year that were registered. They presented that information to the suspect, and he confessed. The victim had had car trouble. This guy offered to help. He picked her up, and raped and murdered her in his vehicle, and then just dumped her by the side of the road.

TRACE ANALYST

Glass

Anytime you have glass from a break-in at a scene, that glass can be *extremely* helpful in figuring out just who entered a home, a business, or a vehicle, to commit a crime.

If you break a window with a hammer, a large percentage of that glass goes in the same direction as the hammer. *But*—a very significant amount of it goes back the other direction. Now, these are minuscule pieces. They're tiny. But they go back on the person who broke the window. Glass, to a certain extent, is elastic, and it springs back.

Have you ever had a broken windshield on a car? Have you ever noticed, as you're walking away from it, sometimes you can hear little pieces flicking off? That's because it's under tension. When it's made, they do these heat treatments to it. It's under tremendous mechanical stress. So when you break a windshield, it continues to release that stress. And with release of that stress, little tiny fibers get pinged off. You can hear it for up to two days.

That's in slow motion of what happens when you break a window. It breaks very rapidly, and it releases the tension immediately, and shoots it, sometimes up to fifteen, twenty feet back. So the person breaking the window can have these tiny shards all over them—on their hair, on every other part of them.

So, with the point of entry in homicides, burglaries, whatever—we take the person's clothing, shake it down, and *look* for these things. Then we go back, take a sample from the window, and compare that to the glass found on them to see if that glass has the same physical properties and optical properties, as that found on the suspect.

GLASS SPECIALIST

What we do: There are a couple of main properties of glass that we use to differentiate glass, one from another. The main one is measuring the glass refractive index, how much that particular piece of glass bends light. And with that we measure the elements that are present in the glass.

GLASS SPECIALIST

There are a couple schools of thought about doing glass evi-dence. In Canada, the United Kingdom, and New Zealand, for example, they've been doing lots and lots of glass cases, for a long time. In the United States, we have so much violent crime, we're so busy with that, that we don't get to the burglary stuff.

But it's been proven, through DNA profiles, that people who are arrested for what are called minor offenses, such as burglary, subsequently these are the same people who turn up doing more violent crimes at a later date.

GLASS SPECIALIST

The LAPD crime lab has display cabinets around the perimeter of its lobby, in front of the various sections. One of them contains a pieced-together vehicle mirror, a right side-view mirror. This mirror was from a vehicle that struck a pedestrian, the pedestrian went over the right fender, struck the windshield, and then kind of rolled around the side of the car. Well, in the process of the victim rolling around, the right side-view mirror was slapped hard against the right-hand window, and broke the window. And the glass part of the mirror broke and fell into the car, except for a couple of little tiny pieces. And then the driver sped away.

The police were able to get a description of this vehicle and eventually found it. You could look at this car and you knew darn well that it had hit something. And from seeing a lot of these, I could tell: "Yeah, this definitely was a body." But that isn't scientific proof.

We got called to the scene on that one afterwards. The officers basically swept up the street and collected all the glass.

And inside of this glass were these two little tiny, I'm talking probably eighth-inch-by-quarter-inch pieces of mirrored glass. And a search of the vehicle showed that the mirror had actually broken off, broken the side window, and fallen inside of the car. So we collected the mirror and brought it back to the crime lab. We put it together, and down on the corner of it were two little missing pieces. And the two pieces from the scene just fit right in there.

When you do a physical match like that—We've got lots of stories of paint chips that have actually fallen off of a car and been left at the scene, and you can basically do it like a jigsaw puzzle—put the piece back into where it came off the car.

But in this particular case—you know, glass sometimes breaks very smoothly and you don't have quite the jagged edges that can fit in like a jigsaw puzzle. However, what glass *does* have . . . It's a phenomenon or a creation called "hackle marks." These are tiny fractures created due to the force that it takes to break glass. And the way you see them is not on the face of the glass, but on the broken edge. And they're just like little fracture lines, and they have a unique pattern to them. It just so happens that the two sides of a broken piece of glass will have the same hackle marks. And in this case, the two little tiny pieces, we took them, turned them on edge, lined them up with the piece of mirror that was found inside the car, and these marks lined up exactly. There was no question about the match.

It places the vehicle at the scene. It doesn't necessarily put the driver behind the wheel. But that's where the information we provide, along with the questioning skills of the detectives, work together. If they can get a person to state, you know, "This car's been under my control," without saying that they'd actually been involved in the accident, and we show that that vehicle was the one vehicle that caused the accident—you tie one piece to the other and usually they end up pleading guilty.

CRIME LAB DIRECTOR

Strange Bits of Evidence

Trace Analysis is the section of the crime lab where, if they don't know where to send it, they send it to us. We get kind of oddball things in here. Feathers. We've had feathers come into the lab. Bird feathers.

One case: A person was shot and killed outdoors, near a garage. The bullet went through the victim's down jacket. And then it hit a garage door and deflected off. In that garage door, in the bullet hole or indentation, there was a little feather. I think the defense's story was that the shooting was accidental, that the defendant had aimed at the garage, and the bullet deflected off it, and then it went into the person afterward. We couldn't say for sure that that feather was from that jacket, but finding it on the garage door corresponds more with the person being shot and then the bullet going into the garage door. The person was hit first.

I've had to analyze glitter for a case. A woman was sexually assaulted. The suspect said he had no contact with her. But she had on a shirt with glitter. I looked at *his* clothing and I found eight pieces of glitter that corresponded in color, size, and shape in instrumental analysis.

When I was preparing to do my paper for a conference, I found seven other cases in the United States where glitter played a role. Sometimes it's craft glitter. Sometimes it's glitter from clothing. You can get glitter from a lot of sources.

TRACE ANALYST

Duct tape. We've had quite a few cases involving duct tape. Of-ten, they use duct tape to bind their victims. The first thing we'll look for in a duct tape is physical match. Look at the ends. See if we can match them. If we can't, then we'll go on and start analyzing the tape itself. In duct tape, there's three different layers: there's the adhesive, you know, the sticky part. And then underneath that, there's the cloth. And then underneath that, there's the backing. So we'll analyze all of that.

TRACE ANALYST

Multiple Elements of Trace Cases

With homicides, we'll get in multiple things, so it can take a long time. For one case, I had to do shoe prints and fabric impressions and duct tape and look at some cords. With homicides, you get multiple things, as opposed to burglaries, where you might get just glass.

TRACE ANALYST

The Heavy Metal Holiday Weekends. The name of the guy who did these homicides was Gary Ackley. He was a relatively unskilled grinder-polisher; worked in a metal company. He was a wannabe rock star, but he wasn't very good. He looked like your classic Rent-a-Suspect. He had a mullet haircut, stuff like that. He'd been living with a woman for, oh, ten years or something, and he had two kids by her.

What happened was, on Memorial Day weekend, I was called to an apartment in a suburb of Seattle; the lady who lived there—she was fifty-six, fifty-seven years old—and she was reported missing. Her door was open, her trash was there, and there was some blood on her bed. We collected the bedding. I could tell from the blood that the sheets had been pulled back up after the blood had dried. In other words, if there was blood on the top of the bed and it was wet and you put the sheets over it, it would transfer on to that. It didn't. So somebody was there for a while.

The victim was a very, very clean lady, The rest of her apartment was wonderfully clean. We didn't have any suspect.

On the Fourth of July, another woman's body was found thirty miles northeast of Seattle in a campground. Both these women were found in fairly advanced stages of decomposition, so DNA was of no use to anybody. They could not determine the cause of death.

Before the second victim was found, we were looking at the first victim's bedding and we're finding all these tiny little fragments of metal. Not just one type of metal. Not just steel—there was brass, there was aluminum, there was titanium. . . . Some were little spirals, such as you get when you cut something with a cutting tool. Some of them were hollow spheres—they come when you grind metal against metal. There was also a hand towel in the first victim's bathroom that I collected. It was soiled; it just didn't look right in that fastidious woman's apartment. There were metal fragments on *it*.

These metal things were caused by someone who was grinding and cutting and polishing metal. The first woman was a seamstress who worked for a sports coat company. In her background, she wouldn't have any metal fragments.

When we got to the second victim, lo and behold, there were metal fragments on her. So the cops started to deter-

mine: Who did these women know in common? It turned
out that the first victim was Gary's common-law mother-in-
law. He had had a verbal altercation with her.

Then, it turned out that the second victim was a child-
hood friend of his. She was the last one seen with him at a
party on the Fourth of July.

We compared the metal fragments from the victims with
metal fragments from Gary. We collected samples from his
clothes. I went to his car and collected samples. We went to
his place of work, collected samples. And did a comparison
with all the other samples we had collected from the crime
scenes. And a lot of the samples were similar to what we
were finding on the two victims.

The other thing we did, which was a wonderful find for
us: He had just bought a secondhand car, a Camaro. The
mother-in-law had never, ever been in it. He even said so, in
a statement, himself.

This guy was cheap. He bought the cheapest possible car
seat covers he could, to make the car look new. When he did
that, of course, those fibers came off real easy. The cheaper
the thing, the easier it loses fibers. So I took samples of those
fibers from his car, and then I used a technique called tape
lifting to connect the fibers: You take a two-inch-wide strip
of clear Scotch tape, about six inches long, you put that on
the material and lift it off. And then you put it on one of
those sheet protectors for files. You just put it onto that, so
then you can look through it. Trace people used to vacuum
up sweepings from a car, but if it's a fifteen-year-old car, say,
you're going to get all the trace evidence from the past fifteen years. But if you tape-lift, you get the very top surface,
the most recent activity.

What we saw was— The first victim was wearing a polar
fleece jacket in a purple-blue color when her body was
found; she had been dumped five miles from her apartment.
Purple-blue fibers from her jacket were found on the back-

seat of this car. We also found fibers from his car on her
jacket at the crime scene. That's what we call a two-way
transfer. He said she was never in that car. But the fibers said
she *was* in that car. He used the car to transport her body.
We suggested that he abducted her from the apartment,
killed her, transported her, and then drove about four, five
miles away and dumped her.

At trial, he had no explanation for why all those bits of
metal were found on the victims. And his defense didn't,
either. The defense did say, "Well, *everybody's* got metal
fragments on them." I said, "Well, let's have a look at that."
The defense even brought in the bag from the vacuum
cleaner from the mother-in-law's house, and said, 'Look!
Look at all these metal fragments!' There *were* metal fragments.

But what they were—I examined the contents of five different vacuum cleaners in the crime lab. I looked at the contents of my own vacuum cleaner. There's a lot of flat, rusted
pieces of metal, mostly iron, which are in the environment.
But all the ones we had found were shiny. They were untarnished. They were brass, they were copper, they were aluminum, they were titanium, they were various grades of
steel. And they were all totally untarnished. If you look at
the average person, you might get a small amount of flat
metal plates from iron from buildings and rust and cars and
stuff, but you won't get what we term "fresh metal."

He was found guilty of first-degree murder on the second
murder, because there was premeditation. They couldn't
prove premeditation on the first one, so that was second-
degree. Prison forever.

The twist in the tale is, he was found guilty. Before they
sentenced him, the woman he had been living with marries
him, the guy found guilty of killing her mother.

TRACE ANALYST

We did the biggest case in United States criminal history here
[in Seattle] and we solved it with DNA and trace evidence.
The Green River Homicides.

The killer was charged with seven homicides. DNA could
only be used on the first four victims found. Paint-spray trace
evidence was used to identify three more. He finally admitted to forty-nine victims, that he was eventually charged
with. He also said in court, "And for those that I don't remember where I buried them . . ." So, in all probability,
there's *more* than forty-nine victims. He killed, more likely,
sixty or seventy, even.

He deliberately chose people who wouldn't be missed.
Hookers. When they went missing, people would just think
they moved on, you know? Apart from the initial victims, the
majority of them weren't found for several years. We didn't
find a lot of them back in the eighties—the first Green River
victim was eighty-four, eighty-five—so when he was arrested,
he volunteered, if he didn't get the death penalty, to lead us
to some of them. We found five or six bodies just based on
his knowledge.

The first victims were called the Green River victims because the first three were found in the Green River, which is
in a suburb of Seattle called Kent. In one day. One woman
was found floating in the river. Police were called and they
found another victim underneath her, in the water. When
they were clearing it off, there was another victim on the
bank. Those victims were killed at different times, but the
two had only been in the river for a day; the one on the bank
had only been there for a day. There was a fourth one found
within a day or so after that.

All the other victims—and it was his own term he used—
he buried them in "clusters." He used to bury them together.
So that's how he was able to find them. Unfortunately, the
Pacific Northwest seems to breed these guys. Like Ted

Bundy, the Green River Killer liked to go back and visit his victims afterward. But he buried them farther and farther and farther away from where he picked them up. They weren't being found. And without his assistance, we wouldn't have found a lot of them. The ones we found—a lot of times, we were just finding bones. A lot of times, we were finding bones with clothing on them.

The first four victims found were the only ones identified by DNA, because the other bodies were exposed to the elements for months and sometimes years after death. So there was no skin, tissue, bodily fluids, anything left.

The samples from the autopsies were frozen. They kept waiting till the technology was good enough. As you know, DNA has taken off now, where you can use tremendously small samples; you can use tremendously degraded ones.

And eventually, in August of 2002, the Seattle lab got a hit on Gary Leon Ridgway. He was one of the top three suspects, but they never had a thing on him. They then kept him under surveillance. On the last day of November, 2002, they found that he had slipped away from their surveillance and tried to pick up a police officer disguised as a hooker. It was like, Oh my God, he's starting up again.

I was called in and had to form a team. Four of us in four days hit every house he ever lived in. He lived with his parents. He then moved to a second house, a third house, and then his current house. We didn't know what we were looking for. Everything. Fiber samples. DNA samples. Looking, going through stuff.

He didn't fit any profile whatsoever. He had finished high school. He had been at the same job for thirty-odd years. He had been married to the same woman for eighteen-odd years and was still married to her when we arrested him. He was a spray painter for a company that makes Kenworth trucks; they're the big semis you see on the expressway. He sprayed those. He was one of their best sprayers.

So we were looking for paint. I went to his place of work, and I collected samples of paint from his work. We got all the records from the company about the type of paint they used back at that time. It's amazing how coincidences turn up. The company was in Seattle, right next to Boeing Field. The building the task force was in was directly across the street from the building where Ridgway worked for twenty-five years before moving to the new factory two years before. So the headquarters was *directly* across the street from where Ridgway worked all the time he was killing. You just crossed the road and you were there.

In the lab, we looked at hairs, I don't know how many thousands of hairs. We looked at fibers, thousands and thousands of fibers. I was collecting samples of carpet from his house. When he put a new carpet down— You know the tack strip that you have along the side, each time you take them up, they split real easily. Most people don't take them up. They leave them there, and what happens is, little fibers get caught in the nails that come up from the tack strip. So you can actually go back to a house and get fibers from a carpet that isn't even there anymore by looking there.

We were looking for every type of trace evidence. This was all done in the Trace Section in the crime lab in Tacoma. We were looking at hairs, fibers, glass, metals—any type of trace evidence. We got Skip Palenik, of Microtrace in Chicago, one of the foremost forensic scientists in the world, to help us. We collected a lot of evidence and shipped it to him.

And Palenik was able to find evidence on three other murders, based on minute fragments of paint. And it was paint spray. When you spray paint, it goes through the air and it forms little tiny balls that dry. They're minuscule; you can't even see them without a high-powered microscope. We found some of those on some of the victims' clothes that the crime lab had stored and cataloged. The paint particles were also found on Ridgway. The paint was part of him; it came off on his victims.

We went to court. Normally, I go in, give my evidence, and leave. Half the time, I don't even know if the guy's found guilty or not, unless the prosecutor tells me later, "Thank you for your time. He was found guilty." And I'm like, "Oh." It doesn't mean anything to me.

But on this one, I was there when the families got to speak to him. I've never seen that before. A lot of them were angry at him. Some of them said, "Hope you rot in hell" and stuff like that. One guy got up there and he called him, "You're nothing but a son of a bitch coward. You'll get your reward at some stage . . . ," and then he broke down and he just laughed. Some people got up there to say something and they just stopped. They had to go back. But a lot of them said, "Thank you. At least we know where she's buried now."

The enormity of it! This wasn't one person, or two persons coming up. This was like *fifty sets* of families coming up to do this. One after the other. The sheer scale of the thing was amazing.

TRACE ANALYST

I worked on a case that had multiple trace elements, but it was ultimately solved by a single hair.

This was a missing persons case. A young lady, Laura. She was just graduated from Harvard. And she had just gotten home to Maryland, gotten a new job over in Virginia. Doing great.

All of a sudden, that October, she's missing. She was living with her mom; the parents were divorced. The mom happened to leave on a conference trip. The daughter was there alone. The son comes over on the Sunday. They do laundry together, watch TV. He said he left about ten, eleven o'clock at night, and she was perfectly fine. He gets a call the next morning, Monday morning, from her workplace stating that she didn't show up for work and she didn't call in, which is very unusual, she was very prompt. Did he know anything? Was she sick? And he said, "No, I saw her last night; as far as I know, she was planning on coming in to work."

The brother goes back to the house and looks around. Her briefcase is missing: that's usually by the front door, ready to go to work. Her bedroom looks like what it normally does. Nothing is missing out of the house. The house is locked. He's just baffled.

He calls back to her work. She's still not there. He calls other friends. They don't know. The mother's nervous; she comes home. By early evening, they call the police. And, of course, with missing persons, you can take the information, but you have to leave a little time.

By the next day, when she still hadn't shown up, the investigators came out to the house and started to ask routine questions. The strange part is— The detective told me that when the mother described the part-time gardener she employed to him, he just froze. Because the name she gave was the same person this detective had investigated about six years earlier for another missing person, a little girl. And they never could pinpoint that he had anything to do with it. But now, here's another missing person, and here's his name again.

They managed to track the gardener down within the next day or so. He mumbled some words like, "I guess I shouldn't have done it," but he never expressed anything past that. And that isn't enough to hold you.

They read him his rights. It wasn't until they got to more direct questions that he said, "I want an attorney."

Laura's disappearance was reported on Monday. Friday, they were able to convince the Maryland State Police to use their tracking dogs. They took scents of the girl and did a radial search around the house, out to about a quarter mile.

I got a call that night at home. I had to meet them at the

crime lab back at police headquarters, because they found something. I get there and the dogs had found a pillow that had blood all over it. The pillow had a pillowcase with Batternberg lace on the end. That's exactly what she had in her bedroom, bed linens with Batternberg lace. That, to me—you don't see that style everywhere—that was enough to make a very strong association with the missing girl.

I confirmed that that was, in fact, human blood on the pillow and on the pillowcase. You have an item for exam—in your notes, you detail it exactly, the item number, then you start describing it, telling, in your interpretation, how much blood is there. You even draw it.

So I draw the pillowcase and the pillow and I draw in where all the stains were. And then, once I was sure I had documented how everything looked, I took cuttings of all the stains to send off for DNA testing.

I was able to determine it was human blood. Again, we don't have a body; we don't know what her blood type was. Except—she routinely donated her blood to the Red Cross. So we petitioned for their records and it showed she was type A. And that blood correlated to what the mother's and son's blood types were; that was enough to give us an associative factor there.

It dawned on me—When we put out a plot of where the house was located and where the pillowcase was found, the residential area led to a wooded area that joined a church and its property. The pillowcase was found at the base of a very large tree in the wooded area.

This is all the information you have. And you're on a time line. Now the person is missing four days. We're hoping she's still alive.

The first question given me in the lab was, "By the amount of blood on the pillow and on the pillowcase, is she dead?" And I thought, Oh, great. They want to know if they should turn the investigation into a homicide.

The thing is, if this was from the head, which you would assume from the pillow, head wounds bleed profusely. It just keeps going, and going, and going. And it'll leave a lot of blood. I said, "If this is a head wound, I wouldn't be surprised by this amount of blood. She may still be okay. But if this is from another location, like a major artery, that spurted *past* the pillow, and this is just drippage, then she *wouldn't* be okay."

The detectives were happy with the thought that maybe she was still alive and that this was just from a head wound and had been rectified.

But I'm looking at it. Why was this found in the woods? Did he stop with her there for a moment and prop her up? Or use the pillow to support her?

He must have handled this pillow quite a bit. I spent the next day scrutinizing the pillow, putting folds in the pillowcase to see if I could find any other type of evidence. It's like those paper puzzles, where if you have the paper flat out, it will show you one thing, but if you fold it in threes, it'll show you something else. So I was trying to do that with the pillowcase, to see if I could find maybe another pattern that was on there if the pillowcase was folded odd.

And, believe it or not, in the corner of the pillowcase I found a print in blood. It was a very faint print. After picking it up, I used a dye enhancer called amino black that they use for latent prints. It reacts with the protein in blood. When I applied that to the stain, it brought up all the other ridge details that weren't seen at first. The Forensics Services Section at the crime lab took wonderful photographs and then sent it for latent examination.

You're on pins and needles. I'm thinking, they've already brought in all this evidence from her bedroom for me to look at. The exam room was just filled with all these items. And all I'm thinking is, "Oh please, oh please, oh please, let them ID the print so I don't have to look at everything."

I've found prints in blood before. And it always turned out to be the victim's. Because the victim is the closest thing to that item. They're usually struggling, they're trying to push things away and defend themselves. And they're the ones that transfer their identification onto other things. I thought, "You know, knowing my luck, it'll just be her print and then we'll be back to square one."

I was ecstatic when they came back and said it matched the part-time gardener. His thumbprint. I was like, "Yes! That's it!" His thumbprint in her blood, with him acting strange—that's it. This case is done. I can send back all this evidence.

Then I found out—Within a few hours, the defense attorneys for this gardener came back with a media interview. They said that their client was being wrongly accused, he's being persecuted because he's a homeless person. And they said he routinely goes around and searches for objects that he could use. That night, he happened to be out walking in the woods because he routinely parked his truck in that church parking lot to sleep overnight. And he must have stumbled across this pillowcase and picked it up. Realizing it was damp and sticky, he dropped it and continued on his walk. And that's how he transferred his print. When I heard this, I thought, if I was on a jury, I guess I'd have to say that *could* happen and I'm not gonna be the one to convict this poor guy.

So, now I'm back to looking at all the evidence that was stored in the crime lab. We had quite a lot because they weren't sure what was going to be the important piece. Most of the evidence I received came from him because he was under arrest. We found out, from his canceled checks, that he had storage facilities that he paid rent on. He had a storage facility in Maryland, another in Rhode Island. When they started digging a little into his preferences, they found that he was infatuated with the book and the movie *The Silence of the Lambs*.

Keeping that in mind, the investigators were now faced with going to a storage facility and opening this door. They were telling each other, "You do it." "No, you do it." "I ain't doin' this."

When they did open it, they found containers filled with all kinds of unusual stuff. He just had tons and tons of stuff stored in these storage units. They brought it into the lab to look at. I had to go through all of that, looking for anything that could be associated with her. It just took forever to go through it.

I looked at piece after piece and I found blood on things. But then it'd come back to be his blood. They found a camping site he used and the tent was filled with comforters and all kinds of knives. The comforters all had blood on them. And he hunts! I found a lot of animal blood on the knives. The media would get hold—"Chemist finds blood on knives." The media thinks the case is solved.

The bottom line: Six months I spent looking at evidence. The state's attorney's office decided it was time to go to trial.

I hadn't even started looking at all the hair evidence on this case. I had to switch my hat to "hair and fiber examiner." I started collecting all the hair and fibers that I recovered from each of the items I looked at. I found some of her hair in the back of his truck. A sideline here: When the police confiscated his truck, they found accordion files in the front seat filled with information involving his life. There was a notebook where he would line-item expenses. On the page for the month of October—four days prior to Laura's disappearance—there's an entry: "$21.13. Laura." There was a returned check from a local hardware store. In the memo part on that check was the name "Laura."

I was still doing the hair exam. We still didn't have a body. I needed a known hair sample so I could tell what her hair characteristics are. The only known samples I had were from

the brushes on her bedroom bureau. I had to obtain a statement from the mother and from her girlfriends that they never
used the brush. I was using those hairs as known samples. My
process is: Take the hairbrush, detail it in my notes, and then
start pulling the hair that's caught between the fibers of the
brush. You look at it under a stereoscope and that allows you
to see the general shape and coloration of the hair. Is it straight
or curly? Is there a slight wave to it? Is the hair coarse? Is this a
natural blond? I'm taking all these notes on these different
hairs, and I've taken out, maybe about fifty hairs.

The next thing you do is mount each hair on a microscope slide. The point of this is to have it in a stable
medium so when I put it under the comparison scope, it's
going to stay still. Then you can slide these microscope
slides on the microscope stage and see the internal characteristics: Does the person have large pigments? What are the
shape of the pigments? Are they dense? Is it lightly speckled
throughout the hair?

So I'm taking notes. She has this kind of pigmentation; it
occurs this often in the hair shaft. Look at another hair. Yep.
Same stuff here. I notice this characteristic in this hair shaft.
I put up another slide—same thing. Boy, she's got very consistent characteristics. This is great. Put another slide up
there. And I pause, and I think, "Omigosh. Let me look at
this again."

What I had under the microscope was a wig fiber. And I
look back at the brush, and I'm thinking, "A wig fiber? Why
do I have a wig fiber coming from her hair?"

At that point, I take all the hairs off the brush. She had
quite a bit in there. I look at every single one. This was the
only wig fiber.

I called the investigator just because—I don't know if the
victim wears wigs. He gets back to me later that day and
says, "She doesn't wear wigs. The mother doesn't wear wigs.
None of the girlfriends wear wigs. They don't have wigs in

the house." And I'm thinking, "Oh my God. From this one wig fiber." As we were talking, I think a light went off in the investigator's head. He said, "I think I remember seeing wigs in his storage facility."

They just beam out there, grab the stuff, bring it back. They bring back a bag that had about twenty-four wigs and little wig pieces. I'm going through these and, sure enough, I hit one that has the same dye, the same internal characteristics as the one wig fiber I have. I do a chemical determination and they're both composed of the same chemical configurations. It was like a needle in a haystack.

This is a couple weeks before trial. The prosecutors were just jumping up and down for joy. I sent the fibers to the FBI, which was able to determine that the wig hair came from a particular manufacturer.

When we gave the defense the information, they actually pled guilty within days of going to trial.

The gardener talked to the investigators. What he said was: He had a great working relationship with the mother at the house. But when the daughter came home from college, she just disrupted everything. The mother paid more attention to her, didn't talk to him . . . He was feeling like an outsider. His thought was, if Laura disappeared, everything would go back the way it was.

He knew where the spare key to the house was kept. And that Sunday night, he gets into the house, he takes a pillow from the mother's room, puts it over the girl's face as she's sleeping. He didn't tell us exactly, but he did say he used scissors on her neck and ears. We said, "Ears?!" And he said, well he had to remove her earrings because he couldn't get them out and didn't want any identifiers.

He took her out and put her in his truck. He didn't know he dropped the pillowcase. Everything else was packed in with her. He had a place already dug up, near his campsite, where he put the body.

He went back to the house. He dressed up, like he thought *she* would have for work. When the investigators talked to the neighbors originally, one of them said she saw her leaving for work that Monday morning. The neighbor said she was wearing a trench coat, pants, and a hat.

When they checked into the storage facility, there they found the trench coat, the pants, and the hat. He had brought these to the house early in the morning, dressed up like he thought she would, and put a wig on.

His mistake was, he brushed the wig so it would look nice, and one hair came off onto her brush.

RESEARCH CHEMIST/TRACE ANALYST

The Private Lives of Trace Analysts

I have a tendency to collect odd things. I'll go shopping and if I see something that looks different or odd, I'll be like, "I want to see what this looks like underneath a microscope" or "I want to see what this fur on this jacket is. Is it really fur or what is it exactly?" Or, you know, I'll go into old buildings and collect paint samples to see what kind of paint they used back then. Another thing: My mom is going through chemotherapy right now, so I asked her for some hair samples because I have a feeling the root will be much different than normal roots, because of the chemo.

Know what I do? This is ridiculous. I brush up the floor in my apartment and, this is ridiculous, but when I brush it up, I look in the dustpan. And I'm going, "Now, wait a minute. There's cereal in there. What cereal was that?" And I find myself, after about twenty seconds, going, "What the hell are you doing?"

My kids visit every other weekend. With my kids, I'll go, it's kind of silly, you know. I've got my computer in my office. And I'll tell them, "You can be in my office, okay. But no eating in there under any circumstances." "Yep. Anything you say, Dad." And after they leave, I'll go in. "Wait a minute! What is this *Cheerio* doing here? Why is this *candy wrapper* here?"

My ex-wife used to work in a travel agency. She had a white phone. There were three other women in the office and they all had white phones. And I noticed that the corner of each phone, on the inside, had kind of a pinkish area. I was: 'What *is* that?' And then I realized. Over a period of time, makeup had built up and it left a little pink mark on the inside of the phone, where it touched the side of the face. And there was probably hair spray on the ear end. Stuff like that.

Those are things you wouldn't notice. But it's things *we* notice.

I don't deliberately go around doing this. It's just it's difficult to switch off, sometimes, what you do. We look at things differently, and that's just the way it is. "Trained observer," as it's known.

Salesmen hate to see me coming. When I go to buy a suit, I'm looking at all these different things in the fabric. I'm asking about thread count, presence of certain chemicals in the fiber, kinds of dyes used, short nap . . . I do things like specify the yarn spacing that I'm looking for.

The last time I bought a suit, the guy who was helping me suddenly put his clipboard down. He looked at me, and said, "Who *are* you?"

Five

THE BODY OF EVIDENCE

The body speaks after death. It does. It does. It's literally dying to tell you what happened to it.
> —Dr. Sunandan B. Singh, Medical Examiner, Bergen County,
> New Jersey

You attend an autopsy. Here's a guy on the table, thirty-five years old. Very good-looking. Looks like he worked out a lot. His heart is beautiful, you know, no arteriosclerosis. The guy wasn't filling up on Philly Cheese Steaks. He was probably eating healthy and working out and all that, and Boom! He's dead.

It always makes me feel like going out and having a Philly Cheese Steak. I think, Hey! Why am I knocking myself out eating diet food? Life is short. Have a Philly Cheese Steak.
> —Ellen Aragon, Deputy District Attorney, Hardcore Gang Division,
> Los Angeles County DA's Office

"SEE THIS? THAT'S HIS TORSO."

A crime scene investigator has pulled out some photos. We're sitting outside a Dairy Queen on a hot July day. He's apologized for not having photos of the victim's head: "In the close-ups, you could see that his throat was cut and his nose was almost completely cut off."

Back to the torso picture. To the untrained eye it looks like a white pillow cut open, with yellow ticking inside. "Nope, that's a torso. That yellow stuff is subcutaneous fat." I consider my ice-cream cone.

"Okay, so you've got the torso. See the stab wounds? Those are stab wounds. Okay, what *don't* you see here?"

I have no idea; I'm still getting over looking at a torso.

"It's *obvious* what's not here. *Where's the blood?* There's no blood from those slashes. These cuts were done postmortem. He was already dead."

The victim, in this case, was an elderly man who was murdered by his neighbor's nephew. The autopsy showed that the man bled to death from having his throat cut. All the evidence from the scene and from the autopsy led to a portrait of the behavior of the killer. As the crime scene investigator said, "When the offender cut the throat, it nicked the carotid artery, but they could determine at autopsy that he probably lived a while after that. This man bled out. Now, this is telling me that not only was the bad guy in the room long enough for this poor man to bleed to death, but he stays there afterward, just cutting into him. See how he'd stab him a couple of times? That's just experimentation. The wound to the throat didn't kill the old man right away. So, in the meantime, the offender is here watching this poor old guy die."

In the end, the offender was arrested because of the victim's blood. The crime scene investigator had noticed, and photographed, an out-of-place ridged pattern on the bloody sheets next to the body. This pattern exactly matched the bloodied corduroy cuffs on the killer's jacket.

A victim's body is at the center of violent crime investigations. The body is the ultimate probative evidence. It can also be considered a voice crying out after the crime. From the first discovery of the body through crime scene processing and autopsy, a host of experts work together on hearing this testimony. Their collective motto could be the words inscribed over so many morgues and medical examiners' offices: MORTUI VIVOS DOCENT, "Let the dead teach the living."

People who speak for the dead in this chapter are medical examiners, forensic anthropologists, forensic entomologists, crime scene investigators, and prosecutors. Medical examiners are medical doctors who specialize in pathology and who have the final word on cause of death. Forensic anthropologists bring the science of analyzing bones to the scene and to the lab. Forensic entomologists can determine the time, and sometimes the place of death, by studying the succession of different insects on the body. Crime scene investigators recognize, preserve, and collect evidence essential to the other scientists. And prosecutors work with the experts to tie the evidence together into a narrative on behalf of the victim.

All these experts, working separately and in collaboration, seek answers: "What happened?" "When did this happen?" They ask: "Who is this?" if the body is unidentified. And they ask, and reask: "Why?"

We start with a forensic anthropologist considering a group of skeletal remains in a forest.

Bones tell a story. Even the position you find them in can tell a story. When police find buried remains, or a surface scatter of bones, that's when we [forensic anthropologists] come in.

There was a case in Somerset County, Pennsylvania. The way I got involved, a coroner in one county heard me lecture on forensic anthropology for coroners and law enforcement personnel. A coroner had us process a scene and we gave him a lot of information. Six months later, he referred the coroner in the adjacent county to us.

So this coroner calls me up. "We're in the woods here. And I see a couple of skulls. There's a lot of leaves, I can't really see a whole lot. We could have a Mafia hit burial, or dumping ground, or something. We could have twenty, thirty bodies."

Luckily, they had put crime scene tape up, didn't try to walk over to the skulls or anything. He had been a coroner for forty years, doing scenes other ways, the old ways. But he said, "We're gonna do it this way, the right way, from start to finish."

When we got there, there were three skulls visible and you could see a few bones sticking up out of the ground. It was late fall, so all the leaf litter in this deciduous forest was on the remains. We removed the leaf litter from this mass of human remains. We removed leaf litter very carefully, in a detailed, hands-and-knees search to expose the surface as well as the remains there.

What we had was three individuals, side by side. What crime scene processors might have done in the past was take a few pictures and go in and collect the remains, as best they could, and take them back to the lab. They would have been able to sort the remains into three individuals—there was a twelve-year-old, an eight-year-old, and an adult male—and give an age and sex and ancestry and stature for each one of them.

But in order to figure out what happened here, you'd have to be at the scene.

Three individuals were dead. Each one of them had a gunshot to the head. Without documenting the context, it might have been a difficult determination. Are you dealing with a triple homicide, or two homicides and a suicide, or what's going on here?

We carefully exposed the remains. We did a detailed map of where all the bones were, where all the physical evidence was. We mapped that out very carefully.

The investigators found out the identity of the individuals; it turned out to be an estranged father and his two girls. But by looking at the position of the remains—the father's remains are in the middle, the older daughter's remains are to his right, and the younger daughter's are to his left.

They were all sitting very close together. The orientation of the older daughter's bones was as if she was sitting there and—instantaneous death. You sort of go limp. Her arms are to her side; her legs are splayed. There's absolutely no signs of a struggle. She was shot in the head, from left to right.

Then, going to the younger daughter, the eight-year-old. She's sort of facing him. And his leg is still lying over her legs, as if he's holding her down. She was shot from right to left. And the father had a gunshot to the head, from right to left as well, as if when he was sitting there, he had shot these two individuals and then shot himself in the head. And then his hand went limp, and the gun went between his legs.

By looking at the distribution of the bones, you get a picture of what happened there.

He picked the older daughter, who would have been bigger, shot her first, out of the blue. She was totally taken by surprise, instantaneous death. And then the younger daughter sees this and tries to get away. He has his leg over her; he shoots her, and then he shoots himself. The whole pattern is revealed by joining the detailed map we drew with the remains and how they're situated with the gunshots. We could also, by how much tissue was there, provide an estimate of how long the bodies had been there. And it matched the girls' and their father's time of disappearance. The father and mother were in the process of divorcing. The result? Two homicides. One suicide.

FORENSIC ANTHROPOLOGIST

Even what may look like a random scatter of bones always has a pattern. Sort of my mantra is: "Patterns will emerge." If you assume they're not there, you're never gonna find them. But patterns are *always* there.

FORENSIC ANTHROPOLOGIST

Question One: What Happened?

Medical examiners on how they determine cause of death

The dead speak through us. When you examine a body, you enter into a dialog with that person. The more careful you are, and the more probing you are, the more they'll speak to you.

When I'm doing my anatomic examination, I'm gathering infor-mation and trying to extract from that person: What hap-

pened? So then I can report that information to those they
leave behind, who really want to know.

For some of us, on a more subtle level, I think that's how
we can do this job on a daily basis. If you think about it just
on the surface, it can be a little unsettling.

This job definitely isn't your typical physician job. Most
people go into medicine because they want to help people.
It's obvious I'm not going to be able to make *my* patient get
better. But my obligation is to treat them with respect while
they're under my care. I always call them my patients. I try
not to refer to them as bodies. And when I talk to families, I
always refer to them by name. For example, I was doing an
autopsy on George just now. He doesn't have any family, but
when I talk to his friends, I always say "George." I don't say
"the victim" or "the body." That's just kind. It's the kind way
to treat them.

You use your eyes. For example, the nourishment of the person,
the stature of the person, the race, sex, how far gone the person is from the time the body was alive. Making notes of the
general color of the skin, the liveliness of the skin, "turgor"
as we call it. Some people may be undernourished, or dehy-
drated. You can check that right away by pinching the skin
and seeing how resiliently it goes back.

You evaluate the injuries. How long have they been on the
body? The trauma on the body will tell you things. A fresh
trauma will look different than an older trauma.

People with less pigment—their injuries are very easily detectable. With dark-skinned people, it becomes a nightmare,
believe me. Sometimes you cannot even see the bleeding under the skin. It's much, much tougher to assess superficial injuries on dark-skinned people.

Bellies, too. Somebody punches someone in the belly, you
won't see much trauma from our side. But you open the
belly and, lo and behold, there is a huge amount of blood

there, probably the spleen has ruptured, or the liver has been smashed. Very easy to miss that in dark-skinned people.

I had a case with a ten-month-old little boy. The story was that he was found unresponsive in his crib by his father. It happened in the afternoon. The baby came to us [the ME's office] with the working diagnosis of SIDS, or aspiration, because they had found some vomitus in the crib.

I remember doing the external examination. This was a black child, so sometimes bruises are not so readily apparent. When I looked at his forehead, it just didn't look right to me. It wasn't flat; it looked like it was a little elevated. And when I took my photographs, the flash just came off the forehead in a very unusual way. So I said to myself, "You know what? Let me not get myself in a dither until I see what's going on. Don't jump to any conclusions. Just take it one step at a time and do your autopsy like you always do and see what you find." Because—there were no clear bruises, no cuts, no scrapes—but just the sense that something was not right on the forehead.

We began the examination. We usually do the chest and abdominal examination first. So I did that, and there was nothing as far as bruising or bleeding or any other trauma. When I got to the cranial examination, it was like, "Oh! I *know* what I'm seeing." There was clearly some impact injury. Particularly in the area of the forehead, which was swollen. That's why it was looking so unusual to me.

This turned out to be a child-abuse case. I called the prosecutor's office and said, "This is not what we thought we were dealing with initially." And sure enough, that started an investigation in which the father did confess, after many hours of interrogation, that he couldn't get the child to stop crying and so he punched the child several times in the head. The baby had no skull fractures, but he did have a subdural hematoma that was the cause of death.

It's those days when I really feel that the work is extremely important.

And you know what? I often give presentations to different groups. Once a year, I lecture the Police Academy recruit class. Part of what I say to them is, "Always trust your gut reaction. If there's something that your gut is telling you just isn't right, don't dismiss it. Check it out."

An autopsy is only as good as the background information that accompanies it. If I were to go into the autopsy room and have a dead body in front of me, and just begin an autopsy without knowing who that person was, or something about the circumstances surrounding their death, it really would be meaningless.

When I was in the New York Medical Examiner's Office, I re-member the ME asking us what was the most important tool that we used. I remember scratching my head, going, I could get away without scissors, I could get away without a forceps. You need a scalpel. But you also need a bone saw. I was trying to juggle which of those two was the most important tool.

The ME went around the room and asked everybody, and everybody got it wrong. He said, "The most important tool of a forensic pathologist is the telephone."

He was absolutely right. I spend a great deal of time on the phone with family members, physicians, coworkers, whoever might have some little pearl of wisdom to share about the deceased. You don't work in a vacuum. Everybody—detectives, investigators, local police, family members, coworkers, hospital people—everybody has a little bit to offer.

And it becomes like a puzzle where we each add our little piece.

The body speaks. The body tells you a lot. But you *can't* just look at the body.

In fact, I heard this a long time ago: "The circumstances surrounding death are more important than the autopsy in determining what the cause of death really was." I didn't believe it. But I *do* believe it now.

If you get appropriate, and complete, information about what has happened, or what was alleged to have happened, then you can correlate it with the autopsy findings. And you'll have a much better idea of what really happened.

Often, the autopsy alone can be misleading, and if you *only* do autopsies, if you isolate yourself from things at the scene, you'll be led astray, not infrequently, and you can come to bad conclusions.

One case I handled was that of a woman who fell down a flight of stairs. That's kind of a common case for a medical examiner to handle. Most of the time it's accidental.

This happened to be a middle-aged woman. You always wonder what happened, if there were no witnesses to the event. And, as much as we can give information about fatal head injuries or fractured ribs and injured internal organs, I always wonder: How do we know, one hundred percent, that there wasn't somebody at the top of the stairs who gave them a little push?

In this case, I had been given the information that she had no family that had been contacted yet. And the next thing I know, I'm getting a call from a funeral home wanting to pick up the remains. My question to the funeral director was, "Who made these arrangements? I was under the impression that the family had not yet been contacted."

The funeral director named a gentleman who had made arrangements for her. He said this was a boyfriend, something like that. I don't know what possessed me to ask if this gentleman had any information about how she had fallen down the stairs. The funeral director said, "Well, yeah. He told me that they were having an argument." I said, "Oh, really? We're not releasing the body yet." And I immediately called the prosecutor's office.

It turns out, what seemed to be an accidental fall ended up turning into a homicide investigation. And he ended up admitting that he pushed her down the stairs.

This guy wanted her buried very quickly so that everything would be swept under the rug, so to speak.

The death certificate is not the last word. If I get more information later on, that leads me to a different opinion, I'll revise the death certificate.

And burial is not the last word. Bodies can be exhumed. Cremation is probably the last word.

Cause of death can't always be determined. Take, for example, serial killer Ted Bundy. Well, Ted was apprehended in North Florida. Before that, he went through Tallahassee and into a sorority house at a college, and killed a few girls. And then he made his way down to Lake City. And Bundy's last victim, last known victim, was a thirteen-year-old schoolgirl in Lake City. He abducted her in his van, took off with her . . .

Her decomposed body was found a month or two later. At that time, there was not much left in the way of soft tissue. They could not find a precise cause of death. So the medical examiner who did the autopsy there was reasonably certain that this was a homicide, but he didn't know what it was for sure. Rather than put "Undetermined" for "Cause of Death," he put on the death certificate: "Homicidal Violence of Undetermined Type."

That seems a little edgy to me, but I think he was probably right. Circumstances were just so compelling. And, likely, it was asphyxial.

When you have a victim, sometimes there are just so many injuries, when you first look at it, you think, "Oh my God, I can't find my way through this." So what you try to do is to look at an injury cluster, to see if there's any kind of pattern that you notice. If you spend the time and look for a pattern, it begins to become manifest to you. You begin to see a pattern there.

I had one case where a girl had blunt-force trauma to the head and she also had a pitchfork and a saw used to try to dismember her. The assailant ended up not being able to dispose of the body, but the marks were clearly there, indicating that he had tried. There were marks from a pitchfork's prongs, spaced at regular intervals.

A lot of times, people will be amazed at the kind of conclusions you can make. If you're not trained to look, you're not going to find anything. But if that's your area of expertise, you can see through all the mess to make some meaningful conclusions.

I've had cases with nearly skeletonized bodies where I worked with a forensic anthropologist, and we found the cause of death. The latest case I worked on was a middle-aged man whose body was found inside a large plastic garbage can. He'd been there four to six months. He had been strangled.

The general autopsy didn't show very much. But when we took out the neck organ block, after the forensic anthropologist x-rayed those, we found that the hyoid bone had been fractured. The hyoid is a little horseshoe-shaped bone in the upper neck, and it gets fractured when you *squeeze* it real hard, like with a manual strangulation. Not with a hanging, but with a manual strangulation.

This man was old enough that the bone was partially ossified; it was pretty hard, so it fractured easily. In early life, children and young adults, the bone is kind of flexible. You can't break it in a young person. But it's much easier to break if you're middle-aged or elderly. Might not happen with a thirteen-year-old girl. But it sure did happen with this middle-aged man.

I responded to a scene—a triple homicide in a home. There were three males that seemed to have been murdered execution-style. Shot in the head, two of them multiple times. We brought the bodies back and performed the autopsies.

The story was this: These three men were dead in the home, and when the young son came home, during the lunch recess, he discovered these bodies and then of course the poor frightened child ran to the next room, he called the police, and I responded as well.

I performed the autopsy on one of the victims. My victim was very interesting in the sense that he had almost sixteen stab wounds on him. Mind you, the other two victims were shot, and it puzzled everybody what happened here. The stabs went through the front of the neck, chest, and even abdomen. And somehow, on the right cheek of this person, there was a very jagged injury. And we couldn't understand what the heck it was—because all the stabs are there, and what's this? Stab wounds are sharp and clean, in a sense, and this was jagged.

We x-ray our victims before we do the autopsy. Lo and behold, we saw that there was an object in the throat of this person which seemed like a bullet. When the autopsy was completed, the prosecutors thought that this person may have been tortured so as to find out where the valuables were: there were valuables missing from the house. Jewelry. And the person who owned the house was a jeweler. So they thought the killers tortured my victim in order to find out where the jewelry was.

I had done the autopsy, but there were some other injuries on this person, particularly on his palms. The injuries seemed as if they originated on the ulnar side, meaning on the side where the little finger is. It came from that side and then went out the thumbs. It was totally shattered. The bullet seemed to have passed through, in between the victim's two palms. It had gone through that and then hit the right cheekbone of this person, and then, of course, knocking out the corresponding molar teeth, then going into the throat, and lodging there.

The three victims were all Indians. And they were Hindus. And Hindus, you know, put the palms together in prayer.

I argued against the prosecutors' belief that the victims were tortured. I said, "On the contrary, I think, by the time they came to this third victim, they were left with just one bullet. The previous two victims had been shot in the head. They tried the same thing with *this* person while he was begging for his life, folding the hands together, and begging them to spare him."

So it isn't that the bullet just happened to pass through both the palms like that, starting with the pinkies, and then shattering the thumbs, and then hitting the right cheek, and lodging in his throat. Just imagine—the guy must have been on his knees when he was shot. The angle of the bullet was such that a person must have been standing over him while the victim was on his knees, literally begging for his life. And then gagging on all the blood, and gurgling and sputtering.

The assailant was not going to leave a witness to identify him. So what the assailant does is goes into the kitchen and brings back a knife and—stab, stab, stab, stab, stab. That was my interpretation. And I really imposed upon the prosecutors to accept my interpretation. I said, "This is not torture. This is the necessity to kill the person so there is no witness."

Pathology is a very broad field. It's literally impossible to prac-tice without a very large peripheral brain, and by that I mean a very extensive, up-to-date, and expensive—library. We all do a lot of booking.

But in television or movies, the pathologist knows everything! Bullshit!

You see all these truly exotic, state-of-the-art, technologically advanced examinations being done on television. That's not how it is in the real world. That's not at *all* what it's like in the real world.

We all have tight budgets; we can't do the unlimited autopsy, "Nothing's too good for this case." You can't do it. You just can't do it.

I'm terribly amused when I see something on TV like, the detec-tive comes to the autopsy. Here is the forensic pathologist; she's sitting there. The body's still on the table, mind you. And the pathologist is talking about the results of the DNA testing.

That's kind of interesting. DNA testing takes a while, weeks or months. But she's got the results already. The body hasn't even left the table.

I love my job. I love the science of it. I love that you're part of a team. You're working with detectives and prosecutors and forensic scientists—it's a team effort.

I just love it. But it's awkward to say that. It gives people the idea that I must be some sinister person who dresses in black and stands at the back door with my scalpel, just waiting for bodies to come in. That's not the case at all.

A lot of times, these are sudden, violent deaths. Families never prepare themselves for anything like this. Their loved one comes here. They don't know what to do. The thing I find most rewarding about my work is dealing with families, giving them answers to the questions they have about cause of death.

Even if it's just— They hear your voice and know that you're the person that's going to be doing the autopsy, and they have some idea that you're not somebody that just cuts, cuts, cuts. I think that really helps them.

Forensic Anthropologists on What Bones Reveal

I am a working forensic anthropologist. I work as a consultant to the medical examiner and law enforcement in cases of unidentified remains. That doesn't necessarily mean skeletonized remains. I also do work on decomposed bodies and burned bodies.

My job is to help determine the age, the sex, the race, the height, and any other physical descriptors of that individual that would aid in identification.

Any case that we work on, we want to examine the bones. It can be the bones themselves, the trauma you examine on them. It can be where they're found, or how they're arranged. It can be: The individual has cracked ribs. He was beaten before death. There may be witnesses who can say, "Yeah, I saw this happen and that happen." That can be corroborating evidence.

If there is perimortem trauma, we want to be able to distinguish among sharp-force injuries, blunt-force injuries, gunshot wounds, and various fractures. To fine-tune that, we'd hope to be able to learn something about the directionality of the injury, the velocity of the injury. If it's a gunshot, what can we say about the characteristics of the projectile?—whether it's a rifle or a shotgun slug. If it's a knife, what type of knife was used?

If it was blunt-force injury, sometimes you can identify things as fine-tuned as a hammerhead or a tire iron. These occasionally are imprinted on the bone.

And where all this becomes important, of course, is in aiding in reconstructing the circumstances of death.

There are lots of misconceptions about bones. I got an e-mail from a crime lab in England. It said, "We train our people that saw marks destroy their own evidence because it's a blade with numerous teeth and each tooth interrupts the consecutive teeth and therefore toolmark analysis on bones is nonexistent here." I've heard that from the FBI, too.

I wrote my dissertation on analysis of saw marks. Saw marks are great, because here you have a repetitive motion, numerous teeth create patterns, and patterns are identifiable. I *love* saw marks. I mean, they do so much more than just a stab wound to the bone or cartilage. There's so little information there. But saw marks leave tremendous information, and it's good stuff, and many times leads to narrowing down the suspect tool. And it narrows down, potentially, the behavior of the perpetrator.

In the eighties, we had lots of dismemberment cases. In the nineties, it really slowed down. Because all the forensic science was coming out, saying, you know, we can identify somebody from just a speck of bone. But now they seem to be coming back again.

There are three reasons people do dismemberment. The primary reason is to deter identification. Another reason is transport. You've got a dead body in your apartment and you need to get it out. You might try to cut it up. The third reason is total abuse of the victim. There's a lot of hate there.

People think it's easier to dismember than it really is. People get caught all the time when they're half done. Or they're just getting started dismembering somebody and they're trying to flush them down the toilet, or something, and it just doesn't work. Really.

I had one of these, years ago in Memphis. First date. Woman picked the wrong guy to go out with. Something went bad and he started to beat her, then he stabbed her. Then he decided well, he needs to hide the body. He did a bad job. He sawed on the arm in one direction, then gave up and sawed in the other direction. I could prove that in court by the cut marks.

He tried to put tissue down the toilet and the toilet got clogged. At that point, his roommate ran out and called the cops. When we arrived, the killer was on the floor, screaming that he had been attacked.

The more evidence you have to look at, the more information you're gonna get. So, in a dismemberment, I like to see a lot of bones sawed up. If someone's died from a beating, if there's more blows, there's more information.

Bones can tell a story. Say, there's a scuff mark on the skull. That may be diagnostic of the tool that hit it.

But if even there's just one blow or one wound—if a bone if compromised, or altered in any way, that's evidence.

Some of the cases that are most challenging that we end up hav- ing to investigate are cases involving Jane or John Does, where the body's found in a very decomposed state.

What it *requires* is taking those remains and, typically, dissecting or boiling to remove the soft tissues in the body so you can see the skeletal elements in a very clean and pristine state. And many times when you look at these types of cases where there is no cause of death, we will end up *finding* a cause of death, such as a stabbing—which may have caused very large soft tissue injuries that are no longer there as a result of the decomposition. As the body decomposes, that evidence goes away.

But stabbings leave very discrete marks on the bone. They may only be a millimeter in length or less. We've had many, many cases where there's no cause of a death, and then we do a detailed examination, after removing the tissues, and we find evidence, you know, that the person's been *stabbed* six or seven times in the neck.

Crime Scene Processors on Their Findings

I've worked so many baby deaths. You can use forensic light sys-
tems, kind of like a laser, to investigate these deaths. Illinois
is unique: every crime scene investigator has one.

One thing the laser is really good on is with dead people;
it shows bruising really well. It works very well on women. A
lot of women get strangled to death and you can't see it. The
laser picks it right up. For some reason, it works two days after people have been embalmed even better.

I've done this with infants and babies so many times. I've
gone to funeral homes and examined these little babies. It's
like an hour before the funeral. What the bulk of them
are—you can see where somebody hit them with a fist.
There will be these little patches, two or three inches square.
And you'll see these all over the face, the chest, the stomach.
It's where they've been beaten to death. It'll show up, with
the laser. You put an orange filter over the camera and then
you can photograph it. I'll take the photos and show them to
a pathologist and the investigation goes from there.

This laser puts out a very intense, bright light, and you put
orange-colored goggles on. If you don't have the goggles on,
all you see is the light. Bruising on a baby will show up as a
darker area. An investigator from Orange County told me they
used this technique on a baby. Once the laser was on, they
could see a very clear imprint of four fingers and a thumb.
The fingers were across the mouth and nose of the baby.

Look for patterns in wounds. Like in skulls? Half-moon shapes
are usually indicative of a hammer. A claw hammer. Because
you don't normally strike the flat surface; it's usually a corner.
So it leaves a half-moon impression. I've seen U-shapes,
which are from pistols—the hollow end where the magazine
goes in. And you're hitting on an angle and you're leaving
these U-shaped impressions. Jagged cuts *can* be indicative of a

serrated edge—knife, saw. Incised wounds are clean; they're usually indicative of something very sharp, like a razor.

The biggest misconception has to do with ballistics. People love to think that bullets go and they bounce around and then they go in some other direction and they bounce and they go some other direction. People forget that these bullets are moving in feet per second. They're gonna go in a straight line until they stop, or they hit a brick wall, or they lose their energy and they turn from feet per second, which is ballistic, to blunt, which is miles per hour. Right before it stops, the bullet loses energy and it can be diverted.

But people have all these theories about the bullet entering the elbow and then going back down and then ending up in the liver.

What you do, if you line those wounds up, you find out that there really is a straight line. If we all stood in perfect anatomical positions when we got injured, it'd be much easier to interpret, but that never happens. The body's always in some weird position, which makes it difficult to interpret.

Question Two: When Did This Happen?

Medical Examiners on Pre-and Postmortem

We often get asked this: "Can you tell the difference between a trauma caused premortem and a trauma caused postmortem?" The main answer is this: If a person is alive and trauma happens, the body reacts in many ways. The reaction of the body is called a live reaction.

This reaction will be lacking in a dead person. You can shoot a dead person and make it look like a gunshot wound. But if it is postmortem, the body's reaction will be lacking. Or a person may be hanged, you know, after the fact, to make it look like a suicidal hanging. Or a body may be burned after being killed. The reaction to the burn marks would be lacking. Postmortem trauma may be to conceal a crime. Or you may have someone like a serial killer assaulting the body after death. You have to consider these things.

We look at postmortem artifacts. For example, when the bodily functions cease, the body becomes subject to environmental influences—external and internal.

Speaking of the internal environment, you know the body has en-zymes and bacteria in the intestinal tract. They are ever hungry to work on the body's resources, and they'll start the decomposition processes, which can be useful in determining the time of death.

External environment includes variations in temperature, in moisture, and other conditions. Hot temperatures, especially, make the body start decomposing early. If it's cold, the body will not decompose as quickly, but that will add to other effects of cold on the body. For example, it might freeze the body and cause damage to certain parts, which might be misinterpreted as being from trauma.

And in the external environment, microbes and termites, flies and larvae, and even small animals, like rodents or other flesh-eating animals, can cause damage to the human body. And they can create certain conditions which may be misinterpreted as trauma. Even little ants, roaches, cockroaches, can do that. So you have to be aware of those things. They can either be used to your advantage, depending on how alert and knowledgeable you are, or they can be misinterpreted.

When Did This Happen? Part Two:

A Forensic Entomologist on Insects as Clocks

The body changes biochemically over time, right? It goes through many different chemical changes. Related to those chemical changes are different groups of insects.

So, if we've done research in Indiana in the summertime, for instance, and we found a body out in the woods and it has species D, E, F, and G, I can say, "Okay, that means this is between day 24 and day 36." That means this body has been out in the woods a minimum of twenty-four days and a maximum of thirty-six days.

What we do in forensic entomology is use standard insect biology, insect behavior, insect growth and development, and apply it in a different way, to estimating time of death. We have two methods. One is taking a specific insect species, one of the blowflies primarily, and by knowing how fast or how slow it grows at different temperatures, then we can determine very precisely how long the body's been there. Insects are cold-blooded, right? They don't have an internal heater like we do to keep our growth rate constant. They're at the mercy of the temperature. If the temperature gets cold, they may not grow at all. But if the temperature's up to ninety, they'll grow in a very short period of time.

The other method we have is to determine— Okay, let's say we've studied the progression and decomposition of the insects that come in and leave over a period of time. It's been known since the 1880s that there's a certain sequence to decomposition *and* there's a certain sequence of insects that come in.

Blowflies are the first ones on the scene. Within seconds to minutes after somebody dies, they're gonna be there. They're gonna be the ones found with the body, unless the body has progressed into the stages where they're no longer interested in the body.

The time of death is one of the most important things to figure out. It tells you the last person who was with the victim. It certainly would indicate where the person might have been last. If you can find out who the person was with just before he died, it may illuminate who killed him.

If you can establish when somebody died, then you can implicate suspects, or you can exonerate suspects. And clearing a suspect is just as important as fingering one. Because if you have five suspects and you can get rid of four of them, and this one guy is left, who's the prime suspect?

Location of death: That can sometimes be established by insects, based on where you know a particular insect lives.

For example, a body was found off of I-75 in Lake City, Florida, dumped there. When the insect specimens were collected from the body, it was realized from the specimens that the species didn't occur in Florida. They weren't found south of Tennessee. They found out that the person had been murdered in Detroit, driven two thousand miles, and dumped in Florida.

I've got a baseball cap I like to wear with the saying MAGGOTS ARE OUR FRIENDS. A coroner gave it to me. When I'm doing PR for TV shows and stuff, sometimes I'll put that cap on.

I want to get a T-shirt made up with that. The T-shirt's gonna have a copper, he's taking notes, the body's at his feet, and there's a little maggot on his shoulder, whispering in his ear, telling him the story. I mean it: Maggots are our friends.

Question Three: Who Is This?

A Forensic Anthropologist on Identifying Skeletal Remains

My specialization is unidentified bodies. I try to help to identify as many people as possible. I may not be able to identify the person, but I'm going to comb through those remains to see if there's *anything* on that skeleton that's gonna help identify that person.

People don't realize that bones tell a great deal about their owners.
Somebody had a broken bone during life—I should be able to see that healed fractured bone. If somebody had a hip prosthesis, I should be able to see that. If somebody had a vertebra that collapsed, or they had arthritis—I should be able to see that. What happens is, the height of the vertebra becomes less with age, and with gravity, and with arthritis, and you can see that in the bone. So, by looking at that, I might say, "Okay, maybe this person had pain in their neck because they have this much osteoarthritis." Or sometimes, the vertebrae fuse together and now the person can't even turn their head.

So, I'm trying to tell a little story about the person, based on their bones.

If you have some information about the buried individual—if that person was a laborer, or a bodybuilder, say—the body may have certain things that are clues as to what the occupation of that person may be.

I helped out on a cold case involving an Olympic boxer from Russia. This was in the late nineties. This boxer was working as a bouncer at a bar in New York. He threw some people out of the bar and they didn't like it. They apparently came back and attacked the guy, put him in the back of their car, and drove him around and ended up in New Jersey. Somewhere along the line, the victim died.

So, he was driven to New Jersey and buried in the back-yard of a house. Several years after he was kidnapped and killed, the FBI in New York had gotten information from an informant about where this body was buried. They contacted the police department in New Jersey in the town where the body supposedly was. They requested my assistance in doing the excavation.

It took us three days to find the skeleton. Completely intact. We did an age, sex, race, and height analysis. We couldn't identify him at first because the dental records we received were from Russia—and they use a different dental identification system.

But I found evidence of healed fractures and other injuries. Things that were consistent with the occupation of being a boxer.

If we have this unidentified body—and I have determined the age, sex, race, height of the person, and any kind of pathology or injury that person may have had during life, and there's a ring found on one of the finger bones, so you know it belonged to the person—I'll use all that in a flier. You want to pack the record. You want to get everything you know about the body out to the public. So you make a flier, you put all your information in the papers, you put it in the national database for missing and unidentified bodies.

But if that person *remains* unidentified, the law enforcement agency may ask me to do a facial reconstruction of that person. Facial reconstruction is a last-ditch effort. So they say, "We don't have any more leads. Can you do a facial reconstruction so we can get an idea of what this person looked like? And we can get that out to the media."

When I do that, I ask for all the investigation reports. And I'm usually at the scene. I want to know about all the clothing, everything that was found with this body, including hair. Hair is very important. If I have *any* hair, I'll send that to the state police lab for hair analysis. Because what they can do is determine the color of the hair, whether it's been treated, if it was recently cut, how long the hair is, and the race.

I ask for the clothing. I want to see if there's anything on the person that would help me determine how big the person was. From the bones, you can't really tell if the person was skinny or heavy. But you can tell from clothing. Unless you have a homeless person and he picks up clothes out of a garbage can or the Salvation Army; he doesn't necessarily have clothes that fit him. I've worked on bodies that have had multiple layers of clothing, because they're trying to keep warm.

So, what I look for: I look for a belt. If a belt is on the body and it's buckled, you know it's gonna be buckled where it's comfortable for the person. So, when the body is found, I want to know if there's a belt and was it buckled. And then we measure the waist. If you have the size of the waist, which can give me an idea, once I determine the height of the person— If I've got a man who is five-foot-one, and he's got a belt around his waist and it's buckled, and it's at size 46, what would that tell you? He's pretty big.

Then I know, when I do my facial reconstruction, I need to make this guy look a little heavier.

If there's no clothing, then I have to do just an average face. And you say on the flier that this is just a facsimile of what the person may have looked like.

Facial reconstruction is a good technique to use on skeletonized remains because other things you can usually look at on the body—such as pierced ears, tattoos, scars—you no longer have.

I work directly on the skull. I use modeling clay. It doesn't harden. I use real prosthetic eyes in my reconstructions. And I use real wigs.

I use tissue thickness measurements on twenty-one points on the skull. Those tissue thicknesses are based upon the sex and the race of the person. Since the late 1800s, researchers have measured thicknesses on different points of the face. Those have been averaged to fit a particular race, a particular sex, and we use those as guidelines.

I cut markers to that tissue thickness for that particular point on the skull. And I glue it on the skull. I cut clay to the same tissue thickness and I put that on the skull as well.

But the skull really dictates to me what the face is going to look like because I'm following the bony contour of the skull. The skull is really speaking to me, in a sense.

Yeah, it really does. It really does. It takes shape under your hands.

I guess it takes me eighteen to twenty hours to do one. I do it for a couple of hours, and then leave it, and come back. The skull is really what tells me what the face is going to look like. It's not like doing a bust, where you're starting from nothing. I'm working directly on the skull, so the skull is telling me where the nose is and how wide the nose is going to be, where the teeth are. And the skull is going to tell me how long the nose is and what the angle of the nose is going to be, what the height of the ear is going to be.

Until I'm working on that particular skull, I don't know what I'm going to come up with. I don't know what face is going to come out until I do it.

A body washed up on the shores of the Hudson River in north Jersey in October of '95. He was mostly skeletonized and decomposed. I examined that body for all the information: age, sex, race, height, and I had determined that he was a Caucasian male between forty and sixty, between five-four and five-seven. He had a partial denture still in his mouth and he had an underbite.

That case went into the national database; there were no matches at all. The prosecutor's office in Bergen County asked me to do a facial reconstruction. I finished the reconstruction in January of '96 and returned the skull to them and they had it on somebody's desk in their office prior to holding a news conference.

A man walks into the prosecutor's office. My facial reconstruction is sitting on the desk. He sees it, and says, "That's my friend!"

He said he had searched for a year, everywhere in New York City, and he couldn't find his friend. He decided, Well, I've exhausted everything in New York. I'm gonna go try New Jersey.

They took his information. His friend had been reported missing in December 1993 by his wife in New York City. They got dental records, and he was positively identified. His cause of death remained undetermined.

The friend that had been searching for him was a doctor, had been out of the country for years, and returned in 1994. He said, "Once in New York I started calling every acquaintance of the victim, but no one knew anything. I was surprised to find out the family kept the landlord ignorant of the disappearance in order to retain their rent-controlled apartment. That took precedence over the search. None of the neighbors who knew the victim had been questioned." He just kept asking everybody who knew the victim where he was. Manhattan police directed him to Missing Persons. They showed him hundreds of photographs of unknown bodies that appeared in all five boroughs of New York City since 1993. They told him that his search was a formidable task. He finally abandoned the search in 1995. In 1996, he was talking to his nephew about his friend, and the nephew said, "Why don't you just search across the Hudson River?" So the doctor called the Bergen County police and they directed him to the county prosecutor. And I had just given them the skull. And it was sitting right there when he walked in.

They still don't know what happened to the victim. His family didn't even bother to report him missing. But he did have a friend who kept looking for him until he found him.

You know, I see all the bad things that people do to each other, because the people I see have ended up deceased. You see this

day in and day out. But you don't read about it in the papers.
You read about the *big* cases, like some horrible dismemberment case, or if it involves a child. You hear about that. But
you don't hear about all the persons that are reported missing. There may be a blurb about a body that's found, but
then you don't hear about it anymore. And maybe the public
thinks the person got identified. But maybe not. There are
more than two hundred and forty unidentified bodies in
New Jersey. California has more than two *thousand*.

There is a lot more out there than the general public
knows about.

Who Is This? An ME's Story

Once every few years, I get a totally unidentified person, either
skeletonized or otherwise. There are set criteria laid down.
We take measurements in all cases: height, weight, age, sex,
race, dental records, x-rays, if there are any tattoos, any scars.
We'll enter that information in the NCIC [National Crime
Information Center] database and we'll take off from there.
There will be some hits. Some misses.

So far, as far as my memory goes over the past twelve
years, there's been only one individual who has remained *totally* unidentified.

It was a woman. And I suspect that the person who killed
her was aware that she did not have any type of fingerprint
record. So what he had done, he had hacked the body—please
don't think that I'm being very cheap here, but this is the best
way to describe what the offender did—and he dumped the
body in a Dumpster, minus her head. So we could not establish from facial features what she would look like and circulate
a picture of her to the media. There was no fingerprint record
to match. And since there is no face, there *is* no person. No
one came forward to ask about her. She's still unidentified.

The person who had murdered her was almost like a professional. We could see that. He exsanguinated her: there was no blood left. He must have dismembered her in a bathtub or something like that. He used a mechanized cutting device. And he went through the *joints*, so he must have had a basic knowledge of anatomy. Say, for example, going through the knee joint, a clean cut like that to sever the lower leg from the thigh, and through the hip joint, so he knew anatomy very well. Sort of like Jack the Ripper. Very anatomic.

The gruesome thing was—when I reached the place where the body was, the name of the place is Hackensack. And it was a perfect case of hack and sack.

The Final Question: Why?

Medical Examiners

There is a case that bothers me as a person much, much, too much. This case has disturbed me very deeply. No matter how much you have worked in this field you never get inured to the pain that you come across. It hurts you. Especially when it comes to children, when they are involved in some type of . . . insane . . . violence, it bothers me a lot. And even to this day, this case haunts me, literally.

In 1992, I was called to a scene where, at first sight, it looked like a double homicide. A father and his four-year-old daughter were found in an apartment, a very nice, elegant apartment. They were dead at the scene. Our first reaction was, Who could so brutally murder a man and his daughter like that?

The girl had been shot at least two times in the head and she was right in the crook of the arm of her father, who was on the bed at her side. But what really was bizarre was that the face and head of the father was swathed in some duct tape on his eyes, on his nostrils, and it didn't make any sense why it would be like that.

But, gradually, you know, things started unfolding. The gun was at the scene, they made the prints on the gun, and they found the prints of the father himself. His were the only prints on the gun.

The subsequent investigation revealed that the father had shot the child first, in the head, and then himself. And he had shot himself through his mouth, into his head. The investigation also showed that the father was some kind of paramedic or male nurse.

You know, the entire event, all this had happened on Mother's Day. Apparently, his wife was on the West Coast looking for a job and the couple was in the midst of a separation.

He had left a note for his wife: "This is my gift to you as a Mother's Day gift." Can you believe that?

I have been absolutely beside myself for a very long time after this event. It really, really, really bothered me a lot. And even to this day, I can't imagine an individual doing something like that to himself and to his child. Just to spite his wife. It does hurt me a lot, very deeply. But, again, there are things that really, really bother you a lot.

We do a so-called psychological autopsy on our victims. I just couldn't understand why he would put tape on his eyes and nose and features. I've seen some people who have shot themselves in such weird ways that they didn't want to deface themselves. My take on this was he probably wanted to preserve his features and not damage them. And probably to make it look like a double homicide.

This was horrid, very horrible. Why kill the innocent child? Kill yourself. Let the wife and child be by themselves. This case was way back in 1992. But for me, honestly, it has not stopped haunting me even to this day.

People often ask me, "Do you take your job home with you? Does it give you nightmares?" I always said, "I do my job. I don't try to pry to that level of personal information. I'm able to do my job. And then I'm able to let it go."

But this one case was very different. Easter Sunday 1996 was an amazing experience. If I practice forensics for a hundred years, I will never have another case like this.

This particular gentleman was an internationally known scientist, a cancer researcher. He was killed in Rockland County, New York, in his apartment, by his wife and her male cousin. After they killed him, they put his body in the bathtub and cut it up into over sixty pieces. Then they had about thirteen big, black garbage bags in which they packaged up all the body parts, and loaded them up in the trunks of each of their cars. This is going on in the middle of the night.

Then they drove the cars down here into Bergen County, New Jersey. The family owned a business here, and the industrial complex it was on was right on the Passaic River. That was the way they were going to dispose of the body parts. That was the plan.

The wife left the cousin there, in the parking lot, to do the disposal into the river. So, he was just going to take bag by bag, go down to the river's edge, and dump the contents.

What happened was, after he dumped one bag of body parts, he was walking back up to get another bag, and he had bloody gloves on. It was an amazing, fortunate coincidence that an East Rutherford police officer was making a routine patrol through that parking lot as the guy was coming up the side of the river. It was like he was thinking: "Now, why is that car parked at the edge of the parking lot and the trunk is open and. . . . *there's a man with bloody gloves on coming up from the river!* This does not look quite right!"

I was working that day. We actually were having a quiet day and we thought we were going to be able to get home to have dinner with our families. Around eleven A.M., we got a call, "Your presence is wanted in East Rutherford. There are body parts in the back of a car."

You know, we often get calls like that. When I was in Newark, they called one of our doctors out for a body in a garbage bag and it turned out to be animal parts. So, I wasn't going to get myself too excited about it. I said, "Are you sure they're human body parts?" "Oh yeah, we're sure."

I went down there with my partner, Colleen. We took four body bags with us. And we spent the next five days working on this case. Because it was Easter Sunday, people were at church, or brunch, so it took a while for everyone to assemble.

And then, honestly, we didn't know where to begin. Because normally when we go to a crime scene, we have the body there, I do a cursory examination, and I have some idea: Am I dealing with a gunshot, stab wound, blunt trauma? And then we process the scene and the body is taken back to our office and we do our examination.

Here I had body parts. And they asked me, "Can you give us an idea of how many people there are?" I'm just flying by the seat of my pants. I have my gloves on and I'm looking through the bags that are still in the trunk. I didn't see any repeat parts. I didn't see two right arms, or anything like that. So I told them, "For the moment, I'm going to assume it's one person." And they said, "Oh, by the way, see that car on the other side of the parking lot? We forgot to tell you there are bags in the trunk of *that* car as well.' So I have to go do the same thing with those bags.

They had called the county Scuba Team to go into the river and retrieve whatever had been dumped. So they're bringing body parts up to the parking lot where we are, and we're bagging them separately. There were five or six or so body parts that they brought to us. We decided it's best to have the cars flatbedded to the East Rutherford Police Department so they could process them for search warrants and so on. By the time we actually got the bags out of the cars, it was about five or six the next morning.

So here comes this body in all these pieces to me. It was a surreal experience, because normally I have an intact body and I document what injuries I see and I proceed with my examination. Here I had to take body parts out of these bags and try to—make a person. Try to make this person whole. And *then* begin my examination.

There were some ax wounds on the back of his head and multiple stab wounds on his torso. I could corroborate this, because I was able to put the internal organs in place also. There were stab wounds on some of the organs as well, so I knew what I was seeing on the body surface was real.

It really was like trying to put a puzzle together. It was awful. The other dimension of this case that made it horrible was that there was a lot of media attention about that case. It was not only national, but international, because the victim was a very famous person in the scientific community. So, every day, I would go outside to pick up my newspaper, and every day, there would be a big front page article about him. I was constantly bombarded by personal things of his. Number one, his picture was there, in the paper, every day. I worked on him from Monday to Friday, before the body was released. He had a very prominent cleft in his chin, in the photograph. And then I would come in here every day and see what had happened to him. And you could see the cleft in his chin.

I made a connection with him unlike any other case that I dealt with. And that was a little disturbing.

This one was very different because he and I were working together for so long, and I was constantly bombarded with information about who he was as a person. That makes it difficult to let go when you walk out the door. I would go home, and on the six o'clock news, there would be the story again. And they'd replay the crime scene, where we found the body, over and over and over again. And it really started to work on my mind, to the point that I *did* have nightmares about that case.

They killed him because he and his wife were in the process of divorcing. She was your classic woman scorned. You know what they say, "Hell hath no fury. . . ." She enlisted the help of her cousin, who was very big and husky. She needed his bulk to help her with her plan.

The trial was conducted in New York State. In this particular courtroom, the defendant was right next to me, within six to eight feet. That really freaked me out. She had the most alarming scowl. To have to sit right next to her in court and talk about what I had to talk about. I *knew* what she did. More than anyone, because I had worked with her husband. I *saw* what she did. And I was about to tell the jury about it, too.

Why?

A Prosecutor's Story

In child homicides, many times you find that the person who committed the homicide is either the stepfather or the boyfriend.

We had a case where I was one of the two prosecutors. The child was the product of the mother having an affair during her marriage. She stays in her marriage, and the child, obviously, is not that of her husband.

Ultimately, the child is killed. The husband calls the cops and tells them that the child fell getting out of the bathtub and hit her head. The child is all of fourteen, fifteen months old. It just didn't sound right.

The medical examiner found a missing series of little beads. She was a child with corn rows, and each little braid had about six beads in it. And one braid was missing beads. And when the braid was lifted up, that's where *all the damage was.* You would not have been able to tell if you weren't trained medically. The hitting of the head in that area was force enough to break the beads. It was so forceful that it caused such internal damage that the child ultimately died of swelling of the brain.

The medical examiner sent the investigators back. She gave them an instruction: "Look for broken beads. Look for broken beads. And, by the way, this child is x number of inches tall."

So the investigators went back the very next day. And they found broken beads. When they looked up—And when they measured to the spot that they found, they found an area in a wall, which was not drywall, it was plaster, so it was even harder than drywall. They found an indentation. And you could have put six little beads in that indentation. It was perfect. It was like a glove, almost. You could have just put that little child's braid and head in that area.

The investigators cut a four-foot by four-foot piece of that wall out, put it in Plexiglas, and then they put it in a box to preserve it. We submitted it as evidence in the trial. I never, ever opened that box for fear of disrupting the evidence. We brought it into the courtroom and it was just awesome. Awesome.

The stepfather was convicted. His motive? He was jealous that his wife had had a baby with another man. And it was those *tiny* beads that the medical examiner noticed on that little girl's body that convicted him of murder.

It was as if that little girl just came out there and spoke about herself and what happened and the—*fist* that sent her into that wall.

Six

DNA

There's a *CSI* episode that's become quite a joke down in our DNA section. In this particular episode, detectives need a DNA sample from a suspect. They can't get it; they don't have probable cause. So they get the suspect angry, and he spits at one of the detectives.

The other detective whips out a swab, gets the saliva off his friend's face, walks through the entire police department laboratory with the swab right out in the open; he's holding it above his head. He gives it to an analyst, who immediately scrapes it off and puts it into a little centrifuge tube and starts to centrifuge it.

No sealing. No documentation. No notes. No description. Nothing—no extractions, amplification, nothing going like that. And it takes no time at all! The analyst says to the detective, "Give me your pager number. I'll call you when it's done."

And then the famous DNA quote. The detective says, "I'll wait."

—Michael J. Camp, Director, State Crime Laboratory,
　　Milwaukee, Wisconsin

Just outside the DNA Section of the Wisconsin Crime Lab, Milwaukee, parked on sills, are about ten model airplanes. They're not fancy. These are little white biplanes with tiny propellers, reminiscent of Lindbergh's *Spirit of St. Louis*. Some of the biplanes have two or three postage-stamp-sized decals on them. Some planes are absolutely festooned in decals. One or two are plain, except for the DNA double helix symbol on the nose.

DNA analysts here are awarded a plane on their fifth "hit," or match of the DNA evidence sample with a DNA profile stored in the national database. Analysts win tiny decals, imprinted with case numbers, for every consecutive hit. These decals are pasted on each plane, sometimes all over, covering the wings and body. One of the analysts is on her second plane, with only a small space left on the tail.

Inside the DNA lab, gloved and white-coated analysts work in silence. "You can't talk to anybody when you're working; that could contaminate evidence. I never go in there and stand over somebody and ask, 'Hey! How's it goin'?' Just *that* could contaminate. Seattle had a *ton* of contamination in its lab. They traced it to one analyst in the lab who talked a lot. If somebody has a cold, we encourage them to stay home. We don't want them sneezing or coughing their own DNA on the evidence," says Michael Camp, the crime lab director.

On a table against a wall facing the DNA lab, are several displays. One is a latex glove from a burglary scene that yielded its owner's DNA. The accompanying court chart shows that the probability of anyone else having the anonymous burglar's profile is one in a number greater than six trillion. Director Camp points out, "This guy is the source of the DNA, except for identical twins. If the defense attorney wants to be dumb enough to ask exactly what the number is, we can give it to him. We'll tell him how many zeroes it is."

Several poster boards propped on a table facing the DNA lab trace the evolution of testing biological evidence. First up is serology, when ABO typing was done on blood samples. Serology, now generally called forensic biology, is still crucial in identifying stains. But the real punch comes with the next level, the late eighties breakthrough of being able to test for an individual's unique (unless that person has an identical sibling) DNA characteristics. This was done through RFLP testing (restriction fragment length polymorphism), a process that requires a fairly large sample of DNA evidence (about 100,000 cells, or a sample about the size of a quarter), and the sample needs to be in good condition. RFLP testing was made famous by the O. J. Simpson case.

Things really picked up in 1994, when the PCR (polymerase chain reaction) technique was introduced in forensic science. PCR is a technique which makes copies of the original sample, so that DNA may be identified from incredibly tiny, or old, or degraded samples. The PCR process can analyze regions of DNA called STRs (short tandem repeats), a typing procedure that provides a great deal of information about the DNA donor.

As Crime Lab Director Camp puts it, "With RFLP, you couldn't establish identity without any doubt. Now, we have this PCR method where we're well *beyond* identity. If we get a match, full profile, and there's just one person in the stain, we're usually able to say something like, 'It matches this person. The chances that two people share the same DNA, other than identical siblings, are one in ten quadrillion.' That's pretty compelling evidence."

Put in evolutionary terms, what the poster boards show is that DNA testing has progressed, in a span of about fifteen years, from the primordial ooze to the Renaissance. In physical terms, it's moved from being able to analyze only large amounts of sample to being able to analyze a sample the size of a pinhead.

And it's still progressing. For example, when DNA from the nucleus of the cell isn't available (as in plane crashes, mass disasters, or cases with only skeletonized remains) mitochondrial DNA (DNA inherited from the maternal line) testing can be done on hairs, bone, teeth, blood, and other tissues. There's a very new technique, known as Y-chromosome testing, which targets regions on the Y chromosome that differ among unrelated males. This testing can pick out the male DNA from an overwhelming amount of female DNA, as in sexual assault cases. And scientists are developing a test which searches for a person's SNPs (single-nucleotide polymorphisms), which are *single*-letter differences in individuals' DNA.

Powering the identification of criminals from these microscopic samples that murderers, rapists, and property criminals leave at crime scenes is the FBI's national database known as CODIS (Combined DNA Index System). The database is evolving too, as more and more state legislatures move to get all convicted felons, including those convicted of property crimes, and even all arrestees, even for misdemeanors, into CODIS.

So. The giant pill of DNA information you've just ingested will prepare you for the power of using DNA in cases where there's a suspect, but scant evidence; cases where there's no suspect at all; cases gone cold; and cases where the wrong person has been convicted and imprisoned. The stories in this chapter are from DNA analysts, crime lab directors, a prosecuting attorney, and a defense attorney. We'll start with a living, breathing example of DNA evidence, a forensic DNA specialist.

I'm one of a set of identical triplets. The DNA thing for me is re- ally cool because, of course, when I became a DNA analyst, I was able to check that, indeed, my DNA is not distinguishable from my triplet siblings' DNA.

In 1994, I was just getting started in the field. Over the holidays that year, I presented my family with the idea of testing all of us for DNA. I collected mouth swabs from my whole family—my parents, my brother, and my two sisters—and I sent them to the crime lab and they did a little study and wrote a little project up on it. It was a cool thing.

I don't just test for DNA with my triplet sisters. One of the big things in forensic science is identification with the exclusion of all others. So I've done tests on my siblings to see things like, Do we have the same ridge patterns in our fingernails? Do our ears make the same image when we put them on a piece of glass? What do the patterns look like on our feet? Are they similar?

Of course, I also did the fingerprint thing with them, too. I *had* to! Come on! I couldn't miss this. And all our prints *were* different. You know, with fingerprints, there's the three main patterns: loops, arches, and whorls. And those correspond to us. Each of our fingers has the same big pattern. But, then, the little starts and stops and bifurcations and dots and all of that, within the pattern, *each* of our fingerprints is different.

My sisters are pretty much done with me. I've collected their hairs and fingernails and ear prints and footprints and fingerprints. One sister, the attorney, she's like, "Ummm, when am I going to get paid for this?"

When I give lectures to cops about why DNA has taken over, I say, "I can tell you that the uniqueness is the big reason. We don't expect people to have the identical DNA pattern, with the exception of identical siblings."

And then I tell the cops that I'm one of a set of triplets. You have to understand, I'm pretty hyper. So when I get to the part of my talk where I tell the cops I'm a triplet, I can see by their faces that they're thinking, "Oh my God. *Three* of them."

A Prosecutor on How DNA Evidence Speaks for the Victim

Detectives came to my office one morning. This is in 2002. There was a ten-year-old girl they believed had been sexually assaulted by the bus driver. She was cognitively disabled. She was wheelchair-bound. She was fed through a tube in her stomach. And really could not verbalize very much.

I felt at the time, from what we had learned, this bus driver probably *did* do something to her. But after I interviewed the little girl, I doubted whether I could ever prove it. And I could not even have gotten to the point of a preliminary hearing because of her—such limited verbal skills. And I'm being generous when I say they were limited. And she also could be led easily.

What happened was that—A woman was in her kitchen, looking out her kitchen window, when she saw a typical yellow school bus pull up and stop right in front of her house. She's looking out her kitchen window and she could see that it was one of those specially-equipped buses. She sees the bus driver get out from behind the driver's seat, reach over and unstrap a little girl who was in a wheelchair. Prior to doing that, he had gone to the back of the bus, got an orange blanket, and laid it on the floor of the bus. He unstrapped that girl from her wheelchair and laid her down on the blanket.

The woman could see all that. And then she saw him kind of go down, out of sight, which would have been below the windows of the bus. He was down, out of sight, for about forty, fifty seconds. Then he got up, gets in the driver's seat and drives away, leaving the little girl lying on the floor.

So the woman figures something is wrong here. She gets in her car and follows the bus. At some point, the bus pulls over again to the side of the road and she sees the bus driver get out from behind the seat, go back, pick up the little girl, strap her back in her wheelchair, then he gets back in the driver's seat, drives around the corner, and there the child's siblings are waiting for her to come off on the wheelchair.

She sees the house that they take the little girl into, and after the bus leaves, she goes up, knocks on the door, and talks to the foster mother. And tells her what she saw. But she says, "Look. I don't want to get involved with this, I had nothing to do with this," and takes off.

The foster mother then talks to the little girl, who could not articulate anything, but was able to take her little Barbie doll, and she would point to her lips and then point to the vagina on the Barbie doll. And the foster mother somehow got from her that the bus driver, whose name was Dennis, put his lips on her vagina.

The foster mother called the police. The child could not be taken down to the Sexual Assault Treatment Center because she was just so frightened of hospitals; she would flail and scream and yell.

So that's basically what we had, that morning in my office. We had basically a nonverbal victim. We knew something went on, but we had no evidence; we had no witnesses. So, a tough case starting out.

I told the police officers in my office that number one, they would make me a very happy prosecutor if they could find the woman who saw the school bus. They had done a search warrant for the bus.

All of that was done. And they combed that area all that night and they finally found the woman by just going door-to-door, knocking on the doors. It was just wonderful police work. They found her about ten thirty, eleven o'clock that night.

The search of the bus found an orange blanket, just as the woman had said.

What they found—the foster mother had used sanitary wipes to wipe the little girl. And they started looking at those wipes. They kept going through them and through them and, finally, on one of the sanitary wipes, they found what is called amylase, which is an enzyme found in saliva. And when they tested it, they got a beautiful DNA profile from that, which was not consistent with the little girl.

Based on that evidence, we did a search warrant to obtain the bus driver's DNA, based on buccal swabbings of his mouth. When the crime lab compared that with the sample from the sanitary wipe, it was a perfect match.

Here was a case where, without DNA, it would have been next to impossible to prosecute. Even though I would have had a witness who could say what she saw, and everything looked very, very suspicious, whether I still could have pulled this off beyond a reasonable doubt, I doubt it, especially with a nonverbal victim.

But when you get a fifty-five-year-old man's DNA on the vagina of a ten-year-old, that solidifies your case. And, again, I can't emphasize this enough, we just never, ever would have been able to charge that case without DNA. And here was a driver in charge of the bus that takes the most vulnerable—the most vulnerable! All children are vulnerable, but children with such severe disabilities are all the more vulnerable. And he would have been still driving those buses, with those children in his care.

Since this case, whenever I talk to crime lab people, I point out that in the work that they do, the wonderful work that they do, they very seldom see the faces of the victims. And I point out to them that, for this little girl, they basically spoke for her. The work they did, they spoke for her, and told the world what this man did to her.

A Defense Attorney on DNA and a Wrongful Conviction

I had a case in the early nineties in San Diego involving a navy man. This man was accused of raping his daughter in navy housing. The story was that he gets up, goes to work; the wife gets up and the daughter's crying in her bed. Her vaginal area is bleeding and she's terribly injured and she's taken to the navy hospital. They said somebody's assaulted her and they call the police.

They suspect the father. The daughter originally said this: "A man came in the window. He put me in a green car and took me to a park and did this. And then he brought me back." Kind of an odd story. She's eight years old. It sounds like the kind of story a little kid might make up.

She's just *brutalized*. She was in emergency surgery. And this really gets to the detectives, like, "Oh my God. Look what happened to this little girl" type of thing. Not uncommon in this business.

They take her out of the home and put her in foster care. She goes to a psychotherapist a couple times a week. She gets physically better, then she gets emotionally better. And she wants to go home. The therapist works with her for a long time, as do the foster parents.

Eventually, they talk to her about what happened and she says, "Daddy did it." So Daddy gets charged with this brutal rape.

But there's really no conclusive forensic evidence. The police collected the girl's nightgown and underpants at the hospital and stored them. There was no vaginal swab done because she was in emergency surgery.

The little girl's father, Jim, is claiming he's one hundred percent innocent. It sounds believable. So I get a person that privately is a tech; we go over to the police station where the evidence was stored and check it out—this is about a year after the assault—and we see some stains. I mean, these stains are on the little girl's nightgown; there was one on her panties. These are not blood stains, either.

We take a very small sample, we look at it microscopically, and we're seeing sperm cells. This is like—home run. The police have missed all of this, probably because when stains are fresh, they're wet, and they're harder to see.

When I interviewed the defendant, he told me he had had a vasectomy, so he's aspermic. And these stains had semen cells in them. I told Jim to get retested because sometimes the vasectomy doesn't hold up. His vasectomy was good. So, right away, we had information that it could not have been Jim.

I proposed that we do a joint test with the prosecution, using Dr. Blake, an excellent forensic scientist, who had been used by the prosecution originally.

The prosecution agreed to it. We agreed to do two levels of testing, where the evidence is tested and then they do the reference samples, so it's very objective. I knew what my client's typings were, and his wife, because they always take the family members. Dr. Blake reports it out that the semen donor was someone other than the father, or the mother, or daughter.

We had been working on this case and had developed another suspect. He was a predator child molester who had been caught attempting to break in to another navy housing project about eighteen months before. One of the odd things was that there was a footprint outside the window of the little girl in our case that nobody could explain. So we were saying this was the footprint of the guy going in or coming out.

When we got to this suspect, he was doing about seven years in prison on this other attempted break-in, where he was going in to another girl's bedroom. It happened seven months after the break-in in our case.

And this guy had a green car, similar to the one the girl originally described. While we were doing the DNA testing, we kept saying, "This is the guy who did it." The prosecution is saying, "Oh! No way! This is totally outside the realm of reality." And the prosecutor told me, "When this DNA comes back and hits your client, Jim Wade, he better plead guilty."

The result comes back. It's not Jim Wade. It's—Unknown Person. And we get the other guy's DNA sample. It turns out to be him. The guy we suspected all along.

These cops—they said they couldn't sleep at night because they were so outraged about what happened to this little girl. You know, it gets the emotions up. And when emotions go up, judgment goes out the window.

Wade is exonerated, the factual finding of innocence is made. He moves on and he gets a civil suit started and he actually collects four or five million dollars from the county.

The guy in prison was eventually prosecuted, and now he's doing like ninety-nine years. The reality is, this guy was your truly dangerous predator child molester that goes into homes and snatches little girls. And he wasn't caught until seven months *after* he brutally assaulted the Wade girl, when he was caught breaking into another home.

DNA Experts on the Changes They've Witnessed

In 1987, I worked on the very first DNA criminal case in this country, a rape case in Florida, which compared the genetic molecules from the suspect with the semen found on the victim.

At the time, there was only one forensic DNA laboratory in the whole country, Lifecodes Corporation in New York. There was no other forensic DNA lab in the country then. None

I was the director of forensic business development for Life-codes. I was the first person to travel around the country, touting the benefits of DNA testing. I lectured about DNA testing to police departments and prosecutors and defense attorneys' offices, and we started getting cases coming in the door.

We went to the FBI and, of course, they kicked us out. They didn't think it was going to work. They really didn't think it was going to work. You know, the FBI has a mentality that is pretty stodgy sometimes. They're pretty arrogant. They have this mentality: If it's not invented here, it's nothing.

This all started in 1987, the forensic use of DNA in the United States. Of course, in DNA time, when you consider all the advances in testing since then, 1987 is ancient history.

DNA SPECIALIST/FORMER LAB DIRECTOR

In the old days, before forensic DNA, when we were doing ABO typing and PGM typing of semen on vaginal swabs, we had mixtures we had to contend with. We had to try to interpret the mixtures. If you had someone of type A and a female of type B, the ABO typing would give you AB. You could eliminate people using this, but you couldn't say a whole lot about the donor.

It was difficult to interpret. And you had the problem of identification. You might have a semen stain that was found in one out of a hundred people, eliminating ninety-nine percent of the population, which sounded pretty damn good, but it still wasn't enough to make an identification.

What DNA was offering was the ability to separate semen cells from vaginal epithelial cells. You could get a semen stain from a vaginal swab and you could separate the semen part of it out and get a DNA profile of that. That was *huge*. You could get the DNA out of the sample and actually relate it to somebody.

And the other benefit, was you could do this on something very, very old. So, our very first cases that came in the door, for the most part, were cases, sort of like cold cases. They didn't know what to do with them. They hadn't gone anywhere. Cops thought they knew who did it, but they couldn't prove it. We started to get these kinds of cases. And we got results in them. This started the whole DNA movement in this country.

SEROLOGIST/DNA ANALYST

The PCR technique is only about twelve years old; it *really* **revo-**lutionized DNA research.

What the PCR method does is allows us to take whatever minute amount of DNA might be recovered from a crime scene and make millions of copies of the DNA to give us enough material to analyze. In twenty minutes, we can make a million copies of—whatever. We simply amplify the amount of evidence we have. It's like a molecular Xerox machine.

Now it gives us all the sensitivity—sometimes too much sensitivity. The technique is now so sensitive that you have to take very, very special safeguards from the moment the evidence is collected. If you get near it, touch it, breathe on it, cough on it, drop a hair on it, that will get amplified as well.

DNA ANALYST

A Crime Scene Photographer Turned DNA Analyst on a Cold Case Showing the Evolution of DNA Testing

The highest-profile case I've worked on was the one where an employee at the 3M Company in Minneapolis kidnapped a female coworker from the office and subsequently murdered her.

The neat thing about this case: It shows all the progressions in DNA testing, from the old serology typing days through the use of mitochondrial DNA. When I think about this case, it really is like watching the evolution of DNA testing.

The victim was kidnapped from 3M in the fall of 1989. I'd just started at the lab. I'd just finished crime scene training as a photographer. I was in the lab on a weekend, working. One of the team leaders came in and said, "We've got a crime scene. And we need a photographer. Can you go?"

I'd been on one other crime scene as a backup, trainee photographer. So this other guy and I, and he'd just finished his photography training, too, we went to the scene.

It was down in Northfield, Minnesota. In a cornfield. It was fall; this farmer had been out choppin' his corn, and found a body. I really don't remember much about the scene other than it was really cold and trying to make sure that my camera was working properly. The one thing I do remember, though, was she was in this tan rain jacket when they dug her up.

The guys processed the scene and we took the pictures. That was 1989. Police had a suspect immediately, her coworker. And, you know, they had done a lot of interviews with him and a lot of search warrants.

One of the search warrants that they did was at his house. The crime scene team members were looking for blood evidence. They used a chemical process called Luminol, which fluoresces in the dark; it reacts with blood. They cut out a lot of the carpeting from the suspect's house. And while they were doing this, they found the murdered woman's car keys.

But when they went in front of the judge, because "car keys" had not been specifically listed on the search warrant, it got thrown out. And the woman's car keys were the main evidence.

They took the carpet back to the lab and did some serology on it and identified that there was blood there. But—this was before DNA testing—it couldn't be confirmed to be human blood. So, because the keys got thrown out of court, and we couldn't get any type from the blood on the carpeting, police didn't have enough evidence to charge him.

The case went cold. Still, police always had a particular suspect in mind. But they didn't have the evidence. What they theorized was, he brought her back to his home, killed her there, and then went and dumped the body somewhere.

In 1993, I'm in the crime lab doing DNA work. We went back to the carpet and tried to do DNA testing on it. I was able to tell that there was human blood present, but at that time we were only doing RFLP testing, and I did not get any results.

DNA testing changed. We were looking at STRs in '96, '97. In 1998, when we were getting close to going online with the new STR technology, one of the investigators came and talked to me and said, "You know, would you be willing to try this if I resubmitted the carpet from the guy's house?" I said, "Absolutely." I was able to find some additional areas that hadn't been tested. I was able to obtain DNA, and, in 1999, I got a profile that matched the victim from blood on the suspect's carpet.

There was some hair evidence that hadn't been resolved. The attorney general's office took the case over. They decided to send these hairs out to a private laboratory for mitochondrial DNA testing. And it came back: One hair found in his bathroom matched the victim. And one hair found on her leg matched him.

This is in 2002. We were having a hearing on mitochondrial DNA testing. Halfway through that, the suspect said he didn't remember anything about it, and he had to go have psychiatric evaluation. Finally, in 2003, he pled guilty.

The woman was murdered and dumped in a cornfield in 1989. The offender wasn't sentenced until 2003, fourteen years after he kidnapped and murdered her. But all that time, we kept returning to the case, and DNA testing just kept getting better and better, and more and more sensitive.

DNA Analysts and Crime Lab Directors Talk About the DNA Criminals Leave Behind

We had a case involving olive loaf lunch meat. The guy broke into a house while the woman was sleeping. He opened up her refrigerator and took some lunch meat out. Took a bite out of it, decided he really didn't care for the taste; it was like, "This is kind of *disgusting!*" and left it on the counter.

And so the woman called and the police came, and she said, "I didn't leave that there. It might have come out of my refrigerator, but I didn't do that."

So they collected it and brought it in to the lab. And we froze it. What you do, with some food items, you want to freeze the food *solid*. Hard. And then you let it defrost just a little bit. Just enough so that the ice crystals on the surface start to melt. And with those ice crystals come the cells. And then you swab up those cells, and then you process them for DNA. If you try to swab food without freezing it, you just get a mess. So.

We got a complete profile from that lunch meat. We put it into the computer system, CODIS, and you turn around and do a search of our felons—and we got a name. This guy was a burglar.

CRIME SCENE PROCESSOR/DNA ANALYST

People, for some reason, get snack-y when they break into other people's houses. We've had soda cans come into the lab. Eating utensils. I'm like, You'd think you'd just want to hurry up and get it over with, instead of sitting there and . . . *snacking*.

They don't realize that the straw they've been chewing on at the crime scene—the one they just sort of dropped on the floor—that straw is perfect evidence for us.

DNA ANALYST

It's amazing. Criminals: They have to smoke at the scene. It's
amazing the number of cigarettes crime labs get in.

They just have to have a cigarette. They break in, they
have a cigarette, and then they take whatever they're taking.

And, in a lot of cases, like burglaries, where there are no
suspects at all, it's amazing the number of hits that we get
from our database, just from analyzing the cigarettes they
leave behind.

DNA ANALYST

In planned crimes, like a burglary, a lot of people wear rubber
gloves, latex gloves, because they know about fingerprints.
Well, you don't walk around town wearing those, so you
commit the crime and you take them off, and you leave them
at the scene, or you throw them in a Dumpster.

Cops check Dumpsters. Or they find them at the scene.
DNA all *over* those things. Because you sweat. And at the
lab, we can also cut off the tips of gloves and dust them and
sometimes get prints from them, too.

They know about fingerprints. They haven't wised up to
DNA.

CRIME LAB DIRECTOR

We're able to deal with smaller and smaller samples. Every year,
the protocols and the companies that make the reagents for
the DNA process and the instruments, they're coming out
with ways to tweak it just a little better, a little more, so we
can use smaller and smaller samples, more degraded samples,
where five years ago, if we had those samples, we'd have got
nothing. Today we can get results.

DNA ANALYST

Ski masks? For bank robberies? A *lot* of DNA can be inside.
They leave them behind a lot. They run out, and they rip
that ski mask right off and throw it. We can get right in

there and get the saliva. The area of a ski mask they have over their nose and mouth is a great source of DNA.

We had one case where there was a single eyebrow hair found on the inside of a ski mask. There was a root on it. We got a profile from that. There's a little piece of tissue on the root that comes out of the scalp, follicular tissue. If that comes out, say if it's pulled out in a struggle, it's skin; it contains nuclear DNA, and we can get a profile from it.

People think when they put on a ski mask, they're totally anonymous. They're not. They leave their DNA behind.

CRIME LAB DIRECTOR

We've had cases involving chewing gum. We had chewing gum in the ashtray of a car that solved a stolen vehicle case. We've processed lip balm left at a scene. Eyeglasses. Shirts. Shoes. One guy went in and apparently decided to switch shoes because he found a better pair, so he left his old shoes. So they swabbed the inside of his shoes and got the DNA pattern that way.

Sputum: A guy spits out the window while the police are chasing him. They stop and pick up his sputum. People leave DNA everywhere.

CRIME LAB DIRECTOR

There was a bank robbery a couple years ago where the bank robber got angry at the teller, apparently for taking a while to get him the money. He started yelling at this woman and ended up spitting on the counter.

This woman was really bright. When police arrived, she pointed out the spittle on the counter. It yielded a complete DNA profile and the guy was caught.

The local newspaper ran a story about the case. The headline was: SAY IT—DON'T SPRAY IT.

CRIME LAB DIRECTOR

We've seen all the fluids in the crime lab: perspiration, urine, feces, mucus. We've had criminals leave Kleenex behind at crime scenes. We had one with a used Kleenex that just gave a *beautiful* DNA profile. If you use a Kleenex— Oh, there's tons and tons of DNA on that from the mucus in your nose.

CRIME LAB DIRECTOR

There was a sexual assault in a park where a guy used a con- dom and threw it into the river. The victim brought the cops back to look and the guy hadn't quite made it into the river; the condom was caught in some weeds on the river-bank. When you get a condom, you've got the male profile on the inside and the female profile on the outside. Couldn't be better.

CRIME LAB DIRECTOR

A really great place for DNA capture is with knives, where the knife blade and the handle meet. A knife is not all of one piece, so there's space. And if blood is present, it's in there.

And guns. Apparently there's a phenomenon where your hand can get pinched in the slide as you're advancing the next round, so sometimes when we get a gun, there might be blood from the shooter. We look for those little, teeny crevices, I mean—we're talking about a *fleck* of blood. So we don't just look at the exterior and say, "I don't see any blood on here."

We try to get folks to take weapons apart, whether we have to bring the firearms people in and they take the weapon apart, or whether we're trying to deconstruct a knife blade from its handle, or shove a clean tweezers in there and let it drop into a petri dish and see what you get.

DNA ANALYST

Even with the technology, we have a big problem getting DNA from guns because—You know what a cop does as soon as he sees a gun? He picks it up. It's a toy. It's a toy. And he shows it to somebody else. It's a toy.

And the cops hand it around. Somebody opens it: "It's a gun!"

Cops. Guns. *God.*

And then the DA says, "Send that gun to the lab so we can link it to the defendant."

For years we told people at scenes, "Don't worry about guns. You can handle them by their rough edges." Well, that's where you're going to find a lot of DNA. So now we tell cops, "If you're gonna handle a gun, put on gloves. And when you're done, bag that sucker up."

CRIME LAB DIRECTOR

Fingernails are *awesome* sources of DNA. They're just awe-some. We've had some really great cases with fingernails. We've gotten full, single-source profiles of the killers under deceased females' fingernails.

Example: We processed evidence from a home invasion. A guy came through the back door. He sexually assaults and murders the woman inside.

The person who worked on this case took a swab and wrapped it around a tweezer head and lightly swabbed up under the nail bed of all the victim's fingers. On one hand, it was a mixture of the victim and the assailant. On the other hand, it was completely just the male. The same male.

They identified where the semen came from. He said that he knew her and they had had consensual sex. But the nails, which were torn and had his DNA under them, showed force. Plus there was the evidence of forced entry into the home. And, of course, she wasn't able to say, "We weren't dating!" But the combination of the semen and forced entry and his DNA under her nails—that was the coolest thing ever. He was convicted.

DNA ANALYST

We had a case solved with just one acrylic-tip nail. One woman killed another woman over a man. Processors found one acrylic tip at the scene. This nail had the female suspect's DNA on one side, from where it had attached to her finger. And it had a drop of the victim's blood on the other side. One drop that fell at a ninety-degree angle on the top of the nail.

DNA ANALYST

We get a lot of "Who was wearing these clothes?" type of cases. Baseball caps are ones that we get a lot. We have pretty good success rate with those. Mostly because people sweat when they're wearing them, and there's a lot of sloughing off of cells inside.

CRIME LAB DIRECTOR

The best sources of DNA from perspiration or handling are repeated exposures to one person's skin. So some of the best sources are baseball caps and shirt collars. We've had cases where people have had contact with the victim, blood gets on their shirt, so they remove the shirt and throw it in an unhelpful place. So it's in a Dumpster behind the Kmart or whatever. Somebody sees them tossing it, and now we've got this bloody shirt.

Now we've got this shirt, but we can't prove who wore it just from the shirt itself. So we chop up the collar or the armpits. What happens is, the moisture from perspiration will pick up the cells from the back of your skin and they'll absorb into the fabric of the garment. We can get the wearer's DNA from that—and we've got the victim's blood as well.

CRIME LAB DIRECTOR

The big advances in DNA are with sweat and saliva. And the best sources come from repeated exposures to one person's skin.

Let's say someone's been kidnapped and we need a DNA

sample from them. If you've got the victim's purse, their DNA is probably going to be on the handle. Their perspiration can probably be gotten from items like their remote control or their hairbrush or their keys or whatever. And toothbrushes, razor blades, cosmetics, things that only that person used, are all great sources of DNA.

Saliva's the other area where the STR method has really taken over. There's not a lot of DNA in saliva. It's not really the liquid we analyze; it's the cells that come off in the mouth when you're talking or eating, say. And it's from repeated use. So, we can get it from a straw because it's been repeatedly brought to the mouth. A cup of coffee is repeatedly brought to the mouth. A cigarette is repeatedly brought to the mouth.

Straws and chewing gum and pop cans and bite marks—they're all good. We had a case—there were two profiles in the bite mark. The major, tall profile is the biter. And the other profile is the person whose skin it was taken off of. That's just amazing. There would be *no way* you would do anything other than forensic odontology off a bite mark five years ago. Now we can get DNA from a bite mark, where there may have been just *one* contact with someone's mouth on someone's skin.

CRIME LAB DIRECTOR

The case I handled with the most extensive DNA analysis was one where a baby was cut from a woman's stomach and the woman herself was murdered. There were five crime scenes, three defendants, three murdered victims, two survivors. I examined 125 pieces of evidence. It was un-un-unbelievable what the perpetrators did.

The crime occurred in November 1995. Prior to the crime, there was a full-term pregnant woman who had told people she was going to be induced into labor about three days later. The fact that this woman was so full-term was part of the plan of the people who ended up killing her.

The victim was part of a large group of people who were

friends with each other, including the people who ultimately killed her.

There were three defendants. There's an adult male who used to date the pregnant woman. He had a female cousin who, along with her boyfriend, wanted a light-skinned baby boy. Sure enough, the pregnant woman is a white female and she's known to be dating a black male. So they knew that the baby would be light-complected. They also knew, from talking with the pregnant woman, that the fetus was a boy.

The female defendant starts faking her own pregnancy. She's trying to match the timing with the truly pregnant woman. When the woman who was faking the pregnancy and her boyfriend found out the other woman was close to going into the hospital to be induced, they find out the schedule of her live-in boyfriend and determine when he's going to be gone.

The male cousin, the female cousin, and her boyfriend all go to the victim's house when the boyfriend's at work. They shoot her in the head. Then they cut the full-term baby from her stomach. Incredibly, the baby survived. There's also a two-year-old boy that the victim had with one of her killers in a previous relationship. The two-year-old survives.

The victim had two other kids—eight and ten years old. They end up getting killed, too. The ten-year-old girl gets killed at the scene, brutally. The eight-year-old boy hides, and then, when the killers are leaving with the baby, he goes with them.

The live-in boyfriend comes home and finds his girlfriend shot, her womb sliced open, and the two-year-old running around the house with blood all over him.

The offenders drop the eight-year-old boy off at the home of one of their friends. He tells these people what happened. It sounds so ridiculous to them that they don't think a whole lot of it. The three defendants come back and pick the boy up and take him away. Then, one of the people who didn't believe the boy, turns on the news. Lead story: A ten-year-old girl and a woman have been murdered. The baby's been cut out of the victim's womb. And there's a picture of the eight-year-old who was just with him, on the news, and yeah, it's true, he was part of the family that was murdered earlier that evening. They call the police. But by the time they get that information to the police, this boy has been murdered and dumped off the expressway.

The apartment where the victim and her family lived was scene number one. The house where they took the eight-year-old boy was scene number two. There was blood in the killers' car, scene number three. Where the little boy was found near the expressway was scene number four. The apartment of the male cousin was scene number five.

The scene that was the wealthiest in evidence was scene number five, the apartment of two of the defendants, the female cousin and her boyfriend, where they took the newborn baby. There were many stains at the home of the two defendants that matched the baby who was cut out. The umbilical cord was not cut or bandaged well, so blood went *everywhere* in that apartment. They had stolen a coat at the scene; the boyfriend was wearing it, and it had blood on it.

We do a paternity test on the baby cut out of the womb because the female defendant is claiming this is the baby she had with her boyfriend. Well, not only is it not their baby, it's not the live-in boyfriend's baby, either. The father is the old boyfriend, who went in with the others.

The detectives brought *everything* back to us. There was a cable cord that had the *tiniest*— this was the stain of my career because I can't believe I found it—the *tiniest* little smidge of blood on it. I swabbed it up, I did a preliminary color test that indicates the presence of blood. It's an oxidation-reduction test using phenolphthalein, which when oxidized turns pink. If blood is present, this reaction is very fast, and the color is very intense and then it was, "Oh my God. What do I do now?"

Normally, the chemicals would be dropped on a small portion of a larger stain, and, when positive, the remaining portion would be sent on for DNA analysis. However, in this case, I didn't have any remaining sample because the stain was so tiny, so I picked up the swab that had the chemicals on it, and sent that along with the samples from the other exhibits to the Springfield crime lab for DNA analysis.

The lab got a profile that matched the eight-year-old boy. The cord was used to try to strangle him. This cord— For whatever reason, they brought the cord with them, up to their apartment after the murders. They had tried a lot of ways to kill him. They tried strangling him with the cord. They tried to poison him with iodine. They were trying to get rid of him because he could talk and he knew all the players. They ended up stabbing him to death in the car before they dumped him.

DNA came into this case in several different ways. DNA obviously played a big role in showing that indeed the baby the two defendants said was theirs was not. DNA came in with establishing paternity.

DNA was found on the coat of the male claiming to be the dad. The boyfriend who came home and found his girlfriend slit open, the good guy boyfriend, said the coat was missing. And this coat had blood all over it. The cord with this small amount of DNA from the boy was found in the home of the two defendants who wanted the baby. There was also a large bloodstain in the back of the car these people drove; DNA established that this stain came from the murdered boy.

I reviewed about 125 items. About twelve were actually presented at trial. The big items were the coat and the cord.

That was eleven years ago. Even with the old methods of DNA testing, we still got enough from all the blood to convict all three of them. The female ended up making a statement, that she was there, but that she didn't kill anyone. She named the other two defendants, who both denied any involvement in any of the killings. She and her boyfriend both got the death penalty and the male cousin got life plus eighty years.

DNA ANALYST

It's astonishing what you can find out from a microscopic sample of blood with the new testing. Case in point: One of our analysts brought in a mosquito he had squished in his bathroom at home. He wanted to know who in the family the mosquito had bitten prior to getting squished.

So he brought the dead mosquito in to the lab and made up a chart tracing the DNA in the mosquito: The Case of the Marauding Mosquito.

Our techniques only amplify human DNA, so the mosquito's blood isn't in the analysis. But you look across this chart: There's the father and mother. They have two daughters. And the first thing that everybody in the lab looks at, of course, "Is he really the father?" And he is.

The giveaway to who the mosquito bit was—the amelogenin—that's the gene present on X and Y chromosomes used to determine gender—was male, whereas the analyst's wife and daughters are female. So it matched up to him. Our DNA analyst was the sole victim of the mosquito.

CRIME LAB DIRECTOR

Prosecutors on Cop and Criminal Maneuvers with DNA

Police sometimes use ruses to get a suspect's DNA. If they have a suspect, but they don't have enough evidence to obtain a search warrant for biological evidence, they might use exceptions in the law relating to abandoned property to get a DNA sample.

For example, this guy was a suspect in a sexual assault. When questioning him, cops tried: "Do you want a Coke?" Then they could get a sample from the neck of the bottle.

But the guy wanted nothing to drink. Then they tried: "Do you want a cigarette?" Yeah, he did. But he put it out and put the cigarette butt in his pocket. So, after he left the station, they followed him. At some point, he spat on the sidewalk. And they *got* it.

More examples: Cops have been known to pose as waiters and waitresses to get the straw or the glass. They vary their approaches. In Washington State, there was a homicide suspect. Police sent him a letter that invited him to join a class-action suit; the deal was, just sign and send it back. The suspect licked the envelope. They got him.

In Michigan, a rapist broke into a home where a woman had some candles burning. He blew out the candles before he raped the woman. And they got his DNA.

The flip side of ingenuity is what criminals do with *their* knowl-edge of DNA. Part of the "*CSI* effect" is that criminals are getting smarter and realizing how powerful DNA evidence is.

For example, we had a serial rapist in Wisconsin—three sexual assaults. He maintained his innocence and kept saying that the crimes were committed by someone with the very same genetic profile.

This guy, Turner, was in jail. He sent a letter to the crime lab saying, "There's been a terrible mistake. Somebody out there, who has my identical DNA, is out there raping women." And then he said, "Check out this rape," and he gave the name and address of a rape that happened while he was in jail. "Check it out. You'll see." I said to the crime lab, "Go ahead. Maybe then there'll be an end to this." They got to the scene, and the semen there matched Turner's exactly. How could this happen? The guy's in jail.

It was *nonsense*. I called the detectives and said, "Find the victim." She was from Green Bay. When they went to question her, "Oh, that." She said she was friendly with the Turner family. She told the detectives that Turner mailed his semen to

her in a condiment package—you know, like those little plastic
ketchup containers—and he told her, "Rub it all over yourself.
Go to a garage (that was his MO), rip off some buttons, get
yourself real dirty." So she did, and she reported the rape. She
did it for $50. She had self-esteem issues, I guess.

The Law and DNA: Getting All Convicted Felons into the DNA Database

Property crimes are probably the richest and the most effective
uses of DNA because the people who are committing these
breaking and enterings, and burglaries of businesses and
residences—they always seem to manage to cut themselves or
leave a little skin tissue on a glass shard, or they go in and
help themselves to a bottle of beer and leave their saliva on
the neck of the bottle. They might urinate. We can find it,
even from a used piece of toilet paper that hasn't been
flushed.

There's a tremendous amount of DNA found in non-sex,
non-homicide crimes. That's what we're seeing right now:
burglaries, armed robberies, bank robberies. A lot of property crimes. And you get more DNA from these, to begin
with, because there's a larger number of property crimes
than violent crimes.

Those cases are a lot easier to do than a homicide or rape,
for example, because usually you're only talking about one or
two pieces of evidence. But that's where most of our hits in
our databank come from, from property crimes.

And when the violent crimes occur, when we make a hit,
we're finding that the reason we've got that person in our
databank is more times than not, because of a prior burglary.

CRIME LAB DIRECTOR

Burglaries are gateway crimes. That's why a lot of states have
moved toward getting DNA from burglars—you know, "Get

the burglars"—because statistics show that property criminals graduate into more heinous crimes.

PROSECUTOR

If a state has a statute that allows us to get DNA every time
there's an arrest, not a conviction, but an *arrest* for a felony,
like the state of Virginia has—every time somebody decides
they're gonna break into the White Hen Pantry and bleed,
and we get that DNA, within a week of it being entered into
this massive national database [CODIS], it will be compared
against 2.1 million perpetrator samples. And this is amazing
to me, the latest count from the FBI, December '04. Now
there is a grand total of 2.1 million profiles—almost 94,000
evidence profiles, and over 2 million offender profiles.

We break it into groupings of numbers, and it is just so
easy to put that grouping into the database and just see if
anyone else has the same grouping. Very simple.

CRIME LAB DIRECTOR

Murder is the *least* recidivistic crime we have. Most murders
come out of a situation that the murderer is never going to
be placed in again, like coming upon his wife in bed with another man. He's probably never going to murder again.

But burglaries are *highly* recidivistic. Car thefts—highly
recidivistic. People are out there doing these all the time.
And if you steal a car, you're back out on the street in a
month, if you go to jail at all. So you really want to get those
people in the database.

Plus, what we know about individuals who commit
crimes: Most of them don't start off as serial rapists. Most of
them start off doing other, little crimes, and they progress as
a criminal. It's a progression. So why do you want to wait till
some guy's killed six women before you get him in the database? Wouldn't you much rather catch him when he's com-

mitting his first burglaries? And that's not enough, so he starts doing rapes, and that's not enough, so he starts killing people? Let's get him early on. It's crime prevention.

PROSECUTOR

The trend now is to expand the database. In the future, it's proba- bly going to be done for all arrests, even misdemeanors. It's probably going to be if you're arrested, taken into custody, you'll be brought down to be fingerprinted and booked and photographed. And they'll swab you. Why not?

PROSECUTOR

The Law and DNA: Prosecutors on Changing the Statutes of Limitations

The law must catch up with DNA. This technology has allowed us to do *so much*. And the technology is so advanced, and it changes so often, it just gets better and better. Oftentimes it leaves us in law enforcement struggling to catch up with it.

When you have scientific technology like this, the question you have to ask yourself is: Does this render the statute of limitations obsolete? When you have something that is so definitive, really, why should we have a statute of limitations for crimes other than homicides, when you can go back and show that this person, beyond a shadow of a doubt, committed this crime?

With sexual assaults, the statute of limitations runs out in six to ten years in most states. Why not stop the statute of limitations by issuing a John Doe warrant, one that identifies the assailant, not by name or physical description, but by his DNA markers? Then, all you have to do is charge the person, not arrest him, within the statute of limitations. You stop the clock and you can work on solving the case and bringing justice to the victim.

The flip side, also, is that you have these postconviction motions that are going on from Innocence Projects all over the country. You have people who have been incarcerated for ten, fifteen, twenty years, and so on. Are we going to say the statute has run out for them? When you have such wonderful DNA technology that can tell you if somebody has committed a crime for which they've been convicted, should we allow time limitations to interfere with that?

No, we shouldn't. We're looking for truth. We're looking for justice, whichever end of the spectrum you're on. And when you look for truth and justice, you're going to have to use this DNA technology. So, by preserving the statute of limitations, by issuing the John Doe warrants, we're not accomplishing anything that is so monumental or wonderful. It just makes sense.

And this is why so many prosecutors' offices around the country are issuing John Doe warrants, and legislatures are changing the statutes of limitations, because it *does* make sense.

DNA is only limited by our abilities to test for, and understand it. The sensitivity, and the specificity, and the information that forensic DNA analysis can tell us is increasing by leaps and bounds on an almost regular basis. Ultimately, in the courtroom, the end result is that the forensic analysis of DNA has truly, in many trials, made the shadow of doubt extremely small. It's a very, very powerful tool.

And we're looking at only about twenty years since it was first applied forensically. Look at us now. We're at a point now where it's not "Can we do it?" it's "Can we afford to do it?"

DNA evidence is such a powerful, persuasive *gift* that we have for law enforcement. DNA evidence is really very probative. If you have a profile of someone, the statistical analysis that we're coming up with today is so rare that you know very well that this person left that DNA sample.

There's so much you can do with this technology. You could really use this technology, and do *so* much good with it. Whether it's putting a guy in prison or freeing a guy who's been wrongfully convicted. Both sides. Both sides.

Seven

CRIME LAB

When you work in a crime lab, there are many positives. It's fun. It's exciting. You're in a position to do society some good.

But there's one negative. And that's the loss of innocence. Before I got into law enforcement, I thought that most people were good. I thought that, at the most, some people were crazy. But when you work in a crime lab, *you learn*: There are some *evil* people out there. And you would never know it by looking at them.

—Barry A. J. Fisher, Crime Lab Director, Los Angeles County Sheriff's Department

THE MINNESOTA CRIME LAB IN ST. PAUL IS EVERYTHING A state-of-the-art crime lab should be. It's new; it opened in November 2003. It has the latest high-tech equipment and teaching facilities. It's one of four state crime labs in the country chosen to operate an FBI-funded, regional Mitochondrial DNA Testing Center.

It's filled with light from a three-story central atrium. It has break areas and kitchen areas with refrigerators, stoves, microwaves. It's the polar opposite of the dark and menacing labs of TV crime shows.

Hanging from the ceiling of the sun-flooded atrium is an eight-foot high, five-foot-six-inch-wide, twenty-six-foot-long, 3-D sculpture of an elongated, dissected human body.

"See the body lying there?" My guide through the crime lab stops at the top of the stairs on the second floor. What you see from this perspective, across the atrium from the sculpture, is a series of giant, Sherlock Holmes–style magnifying glasses held, glass side up, by thin wires from the ceiling. Focus your eyes a little differently, take a long view, and you see red and gray and beige and brown splotches inside the magnifying glasses, which, you gradually realize, form the side view of a skinless human body.

My guide crosses the atrium to the glass containing the dissected feet of the corpse. From this view, you look across feet, skinny legs, bulging torso. Walk its length to the head, and you peer through cross-sectioned brain, shoulders, back, buttocks, legs.

"Look at it like you're trying to solve it: There's a body lying in there and you're trying to solve it. Look at the different pieces of the puzzle."

And there *are* puzzle pieces in each magnifying glass, bits of metal welded to form shorthand symbols of different forensic specialties. Among them: a set of tire tracks and a piece of shattered glass, representing trace analysis; the outline of a computer and a floppy disc for the DNA, firearms and latent print databases; a few insects for entomology; a marijuana leaf for drug analysis; beakers and chemical formulas for chemistry; a microscope and a fingerprint for latent prints; a line of handwriting for questioned documents; and a baseball bat, a knife, a screwdriver, and an ax, representing both weapons and toolmark analysis.

The sculpture, designed by the nationally renowned team of Helmick and Schechter, begins and ends with the double-helix symbol of DNA. The massive installation is called *Exquisite Corpse*.

"So, you see the body. You have all the different little pieces of the puzzle. The way it works: We try to use as many of those puzzle pieces as we can."

Crime labs started in the United States in the twenties, with the very first lab launched by the LAPD in 1923. "I was on a tour of the FBI Lab once and the guide said the FBI was first. Typical FBI," says one crime lab director. "The FBI Lab didn't start up until '26."

Crime labs sprang up all over the United States in the seventies, backed by federal grant money to fight the war against drugs. They vary in size, funding, capabilities, degrees of being rundown or resplendent. They're just about all, great and small, challenged by backlogs created by the success of DNA and other new technologies and by public expectations fed by shows like *CSI*. Crime lab directors and forensic scientists who work in labs across the nation speak in this chapter about the realities of life in the crime lab. And the scientists who have worked in labs for more than twenty years can hardly believe the changes that have taken place.

Crime Lab Directors on the Old Days of Forensic Science

I try to point out to people how fast we've moved in the last ten or fifteen years. I don't think *anybody* has put in perspective how crime labs play such a major role in law enforcement now. And how fast it happened.

I remember, when I started teaching in the early eighties, no one knew what forensic science was. I had to ask: "Does anyone know what forensic science is?" Maybe one person would put their hand up. And then the Atlanta murders happened, with Wayne Williams, and everybody started to know about forensic science. *Quincy* was on. They knew about fiber. Back then there wasn't forensic DNA—it was serology.

When DNA started to come in, you'd ask what people knew; nobody knew much. And then O. J. Simpson's trial came on, and then *everybody* knew. You didn't even have to explain it.

And now, with *CSI* on TV, you don't even have to say anything. People are just asking you questions. That's amazing to me.

When I walk around our crime lab, one of the thoughts I have most frequently is, our new scientists don't know how well off they are. With all the automation, and the nice equipment, and capabilities that were totally beyond our expectations or even dreams back in the sixties and seventies.

I grew up in New York in a very liberal environment. Everybody I knew hated cops; they were called "pigs" at the time. When I told my mother I was going to work in a crime lab—this is 1963—she said, "You're going to work for *them?*" It was like—not a badge of honor. It was like, "What are you *doing?* We didn't raise you to become a cop." "It's all right, Ma. I'm gonna be a chemist."

Back in the late sixties, I worked with a chemist in the crime lab who really liked explosives. He used to work for the Southern Pacific Railroad. And I guess one of the things they did there was get involved with dynamite and stuff.

He used his own little procedure to test for TNT whenever it came into the lab. This TNT stuff was made up, basically, of sawdust and nitroglycerin. He'd cut open the TNT and it was very oily—wrapped in sticks with heavy paper. The nitroglycerin would be kind of oozing out of it. It had this oily stain.

He'd take a pair of scissors and cut it open and take a couple of scoops out with a spatula, a little laboratory spatula. He'd put the nitroglycerin into a beaker; he'd add some solvents, usually petroleum ether, and swirl it around. He'd filter out the sawdust and put the liquid he had made, which now contained the nitroglycerin, on a piece of filter paper, which is usually about four inches in diameter. And then he'd hold it with kind of a salad tongs.

He kept an I-beam, three or four feet long, under his desk, and he would kind of wrestle it out and hold the filter paper at the end of the tongs and take about a three-pound sledgehammer and—*whack!*—he'd smash the filter paper.

We knew it was TNT when it would explode. One time there was a fireball. It actually burned his eyebrows.

I still have no sense in my fingers. You were constantly touching these parts of gas chromatographs that were at 250 degrees

Celsius, or about 400 Fahrenheit. We didn't have autoinjectors back then. You stood over the instrument and you hand-injected everything.

Most people who have worked the gas chromatograph have no problem touching hot things on the stove because, over the years, instead of doing something appropriate, like grab the oven mitt, you'd just grab it, lick your fingers, grab it, twist it, wait a few seconds and then do it again.

You had all these instruments. You weren't quite sure *why* these instruments existed in the lab. Somebody gave it to you, or you found it somewhere. So you kind of worked with what you had.

When I started in Arson, there was something called an emissions spectograph that we had. And it was about the size of a car. What it did, it allowed you to do elemental analysis by burning this material at a high temperature. And, as any element burns, it gives out certain wavelengths in the light spectrum, so you can identify different things. I learned to use that. I'd never even heard of one before. Of course, now they're down to about the size of a shoe box and the computer does everything for you. *Everything* now is quite a bit smaller and quite a bit more powerful.

Back in the early days, you didn't necessarily have all the instruments that would be the best for you, but you worked with what you had. You did the best job you could.

When I worked in Toxicology, we had a lady that was poisoning her husband with arsenic. It was kind of an *Arsenic and Old Lace* case. He would go into the hospital and get better, and then come back out, and then he'd get a little bit worse. They tracked it down by looking at the level of arsenic in the hair. Hair shows a lot of things. Even before we could do nuclear DNA testing on hair roots, or mitochondrial DNA testing on the hair for exclusion, we could tell a lot just by examining hair.

With this man's hair, as the roots grew out, you could track how much arsenic was there. Nothing fancy, but you could reconstruct when he'd been poisoned.

We used to have a crime lab director who believed that you should build your own equipment. He didn't think you should buy things on the market.

Back then, you washed all your glassware. If you broke something or had a crack in it, you'd fix it. Nowadays, most of the scientists, with disposable glassware and pipe heads, they wouldn't reuse anything anymore. Baling wire, shims, and duct tape were a reasonable part of the forensic tool kit back then.

It was bootstrap forensics, basically. Labs were smaller. We were just learning things. As we went along, we were learning things.

In some ways it required a whole lot more creativity than it does today, but we're much more precise in what we do today than we were.

This was before computers. Before copy machines. You'd type reports and you'd actually use something called carbon paper.

Computers have had a huge influence. Databases. And coupling those with the instruments we use and how they can manage large amounts of analytical data that the instruments produce. DNA is a good example of that, with the gene sequencers, and the computers that are attached to that. *None* of that would have been possible in the early days.

The big change is everything's so much more automated now. Back when I did toxicology in the late seventies, it was one sample at a time. Blood or urine. You would take this tear-shaped glass called a separatory funnel, put in a portion of your blood or urine sample, along with some chloroform and either acid or base, depending on what you're going after—and you would stand there and—shake it. That was the procedure.

Now we have robotic systems, where you put in a small amount of the sample and make sure all the right tubes are hooked up, step back, and after a while it gives you something you can test, and you enter that in another instrument and it tells you what's there.

We never used to wear gloves. When we talk about what it used to be like in crime labs, back in the primitive days, and we tell the new criminalists that we didn't wear gloves, they get totally grossed out.

I got a call from the serology unit about six months ago on a case that I did the original work on. It was a bedsheet that was under a woman that had been found murdered. She had decomposed somewhat, so there were a lot of body fluids on the sheet.

At the time, I had found three different semen stains on this sheet and had marked them, so that we could go back to them again. The criminalist working on it now has been around for about three years. I went back there. Seeing the sheet, I remembered it. She's standing there, in her lab coat, her booties covering her feet, and she's got her gloves on, and she's got protective sleeves on, and she's got her white cap over her hair, and the face mask on, and I'm looking at her, going, "You know, when I first examined this, I *did* wear a lab coat. But that was about it."

In serology, we used to believe that, particularly when you're looking for semen stains, the best way to do it was just to feel the garment, because it had a little stiffer feel to it, even if you couldn't see it, but you could feel it with your fingers. This was pre-AIDS. We didn't start requiring gloves until the mideighties. And, much as I hate to admit it, I was one of the ones saying, "Don't make me wear these things!

They're going to make me clumsier. I'm not going to be able to process this stuff." And then you get smart and think, "Hey, wait a minute. My health's at issue here."

Luckily, things have changed. Looking back, that wasn't the greatest way to do business.

One of my old cases: There was a guy in prison who had the nickname of "The Butcher." He worked as a butcher in prison. He found out that a guy had been cheating on him with his girlfriend. When he got out, he killed this fellow. He also dismembered the body.

Then he and his buddies—they decided, okay, they had this body, how are they gonna get rid of it? So they went out and got a fifty-five-gallon drum of sulfuric acid, figuring that they would just dissolve the body up in the bathtub. Unfortunately, it didn't work. They just ended up making a lot of soap.

The district attorney on the case wanted to get an idea of what happens when you dissolve flesh in sulfuric acid. The first thing he suggested to us was that we ask the coroner's office for an unclaimed body. I told him, "That's not gonna play in Peoria. That's just disgusting."

I suggested that the DA have somebody go down to this large meatpacking plant just south of downtown LA called Farmer John's Market. I said they could just get a little piece of pig from the market for us to work on in the lab.

A couple days later, this homicide detective walks into the lab with an entire *leg* of pig just hanging over his shoulder, with a piece of butcher paper draping over it. And he *slams* it down in front of me on the laboratory bench and says, "Here's what you asked for."

I had to take a hacksaw to it and cut out a chunk. I cut off about a two-inch piece of leg, you know, kind of salami style? Just about a two-inch wedge. And put it into a beaker with sulfuric acid to see what happened. Nothing much. It just kind of got really messy and soapy-looking.

So I testified about that experiment. I don't know how much of an impact it had; it was all kind of bizarre, as many of these things are.

We're much more safety conscious than we were. Years ago, we didn't have lids on thin-layer chromatography tanks, the developing tanks. So the solvents were just out in the open.

We used to eat right where we were working. Lunchtime. You'd go get your lunch and sit back down at your lab bench and eat. You know?

That kind of stuff. That doesn't go on any more. It's a much safer place to work.

We found some old notes from back in the sixties, when they were testing for cocaine. One of the scientists wrote, "Numbs the tongue." He had actually put his finger in the cocaine and touched his tongue with it.

A huge change is in documentation. I'll go back now to these old cases and see a set of serology notes that might be five pages long. That was considered extensive note taking. Now, a DNA case of the same type might be fifty or seventy-five pages. Documentation is just a lot better now. Not that we didn't know; you just didn't see it as important. You didn't take pictures of everything like we do now; now that we have the digital stuff, you can shoot to your heart's content, and it doesn't cost anything. It isn't an issue.

The O. J. Simpson case taught us a lot. We [the LAPD and LAPD crime lab] really *did* do the right thing, in ninety-five percent of the situations where we were criticized, but we couldn't prove it. We didn't have the documentation. We couldn't say, "Yes, we did it right. This is why." We learned a lot from that.

The major changes have come in with the sophistication of the
instrumentation over the years, and the ability to do more
and more with less and less. We can throw smaller and
smaller samples onto, or into, the instrumentation we have
now and get so much more information out of it. The skill
now comes in the training, because you have to understand
how to interpret this stuff.

Advances in instrumentation have been absolutely crucial in
firearms and toolmark examination. We use a comparison
microscope as our main tool. That's two ordinary compound
microscopes that are hooked together by an optical bridge, a
series of mirrors that allows the viewer to look through two
oculars and look at two objects simultaneously, in the same
field of view.

The comparison microscope has gone through significant
changes in the thirty years that I've been doing this. The optics are much better today. The manipulation of the comparison microscope is much more precise and easier to work
with than it was. Thirty years ago, your optics were okay for
the human eye to look at objects, but the resolution was not
good enough for very clear, precise photographs.

In the late seventies, we had a 35-millimeter camera that
we mounted on an extension tube to the system. We'd take
some pictures, go into the darkroom, develop the roll to see
if, first of all, it was in focus, and then to see if it captured
that area we were interested in. If it didn't, we'd go back and
try to tweak the system a little bit and try to get a better picture. Essentially, it was back and forth to the darkroom.

Very, very labor-intensive, very time-consuming to produce
even a single photograph of a portion of a bullet or cartridge
case identification. And now you can put recording devices,
digital cameras, on the system and have it take pictures in real
time as you're looking through the microscope. Today, as we
are looking at the objects in our field of view, we also have a

real-time image appearing on the monitor next to us, and if we find a point of interest we want to save, we just click on it and we can print out a hard copy for our files as we go along.

And now we can enter images of cartridge cases and bullets into a system that both stores it and compares it against all other images stored in the system from multiple laboratories, called NIBIN, the National Integrated Ballistics Information Network. This is much like AFIS for fingerprints, same principle, but this is for firearms, cartridge cases, and bullets. We've made many cold hits with this equipment that thirty years ago just weren't being made.

Over the years, different things have been touted as the panacea for forensic science, and they've come and gone. The paraffin test, for example, used to be pretty popular.

This test was one where you put hot paraffin on somebody's hand, you let it solidify, you peeled it off, and then you tested it for gunshot residue. That was developed back in the thirties and discredited in ten years, but was still used even through the sixties in a lot of laboratories. People thought this was going to be *it*, that you were going to be able to tell that somebody had discharged a firearm by running this paraffin test.

I don't think anybody is using it anymore, except for interrogation purposes. You know, you tell a suspect, "I'm gonna stick your hand in this vat of boiling hot wax," it has a certain weight. Paraffin heats at very low temperatures, so, actually, there's no torture involved.

One of the things I appreciate about crime lab work is, it is a very creative enterprise. I think people who thrive at it are creative people. The British have a beautiful term for crime lab work. They say it deals with what is "one-off" in nature. One-off! In other words, every case is unique.

Fingerprints, for example. They are unique to each person, from the womb on, throughout their entire lives. Even identical siblings have different prints. And when you analyze prints, the deposit of a fingerprint will vary, as to what its constituents are. The substrate, the surface the print is on, will be different. In one case, it may be check paper; in the next, white bond paper; next time, it's plastic. That substrate will be different, and that will determine which techniques will be valuable and which ones just can't be used because they could destroy the print.

The amount of time that may have transpired between deposit and your attempt to find that print will be different; what may have happened environmentally to that surface in between may be different. Maybe in one case, it sat in a desiccated, desert-type environment. Maybe it was a check that sat in a safe, and burglars took the safe out into the country, beat it open with a sledgehammer, and dumped it into a creek. We get the safe into the crime lab and it's full of *wet* paper. Guess what? There are techniques we can use on paper that's been submerged. We can develop fingerprints that are every bit as good as if the surface was dry.

You're taking the totality of the circumstances. Each one of those variables lined up makes it almost a statistically unique examination.

It's the *creative* people, the ones who are thinking all the time, who thrive in crime labs. The ones who are saying, "How am I going to get everything out of this that I can? How many bites of the apple can I get?"

We had a case here in South Carolina, about twenty years ago, that drew just about every field of forensic science into it. About the only thing it *didn't* have was ballistics.

It had toxicology. We did serology; at the time, DNA wasn't available. Questioned Documents was one of the key sections that broke the case. Latent prints from the crime scene were heavily involved. And, of course, trace evidence,

particularly with hair comparisons. Hair was the only thing
that was left, when we located the body, by which to identify
the victim.

There was a young lady—high school student—who was
abducted from in front of her home. It had a long, a fairly
long driveway from the home to the road. Country road.

She was abducted. Over the next several weeks, the fellow
that abducted her taunted the family with phone calls, saying
what he was doing, what he wanted to do with the young
girl. He forced her to write a last will and testament and mail
it to her family.

He played games with the family and with law enforcement for a period of two to three weeks there. We had a task
force put together, trying to locate the victim and the suspect.

He was very . . . very sadistic and he wound up. . . . He
wound up suffocating her with tape over the mouth and nostrils. We're fairly certain he molested her, but we can't prove
it, because there was nothing left when we found the body
sufficient to do anything with.

As it turned out, the piece of paper that the last will and
testament was written on had some indented writing on it.
Indented writing means the marks that are made on a piece
of paper that is *under* the paper you're writing on. Our
Questioned Document laboratory was able to identify some
phone numbers, a grocery list, and a few names from the
markings that appeared on the girl's last will and testament.

One of the phone numbers was to a family in another
state. We contacted them, wanted to know if they had any
acquaintances in South Carolina, and they did.

It turned out that the family they were acquainted with
had a home here, in South Carolina, and had just recently
visited on their way back. When this family got back home,
our investigators went to talk to them. We found out they
had been out of town during this period of time in which
the young lady was abducted and her abductor was torment-

ing her family. They said that one of the husband's employees was house-sitting for them.

It turned out, it was the employee who had abducted the
young girl. All this from indented writing on a piece of paper
from a tablet. Once we identified the home, of course, we
were able to recover the tablet. The piece of paper that the
house-sitter had forced the girl to write her will on was from
an ordinary tablet of paper, one that the family used just to
make routine notes.

The kidnapper eventually told us where she was. The
body was located out in the country, in the woods. She had
been left in the woods through July and August in South
Carolina, in hot summer heat and humidity. There wasn't
much left of the body for identification purposes. I don't
think there was much they could do with dental records
then. Her teeth were still in pretty good shape, nothing to
identify them.

The crime lab worked in just about all the forensic disciplines on this case. Toxicology tried to do some extractions,
but the body was too putrefied. Serology tried, too.

Trace evidence figured in. We found some of her hairs.
Her hair was somewhat unique. She had very long hair,
probably in the neighborhood of twelve, eighteen inches
long. She did a lot of coloring and pinning and whatever.
And all along the shaft of the hair you could see color
changes, so analysts could see what she had done to the color
of her hair at a particular time. We were able to identify her
hair back to the time when she had been in the house and
also hair from her original home, from hair found in her
hairbrush.

And latent print evidence was important. The examiners
found the killer's prints in the house, which corroborated the
homeowner's testimony that he had been in the house.

And Questioned Documents, of course, is what allowed
us to solve the case in the first place.

What led up to the murder: The house-sitter had been stalking the young girl. Unbeknownst to her. He had a fixation on her. And she was abducted and murdered just by the chance of this guy house-sitting for his employer. This case didn't have a lot of evidence. It was pre-DNA, pre- a lot of forensic advances. But we used just about every forensic discipline we had to put all the pieces of the puzzle together.

In 1984, I was asked to come from Texas to Alaska in order to set up a crime lab. The lab at the time was a makeshift facility. It was basically two rooms in the basement of the state trooper headquarters in Anchorage. Five people worked there, including the administrator.

The lab was only doing blood for alcohol and very minor analyses. We didn't really have the capability of doing what's generally done in a laboratory nowadays. We didn't even have a standardized rape kit. Let's say you had evidence in a sexual assault case. That had to be packaged and shipped off to be analyzed by the FBI in Washington, D.C. Chances were that it would sit in a mailroom over night or over a weekend, so the degradation of the evidence was a factor.

Before I got up here, they had indicated that they had money to build a new lab. For some reason, at the last minute, the legislature hadn't passed that appropriation yet. So I had to finish up that business and oversee the building construction, equipping the lab, and hiring scientists for a full-service laboratory. Hiring was a problem. Sometimes people want to come to Alaska. Sometimes the men folks want to come here to hunt and fish and the women don't want any part of it because there isn't a whole lot of Nordstroms around.

Now, though, we've got a full-service lab, with a DNA section, fully accredited by ASCLD (American Society of Crime Lab Directors) and we've gone from two basement rooms to seventeen thousand feet.

Forensic Scientists on Working in Crime Labs Today

When I tell people what I do, they say, "Oh, you look at dead bodies." No, no, the closest I get to a dead body is a person's hand. Every once in a while, they'll find a John Doe or a Jane Doe—they find a floater. Somebody's been found in the river or the lake. They bring the body to the ME's Office; they need some kind of identification of this person. What they would do is, they cut the hands at the wrist, put them in the equivalent of a chrome paint can, and bring them to us. We open the cans up in a biohazard area and try to lift the finger-prints off the skin. We powder the skin, we roll the fingers of the hand in printer's ink, and then roll it onto a fingerprint card or lift, and then use that to trace all the information out. Then we enter it in our AFIS system to see if we can identify that person. They may have been arrested before, or have a job application on file with a company that's in our database.

But that's as gross as it gets. I mean, we've had fingers and hands in all different stages of decomposition. Obviously, the ones in the river . . . rivers being cold, that preserves the hands a little bit more. You get a hand in from a river, it usu-ally isn't too bad. But if a hand's been found in like an aban-doned building, then decomposition is pretty severe. Sometimes you *can't* identify the person from the hand.

In terms of cleaning the hands up, there's really not much they [the Medical Examiner's Office] can do. I mean, it is what it is when they find it. So, they remove the hands. Keep them refrigerated so there's no more decomposition. And send them to the crime lab.

And we work those cases—pretty quick. You want to get them in and out. It's a biohazard. They could decompose if they're left out.

But there are certain techniques we use. I mean, in some

of the cases where it might be difficult to get the ridges up, or to try and see the fingerprint left on the skin, sometimes we have to soak the fingers in—now, don't laugh— Palmolive. Palmolive and water. And you know the commercial: "Your hands are so soft, you must be soaking them in Palmolive"? Well, I mean, it works! It brings out the ridges a little bit more. We try to rejuvenate the ridges of the skin and try to bring them up.

You've got to have a sense of humor, working in the lab. So, for example, when you're dealing with hands, you know, you're on the bench and you need the next set of hands out of the fridge, you ask one of the other examiners who's going to the fridge, "Hey, can you give me a hand over here?"

LATENT PRINT SPECIALIST

We look at things that nobody else looks at, that nobody else cares about. This is why we're a unique science. A lot of people will say forensic science is just a "borrowed" science; it's just an applied science: "You're just applying chemistry," for example. We're not. There's a unique body of knowledge that goes with forensic science that isn't covered by anybody. And every type of evidence requires its own methodology.

We're testing stuff that nobody knows. Nobody keeps track of it. You think the manufacturers of Converse All-Stars worry if the prints of their shoes are unique? The fiber manufacturers know that they put delustrant, little particles of titanium dioxide, to break up the light so the fibers have a matte finish to them. But they don't know what the distribution is. They don't go in and look at it like we do and go, "Wow! There's big clumps of it!" Or "It's evenly distributed." Or "Look! These are really *small* granules." The manufacturers don't care. *We* do. It might solve a case.

TRACE ANALYST

I have a theory about forensic scientists. If you are in the field for more than about three years, you'll never be satisfied doing anything else. You'll know immediately if it's not for you.

When I joined the sheriff's office crime lab in '72, there was another gentleman hired at the same time. He lasted about a year. It wasn't for him. He was scared to death at the prospect of going to court and having to testify and having to be cross-examined. He didn't like the work. But I just fell right into it and knew right away this was what I wanted to do for the rest of my life.

I've always said, "I'll do this till it stops being fun." And it hasn't stopped being fun yet.

RESEARCH CHEMIST

You do get a little obsessed. There's a web site for latent finger-print examiners. It has a section called "You Might Be a Latent Print Person If . . ." It quizzes you on things like "When you go through the line at a buffet, do you examine the Jell-O cubes for fingerprints?" I *do* that! I scored an eighteen out of a possible twenty.

What we do *does* have an effect on how we look at things in our own lives. When my first son was born, you know, the hospital takes the newborn's footprint. And they took my son's footprint and handed the card to me. I put my glasses on my forehead—I'm nearsighted, so I had to get in really close to magnify the footprint—and I examined it *carefully*. And I'm standing there, in the middle of the delivery room, and I'm pointing out to everybody that the footprint had no ridge detail. "Look at this! You can't distinguish anything!" And they said, "Hey! You should be happy he only has five toes. Do you have any idea how *squirmy* newborns are?" But I wanted them to retake the prints. I said, "These are of no value."

LATENT PRINT EXAMINER

The job is probably dripping into my private life. I was washing my hands at a friend's house one time and she said, "What are you doing—surgery?" I just got in the habit, you know, scrubbing under the fingernails, really, really scrubbing when I was doing DNA casework and I was washing my hands many times a day. And when I left the bench for a management position, I can tell you it felt totally weird not to have gloves on all the time.

DNA SPECIALIST

It's always different. Your background, the science that you learned in school, is the same science, certainly, but you approach problems in different ways, because the problems themselves change from day to day.

My first three or four years in the field I was doing drug analysis, partially because that was the main reason this lab was opened, to serve as a regional drug analysis laboratory. I really didn't care for that. It was routine. You know, marijuana is marijuana is marijuana. The packaging was different, the mode of transmission was different, some of those things were different—that kept it interesting, but it was still kind of routine.

When I was moved out of that section, and ultimately ended up in Firearms and Toolmarks, it was a lot more varied. You never knew what you were going to encounter from one day to the next. And it requires you to just not know a chemical process, or an analytical process, or a scientific process. It requires you to figure out how to apply that. Which process do I choose to do what I want to do? What do I expect to get out of that? It's always different and it's always interesting.

The second thing—in the beginning I think I was just saying it to say the words, but I really believe it now—is that I'm actually making a contribution to the public. It doesn't pay as well as private industry would, but I'm giving something back. I'm a public servant.

The third thing is that you always are in the know. You're right in on everything. As things happen, you're one of the first people to be called in. You see stuff on television or in the newspapers, and you can turn to your significant others at home and say, "Well, that's not the way this really happened." There's a little bit of an ego deal that goes along with it.

FIREARMS/TOOLMARK SPECIALIST

Crime lab work often has all the scintillating aspects of watch-ing paint dry. It is a very detailed job. You are doing the same activities over and over again. And there's not a lot of gross motor skills involved.

But in the shows—particularly *CSI*—crime lab people are running around, they're wrassling down the suspects, going out to crime scenes, making arrests, throwing on the cuffs. That is not forensics.

There may be some crime scene work, but there's no contact with suspects. Actually, most of the people who work in crime labs *pray* there won't be contact with suspects.

People shouldn't see this as a glamorous job, or as an active job. I want to reduce people's expectations.

On the other hand, I've been doing this for about thirty years. I have never once regretted that I chose to go into this field. I characterize it as routine, but rarely boring. While you're not going to be doing those gross motor running-around things, when you make that identification, as a fingerprint examiner, or when you make the DNA match, for the DNA folks, it's a *yes!* kind of moment.

LATENT PRINT EXAMINER

People think of scientists as walking around in white lab coats, with the pocket protectors and the pens sticking out, coming in to the lab and sitting down and peering into microscopes for eight hours. The truth is, we're all human. And it's the stories and the personalities in the lab that bridge the gap between cases and make us . . . human. And not just people who sit in a laboratory all day doing scientific experiments.

DNA ANALYST

Friendships develop in the lab. Stories develop. Times: "Remember when we were working that case and we had pizza and we ordered it from that place and me and Frank went out and the neighborhood wasn't that great and Frank walks into the pizza joint with his money held out and I said, 'Frank, you may want to keep the money in your pocket till we get the pizza?'" Little things you remember that you tell stories about.

LATENT PRINT EXAMINER

Most crime scene people who have children will admit that, throughout their careers, the scenes that are probably the most difficult to go on are the ones that have children as victims, and the children happen to be, at that moment in time, the same age as their own children. Does that make sense?

Many times, I've been on scenes where there was a child. And the child happened to be the age of one of my sons. It, uh. . . . You go home and give them an extra hug.

CRIME SCENE ANALYST

You know, when I was young, I used to hunt. I'd go out with my father-in-law, and we would hunt deer and rabbit, pheasant, that kind of thing.

After I got into the crime laboratory in the seventies, and then probably more in the eighties, after having been on a number of crime scenes, I tend not to go hunting anymore.

FIREARMS EXPERT

Crime Lab Directors on CSI *versus Reality*

There's a couple of things about *CSI*—this isn't meant as a criticism—it's a TV drama. The real thing would be ninety-nine percent boredom interstitched with a few bright, exciting moments.

You get the impression from these shows that there are two or three people who do everything. And it's like they're waiting for the work to do, and they jump on every case when it comes in the door. I wish that were the case. I wish that every case could be given the resources and attention that the *CSI* shows portray.

We just don't do it in forty minutes. And we don't treat every case the way *CSI* does. And our laboratories are much better lit than *CSI* laboratories. You know, they're constantly moving around in the dark with their flashlights.

The crime labs in the United States are, in general, totally under-staffed. They have inadequate facilities. Inadequate funding. You're constantly behind the curve in terms of trying to do cases.

***CSI* gives people the impression that crime labs are incredibly** well funded and staffed. They seem to always be at the ready. They just jump on cases. And they work one case at a time.

You don't hear the normal exchange between the investigators and the lab people. You don't hear: "Okay, I'll give you a call when we get to this case. And it'll be in a few months."

The way it really works: The police submit *hundreds* of pieces of evidence. "Look, anything you can come up with—a fingerprint, a DNA, a fiber, hair . . ." All the evidence is looked at with a modern eye. And it's often fruitful.

But *CSI* creates false expectations. There's the expectation that all these techniques will apply to a particular case and that they'll be done *instantly*.

Our biggest problem now is that we can't meet *priority* priorities. The examiners are plodding through cases. It's hard. You want to give each case every chance, but it's hard to pull out all the stops on every case. That's the implication you get from *CSI*. But that's not the reality.

The "*CSI* effect" is a real challenge to crime labs. There are such high expectations now. We went from nobody knowing what forensic science was—to now, because of CSI, everybody thinks that we can solve a murder in thirty minutes.

The technology that the crime shows exhibit doesn't even *exist*, in many cases. Fingerprints rotating on a screen, for example; that technology doesn't exist. The idea that they have these bullets—a noise comes across: *did, did, did, did*—and they can fly these bullets across a screen. That technology doesn't exist.

They *do* have ballistics matches in labs, but that's in black and white, not in color, and they don't merge the two bullets together. It takes hours of work sometimes to get that.

But to have someone sit down at a desk and an hour later, he's got the result? What the hell do you need a scientist for? Anyone can do that. Anyone can sit and push a button.

It's like, one of the *CSI* guys recovers one fiber from a crime scene. So he clicks it into the computer database. Instantly, "Oh, I *see,* this was manufactured in Peking, China. They stopped production in 1999. And now I'm gonna check all the databases. Oh, this matches an unusual make of afghan that was only sold in certain stores." And then, to go with that one fiber, they'll have one other piece of evidence—the credit card receipt for the purchase. It doesn't happen like that.

It's fiction. It's distortion. There's the distortion of the time factor. There's the fantasy of all labs having the latest, high-tech gizmos. There's no consideration of how much money it costs to do some of this stuff. And these characters have the whole—lab—to work just one murder case. In reality, there's a four-to-six-week backlog before the lab can even start working on it.

Real crime labs aren't that sexy. People assume, from the shows that take place in big, beautiful labs, "Wow, look how great crime labs are."

Our crime lab is very old. It's beat-up. The equipment's pretty old. Some of the labs are new and high-tech. There's been more money coming in for the last few years, and you see some improvement in the infrastructure.

But most crime labs are beat-up. The average facility is more like Andy Sipowitz in *NYPD Blue* than Gil Grissom in *CSI.*

I don't want people to get a false notion of what we actually can do. If you watch the *CSI* shows, crime labs have all the latest in technology and the most expensive equipment.

Many laboratories don't have that. I'm coming from a system that is very state-of-the-art, but if I talk to other fingerprint examiners from different labs, they don't have new lasers, or new super-glue chambers, or new humidity chambers. They can't buy all the new chemicals coming out.

It's just tough. A lot of money isn't going into forensic science. There are grants out there that help pay for DNA because that is *the* hot topic now. A lot more money goes to that particular section, but it would be great if we could get more money in the forensic science community as a whole to give more people the chance to have the equipment they need to do the work. But people think everything is fine with labs, because that's what they see on TV.

First, you need money. You need money to build labs to have room to hire scientists. But then the problem is, there's a shortage of scientists. There's no shortage of kids who want to be forensic scientists today. Everybody wants to be a forensic scientist. I get ten calls a day. My *daughter* wants to be a forensic scientist.

But. Forensic science covers all the natural sciences. So you're always looking for chemists, biologists, physicists, but the only thing a lab can do is—get a bunch of new positions, hire some of these kids. Then it's two years to train a firearms examiner, three years for a questioned document examiner, one year for a forensic biologist. On-the-job training has to be completed before these people can begin to make their presence felt.

Even once they start doing cases, they're new and inexperienced, so they require a higher degree of supervision. So you can throw money at the problem, and money is being thrown: there's better funding today, especially with DNA, than ever before, but it's going to take a long time for the development of the five thousand to ten thousand forensic scientists needed today to cope with the demand. It's not an easy fix.

And there aren't a large number of private, full-service, forensic science laboratories. We can't send all our evidence in our overflow cases to Forensics 'R' Us.

It's money. Facilities. Equipment. And the real key is people. It requires experience. And a lot of that experience is retiring with the old-timers who came on in the seventies. That's a major stumbling block.

The whole "*CSI* effect" is a two-edged sword. On the one hand, it does educate the public in terms of what the technologies can do. On the other hand, there is this expectation now— on the part of the media, victims, and families—that their case is going to be handled as expediently and completely as they see on *CSI*. The fact of the matter is some of the testing will take months. And, at the end of that, there may be inconclusive results. Things don't always work. There isn't the

Eureka! every day. And these expectations spill over into what evidence is considered valuable in court.

The Dangerous Side Effects of Crime Lab Backlogs

Forensic science laboratories are victims of their own success. Crime labs are overwhelmed with evidence. We're dealing with an explosion of new potential probative evidence being collected at crime scenes. Five years ago, nobody would have thought to collect saliva from beer bottles or straws. They wouldn't have thought to collect a ski mask for epithelial cells, to test for DNA. But now each and every case may have dozens or even hundreds of pieces of evidence.

So, you've got an explosion of evidence versus limited capabilities within the labs. The labs aren't growing at the same rate as public awareness and law enforcement's training and knowledge of the power of DNA technology.

We have this growing rift. Labs must expand their capabilities not only to meet the current caseload, but the future caseload. And it's only going to grow.

CRIME LAB DIRECTOR

The whole phenomenon of the courts depending and relying on forensic evidence much more than circumstantial evidence or eyewitness testimony or other kinds of evidence has put a new burden on crime labs. And the new technologies have created an explosion of work for forensic labs.

CRIME LAB DIRECTOR

I don't think there's a crime lab in the country that doesn't have a backlog. The problem is, there's almost an infinite variety of items that we can test and have found extremely important results. But you never know what you're going to get results from. That's why sometimes a case will come in with literally hundreds of pieces of evidence and take months once you start it.

FORENSIC SCIENTIST

When I was in the FBI Crime Lab, we got everything. Literally, the kitchen sink. One time, agents *did* send in a kitchen sink, because they thought the perpetrator had cleaned up afterward and they wanted us to look for hair. I've had the interior of a car submitted, in pieces. We used to joke: The FBI has trained teams of crime scene technicians. They're called ERTs for evidence recovery teams. They would routinely collect huge amounts of evidence. And then they'd figure, "We're not really sure if this is meaningful or not. We'll let the lab figure it out!" So, in the lab, we used to joke that ERT stood for "empty residence totally."

TRACE ANALYST

The problem with backlog? It's not the delay itself; it's the fact that someone may commit another rape, or another murder while the evidence is still sitting in the crime lab.

When you're dealing with a technology as effective as DNA is, or anything as effective as DNA, how quickly you move or you don't move with it, can literally be counted in people's lives. If you don't move quickly, you have perpetrators out on the street, committing more crimes, raping women, murdering children, who *wouldn't* be raped, who *wouldn't* be murdered, if you had moved more quickly, if you had integrated the technology more quickly.

PROSECUTOR/DNA EXPERT

There was a young lady who was murdered, arguably, as a result of delays in DNA analysis. This is a case that, sadly, points out what we've always said should be obvious: Delays, backlogs in analysis can result in perpetrators continuing to be free to commit other crimes.

This case goes back to '99. A woman was raped in Virginia Beach, Virginia. The police developed, very quickly, a suspect. It took them a while to get a known sample from that suspect.

They had the suspect. They were holding him on shoplifting charges, but they couldn't hold him much longer. The hearing on the shoplifting charges was held, the prosecutor and police didn't show up, and he was released. They didn't have enough to hold him on the Virginia Beach attack because the DNA results weren't in yet.

Ten days later, another young woman, Gemma Saunders, was raped and murdered in Norfolk, Virginia. The Virginia Beach police were upset with the crime lab, understandably, because, sure enough, the results from DNA in the Virginia Beach rape case were identical to the suspect's profile in the murder of Gemma Saunders.

The moral of that story is that if we had even a thirty-day turnaround time, we could have identified him, and he wouldn't have been out to attack and murder Gemma Saunders.

CRIME LAB DIRECTOR

Is DNA Muscling Out Other Disciplines?

DNA probably accounts for ten percent or less of the cases that we work on in our laboratory. In most laboratories. But it gets all the attention.

There's more to forensics than just DNA. You need all the tools, all the different specialties. You want to get as many different pieces of the puzzle as you can.

CRIME LAB DIRECTOR

In forensics, a broad knowledge of all the possibilities is so im-portant. I mean, we literally make use of just about every "ology" out there when it comes to analyzing a case. You never know where it's going to go.

However, the technology that's required to do the work

now is becoming so complicated that specialization is being required. Through my career, I went through three units in the lab. Somebody else might have gone through five. Now, we might get somebody that spends their whole career doing DNA. That's their total focus, because of the long training required, and that makes it more difficult to rotate people around.

So crime labs are going to miss out somewhat on this broader knowledge of the capabilities. When you're looking at a piece of clothing from the crime scene for semen stains, you need to also be able to recognize, "Hey, that hair means something. That fiber means something."

It used to be that when our firearms unit received a bullet, the first thing they'd do would be they'd wash it off so they could see all their little grooves and markings so they could do their comparison. Guess what? There might be blood on there that's important. There might be drywall debris on the nose of it that proves that it went through a particular wall.

You don't want to push those things aside to get to your piece of information. Directors of crime labs have to be very, very aware of that and not lose the ability of people to recognize evidence beyond their one little specialty.

CRIME LAB DIRECTOR

A big issue we're seeing now is, which way do we go with the evidence? Do we go with DNA, or do we go with fingerprints? Let's say, a beer bottle. Do we go with DNA? Fingerprints? Which? We're seeing more and more evidence diverted to the DNA section before it comes to latent prints, or firearms, or the other sections, just because it's asked for more and more as evidence.

LATENT PRINT SPECIALIST

We've tried to get fingerprint examiners and DNA analysts to talk and come to a common ground. We've talked to the DNA people: "Can you get DNA from the mouth of the bottle?" "Yes, that's possible." "Okay, well, what if you get DNA from the mouth and we process the rest of the bottle for prints?" So then we have two chances to find who may have touched or handled that particular item.

A lot of it has been working together between different sections in the lab. I've seen forensic scientists, homicide investigators, and prosecutors become a lot closer and more of a team now, instead of people just working in their specific disciplines and just concentrating on what they have to do. It's become more of a collaborative effort.

LATENT PRINT SECTION SUPERVISOR

It's not a matter of which section is better than the others. It's what's the best way to go? I had a case where the murder weapon ended up being a hammer. There was a bloody print on the hammer handle. Okay? The blood was the victim's and the print was the suspect's. I mean, you *dream* of cases like that. That's a case where we first processed the print, made the match, and then DNA-swabbed that blood and matched it to the victim. That was a case where both of us came in. You work together.

CRIME LAB DIRECTOR

We have *dozens* of different examiners involved in a single case—trace evidence examiners and serologists and DNA people and handwriting people and firearms people and latent fingerprint people. They all come together, so to speak, and all that work comes together.

Sometimes I think of myself as the conductor of an orchestra, where each of the different instruments—strings and horns and winds—come together and *do* make some beautiful music.

CRIME LAB DIRECTOR

Two Crime Lab Cases

The following cases, one involving the largest forensic case in U.S. history, the other involving a murder in a small Midwestern town, show the resourcefulness and persistence of crime lab scientists. In the first, Robert Shaler, former director of the Office of the Chief Medical Examiner, New York City Department of Forensic Biology, DNA Lab, talks about the challenges of obtaining forensic identification of the victims of the attack on the World Trade Center.

Crime Lab Case One: World Trade Center

We identified one thousand five hundred and eighty-eight out of the two thousand seven hundred and forty-nine victims. That's about fifty-six to fifty-eight percent of the victims.

If there was no DNA, we would only have been able to identify seven hundred and thirty-six people. These victims were identified through conventional methods: dental identification, fingerprints, personal effects, tattoos, visualizing the body, as in somebody coming in and identifying them.

Most of our DNA identifications came from either kinship analysis or direct matching to a personal effect from a victim. With kinship analysis, like a paternity test, where you're looking at a mother-father-child trio, or brothers and sisters, or from mitochondrial DNA, to take the maternal lineage—we're looking to find the genetic structure of a family and we're looking for a piece obtained from a disaster sample that fits into that genetic structure. The goal is to be ninety-nine point nine percent sure that it matches.

The DNA we had to work with was badly degraded. That's because warm, moist environments are hostile to DNA. And that's exactly what we had at the World Trade Center. Those buildings burned for three months, and they were squirting them with water. They had to put the fires out, and they had to make it safer for people to walk there, because those girders were hot. It just had to be done.

We knew right away this was going to cause a problem. When we started seeing the remains coming in and we started doing DNA testing on them, within a week or so, we were getting profiles that weren't giving us good-quality DNA.

So I started thinking, "What can I do about this?" I knew about a guy named John Butler, who now works for the National Institute of Standards and Technology, who had developed a test, a couple of years earlier, where he was looking at different ways to look at STRs (short tandem repeats). Our initial approach was to use the normal forensic STRs that we use in our normal casework. Because that kind of testing can look at DNA fragments that are about four hundred base pairs long, so it can look at extensively degraded DNA.

But we were getting partial profiles—which meant that we were seeing DNA, less than four hundred base pairs, but still getting some results, which meant, we were looking at fragments probably in the neighborhood of a hundred base pairs. And a lot gave nothing.

I remembered this John Butler, and the work he had done. We talked, and he agreed to adapt his work to the World Trade Center effort. At first, it didn't work as well as we thought it would. A scientist named Jim Schumm, who works for the Bode Technology Group in New York, asked, in March 2002, if he could pick up on this idea and rework it. He did, and by December 2002 we got the first data, and we got five new identifications from it. Butler had the original concept a couple of years before, but it had never been used in forensics. I wanted to adapt the concept to the World Trade Center. And Jim Schumm was the one who did the final adaptation.

These are called miniplexes, and what they do— Instead of having the range of usable DNA go as much as 400 base pairs, this technique lowered it to between 89 and 218 base pairs. That enabled us to get more genetic information from samples that weren't giving complete information before.

We also did SNPs (single nucleotide polymorphisms), the smallest mutation on the DNA molecule. It's basically a change in an individual base pair; you can't get smaller than that. I thought that if we could design a test to look at those individual base pairs, then I could begin to look at even more degraded DNA. So I called Orchid BioSciences in Dallas, Texas. Turns out that they had a SNP panel that they had devised for paternity testing. The panel had to be completely redesigned to look at small base pairs, but they ended up redesigning the panel, and they were able to look at between fifty-five and eighty-five base pairs. So that ratcheted-down the size of the DNA that we could look at.

Mitochondrial testing helped us, too. I don't think it gave us *per se* an identification, because it's not statistically relevant enough, so we used it in a couple of ways: We used it where the SNPs and STRs didn't make the statistics, but with the mito, we were able to pull the statistics over the top. And we used it for quality assurance problems. If we could look at the mitotype and see a difference where there shouldn't have been a difference, that helped us.

Samples taken from the original remains are at minus eighty degrees Centigrade, awaiting future technology.

I believe that working with families of the victims was a critical part of the whole process. What we learned is this: Families can become very, very vocal, very angry and very hostile, very fast—especially if they're kept in the dark. They want information. Their loved ones are missing or they're dead; they're not identified yet, and they need information.

And it's the responsibility of the political body in that community to provide information. Although I think Rudy Giuliani did a pretty good job with that, it wasn't enough. And there was a perception that there was favoritism shown for the members of police and fire departments who had died versus the civilian deceased. And I think there was. This angered a lot of people. We had been going to these meetings in the mayor's office, the meetings with families, and the anger was just palpable.

At one point, I invited one of the family members to come back to the ME's office. And I showed her around the lab. You know, she's not a scientist, but her husband was missing, and she just wanted to understand.

I spent a couple hours with her late one evening, just talking to her about DNA, and the processes we were going through—this was probably in late October of 2001—and just explained to her what was going on. And she was eternally grateful. She felt very much better. She felt, number one, it wasn't as mysterious as it was before, plus she had talked to somebody who was in charge, and I answered every question truthfully, as best I could at the time. The idea that someone was willing to spend time with her and bring her into the bowels of the medical examiner's office, and show her what's going on—she was grateful.

This started a whole weekly meeting thing, where we met with families and representatives of families for years. They came here. We got a conference room at New York University, which is next door to the ME's office.

It turned out to be the best thing we'd ever done. We found out that the families just want to know what the facts are. They want to know. And they can deal with it. They have loved ones who have died. And they want to be a part of it. They want to be in the loop, you know? *Everybody* wants to be in the loop.

There was a point— We were getting a lot of identifications in April 2002 and in the summer of 2002. I hoped it was going to continue, but I *knew* it wasn't going to, because I knew we were going to run out of DNA in those samples coming up from the World Trade Center. I knew that eventually we would exhaust the samples which had good-quality

DNA and we'd end up with the rest, which was not the best. I knew the identifications were going to fall off, and I knew it would bother the families.

But I had to tell them. I spent a long time explaining that, and that there was a plan beyond that. I had to explain to them what mitochondrial DNA is, and what SNPs are, and how I thought that this was going to work. But, "No, I can't tell you how many identifications might come out of this. There may be none. There are no promises here. It's just that we're working to get as much as we can and these, we think, are the best ideas. For now."

So, that's what we did. I think it went well, because these families *still* come to us. They're terrific. We had a hotline for people to call in, so they could speak to someone to find out if they had enough of what we call "antemortem DNA" just in case we found their loved one: Would we have enough DNA from the families to make an identification? And we found that lots and lots did not. We had to outreach to them again, and collect new samples. We collected an additional thirty-three hundred buccal swabs from family members, because they hadn't been collected properly the first time.

Meeting with the families had a profound effect on all of us. Normally, forensic scientists—You don't often deal with the families. You don't meet the victims. But this was a forensic investigation where we *did* deal with the families. Had to.

It does something to you, which is a no-no in science. Emotions creep in. You can feel hurried. Absolutely. Your instinct is to say, "Ahhh, that's okay. There's really nothing wrong here"—even though you know you should do this test again—"I know that those results are good. Let's turn out the ID." Instead of waiting another three months for a whole new round of testing to get to that ninety-nine percent degree of being sure you've made the right identification.

But when your emotions are ruling your decisions, that's when you have to step back. That's when it's good to have other scientists around saying things like, "Are you sure you want to do this?" You have to step back from your emotions. You're a scientist.

Crime Lab Case Two: Murder in a Small Town

A twelve-year-old girl was found murdered in Waseca, Min-nesota, in 1999. This town had never had a homicide in its history before. The seventeen-year-old sister comes home and finds her. The younger sister has two ligatures around her neck: one was an orange, outdoor-type extension cord; the other was black. Her hands are bound behind her back with white cord; her feet are bound with white cord. She is suspended from the stair railing. She has a top on, but she is naked from the waist down. The cause of death is a single stab wound. She bleeds out internally.

Here is your classic whodunit. This is scary. When you get there with your crime scene bunch, you know, we all have kids. This affects *us* just like it would anybody else.

And here's this twelve-year-old. She's a cute kid. She's dead. She's hanging from the stair railing. I mean, My gosh! Just a terrible scene.

But you have to . . . There comes a point where the adrenaline kicks in. You say, "Okay, we're gonna catch the SOB that did this." You have to work that way. Usually, when I give this presentation—I have a whole presentation worked up on this case—I can't make it through because it bothers me so much. Still, you have to work around that.

We did some vacuum sweepings. The cord used to bind her feet and hands were Venetian blind cords; they came right from the house. You could see where the curtain had been drawn back and the cords snipped off. We painted that area with fingerprint powder; didn't find anything.

The residence had been ransacked. Drawers had been taken out, more or less like a burglary. The indications were that this was probably a burglary that got interrupted. The girl came home from school, the burglar was there. He never killed before. But he decided to do it this time.

We processed the entire house for fingerprints. In the end, every fingerprint and palm print that we had was matched back to the family that lived there or to friends who had legitimate access. There were no unknown prints at the scene.

We had a couple of unknown hairs. One hair was taken from the top of the stairs and one was taken from the girl's body. But we couldn't do full DNA profiles on them because they didn't have the hair roots. There was a tissue under the stairs, under where she was hanging. We processed that to see if it might have biological evidence; that came back negative. There were no other biological fluids in her body. Later on, it was determined that she was probably sexually assaulted, but there was nothing biological left behind for us to collect.

I superglued the extension cord for prints. Nothing. There was another cord that was around her neck. We found that that had been ripped off a clock radio that was at the top of the stairs. Superglued that. Nothing. Those Venetian blind cords had little caps on the end, very small, but we processed them anyway. Still nothing.

We're basically done. We compare all our prints, and there's nowhere to go. This was in April of '99.

In February of 2000, there was a spate of burglaries in Waseca, so the officers were very much aware of the burglary the previous year. And in my opinion, that's what was responsible for solving this case.

An officer down there by the name of Kris Markenson. He was patrolling the streets one winter night. He's driving down the street and sees this guy walking around, it's about eight thirty. He thinks, "Well, he looks kind of out of place, but I don't really have a reason to stop him. I'll go to the end of the street, turn my squad around, and just keep an eye out."

When the officer turned his car around, he noticed that this guy decided to change *his* direction. That gives the officer enough reason to stop and talk to him. He gets out of the squad and starts to chat with the fella. "What are you doin'?" "I'm going to see a friend." "Oh, I see. Where does he live?" And the guy points in one direction, kind of vaguely. "So how did you get here?" "Oh, I drove." "Where's your car?" He points in the opposite direction, again vaguely.

While this conversation is going on, the officer looks down and notices the footprints left in the snow by this person's shoes. And he recognizes the pattern that's been left behind at other burglary scenes. Okay. Now it's time to ask this guy who he is. The guy shows him identification which doesn't happen to be his. However, the officer runs it and finds out he's wanted for a failure to appear on a DUI. Now he can arrest the guy. He puts him up against the squad and removes a flashlight and a screwdriver. Those are burglary tools.

So, things are getting a little more interesting. They take him in, impound his car, and find in his car items taken from burglaries in Waseca.

This is a classic case in law enforcement where every little step ratchets up another notch for probable cause to do the next thing. So, based on all of this stuff, they get a search warrant to go to the trailer where he lives.

In that trailer, they find the mother lode of all this stolen stuff from homes in Waseca, including—on the bottom of a floor of a closet—two vinyl CD cases.

The investigators show photographs of the stolen items to Mrs. Larson, the mother of the dead girl. And you know, she said, "Cally Jo had a pair of CD cases." There were no names on or inside the cases. There was nothing to tie them with her.

Our investigative agent called me up and said, "What do you think? We found these things. Mrs. Larson thinks they might be Cally Jo's." He described them to me. The outside was vinyl and very pebbly. I told him that surface was going to be very bad for getting any prints on; we've tried that before, and it's just not conducive. But I said, "The sleeves on the inside, maybe it's worth a shot. I can spread those out in the superglue chamber and see what we can get." Initially, I wasn't going to do it, but then I decided, this is a homicide; we gotta see what we can do here. So I told him, "Send them up."

There's a quote by a forensic scientist: "What is not looked for will not be found." When I do my presentation, you see that on the screen and I tell people, "You're gonna look at the screen and look at me and go, 'Well, duh!'—but we almost didn't process these CD cases." By the way, they were full of CDs, but they belonged to the perpetrator and his buddies.

I superglued the cases. I know this sounds very melodramatic, but I'm relating the following exactly as it happened. I go through every page of the first CD case and I find absolutely nothing. So, I go through every page of the second CD case and at the second-to-the-last page, I turn it, and there's a blond hair. Cally Jo was blond.

My heart starts racing. I just about had a fit. Think about this: This is February. The murder happened back in April. So the cases have been sitting in this guy's trailer since this time.

I photograph the hair, take it out, and eventually, through lab work, we determined that that was Cally Jo's hair.

On the next page, there's one lone fingerprint. I knew right away it was Cally Jo's because I'd seen it so many times. It had a unique loop formation and it was her right ring fingerprint.

So now, we have the perpetrator in possession of something stolen from that house where the girl was murdered. And now that we have a suspect, we can go back to the two hairs that were found at the scene and do a mitochondrial DNA test on them to exclude his mother and siblings from the scene.

What we had to do was go the alibi route. Where was

everybody in the suspect's family on the day of the murder? The suspect's real name was Lorenzo Sanchez. He was here illegally from Mexico. He had a mother, a sister, and two brothers. It was determined that his mother and sister were in Mexico the day of the murder; they never left the country. He had one brother who had since come to the States, but was still in Mexico at the time of the murder. That left one other brother who was actually here legally, but he was working the day of the murder. And that was verified by coworkers, employees, and work records.

So our guy was left standing alone. No explanation for his being at the home. He ended up confessing to murdering the girl.

This is a different kind of a case, where a lot of things were done kind of in reverse. But it has so many forensic elements: The Locard principle ["Every contact leaves a trace"] is very important here. He left those hairs behind at the scene. And Cally Jo had left one hair in her CD case. DNA came in, with the exclusion of the rest of his family from the scene, which disproved his alibi. He didn't leave any fingerprints behind, at least not that we could determine. But the girl's fingerprint, found in one of the CD cases he had stolen, was crucial in proving he had been in her home.

I was involved in this case, both at the scene as a crime scene team member, and back at the lab, where I worked with the prints.

But the officer on the street—he turned it. He identified the guy. We wouldn't be *anywhere* without him.

Yes, the loose ends were tied up forensically. But it's basic police work that turned this case. And you know what? The crime shows all miss that.

We all have different responsibilities, but in the grand scheme of things, as far as law enforcement, it's all a team. We're a team.

CRIME SCENE PROCESSOR/LATENT PRINT SPECIALIST

Eight

COLD CASES

A cold case means the investigation has come to a dead end, you have no new leads, you've interviewed everybody, you analyzed the crime scene, and you came up cold. A case can grow cold almost instantly. And it can be solved by going back years later.
>—Norman Gahn, Assistant District Attorney, Milwaukee County, Milwaukee, Wisconsin

A murder investigation is like putting together a thousand-piece jigsaw puzzle when you only have a few pieces. Maybe a hundred, a hundred and fifty pieces. If they're the right hundred and fifty pieces, you got it. But if they're the wrong pieces, say they're out around the edges, or off in one corner, you're lost.

A cold case investigation is like putting that puzzle together in a gymnasium in the dark.
>—Sergeant Jim Givens (Ret.), Commander of Cold Case Squad, Phoenix, Arizona

THE REMAINS OF A CHICKEN DINNER AND AN EX-GIRLFRIEND'S report led to murder charges against two men nine years after seven people were found murdered, shot and stabbed to death at a Brown's Chicken and Pasta Restaurant in Palatine, Illinois, in January 1993.

The bodies of the victims, all workers finishing up the last shift, were found in two separate walk-in freezers at the back of the fast food place the following morning. Crime scene technicians scoured the restaurant. One forensic analyst, Jane Homeyer with the Northern Illinois Police Crime Lab, discovered the remnants of a single chicken meal in the bottom of a plastic bin in the customer part of the restaurant, the only food not already disposed of as part of the last shift's cleanup. The analyst collected and preserved the remains of this meal. The cash register tape was collected, too, giving an exact time of the last chicken order purchased.

This was 1993; DNA testing was still in its infancy. The collected food was frozen and preserved at the Northern Illinois Crime Lab. The hope was that something could be done with the meal when bite mark testing became more viable. The cash register tape was stored, too, as a record of last meals purchased at the counter.

No weapons. No prints. No witnesses. The case was as frozen as the chicken meal stored in the Crime Lab. At the same time, DNA technology was rapidly becoming more and more sophisticated, able to provide matches from smaller and smaller pieces of evidence. In late '99, the Crime Lab submitted the chicken meal for DNA testing. A tiny bit of saliva was found on one chicken portion. There was a DNA profile, but no match to anyone in a computer database.

In March 2002, a woman contacted the Palatine Brown's Chicken and Pasta Task Force telling the police officers that a friend had told her who killed the Brown's employees. This friend, a former high school girlfriend of one of the men later charged with the execution-style slaying, told police, after they contacted her, some details of the crime that had never been made public. The former girlfriend later told prosecutors that her former boyfriend called her up the night of the murders and told her to watch the news the next day. "I did something big," he said.

In April 2002, the former boyfriend, James Eric Degorski, and one of his friends, Juan A. Luna Jr. (both of whom had been identified to police by the girlfriend) voluntarily submitted to buccal swab testing. The DNA present on the frozen chicken bone was a conclusive match with Luna. And the boyfriend's DNA matched the DNA from the chicken leg. Both men were arrested and charged with the murders in May 2002. As of this writing, the case has not yet gone to trial.

The Brown's Chicken Massacre, as it has become known, shows

how cases, long cold, long thought of as hopeless, can suddenly revive.

DNA, certainly, can breathe new life into old cases. Cold Case Squads have sprung up all over the country in the past ten years largely because of DNA and computer databases.

But DNA isn't the whole story behind the resurgence of Cold Case Squads. Seemingly intractable crimes can move into the solved column with time and investigative tenacity, sometimes with the presence of DNA, sometimes without. As Cold Case specialist Joe Murphy of the Chicago Police Department says, "It's not just technology. It's not just one set of skills. All these things work hand-in-hand: DNA, psychology, and the interviewing skill of the investigator."

Experts involved in cold cases: homicide detectives, prosecutors, forensic scientists, and cold case specialists themselves, discuss the science—and art—of solving cases that have long seemed hopeless.

A Case Still Cold

This murder was in 1996. A man was murdered in his bed. His girlfriend was with him. She said a guy came in, fired a weapon across the room at the boyfriend; she rolled under the bed. The blood spatter expert said his wound was a close contact wound, but they couldn't find the gun. Nothing really went anywhere.

I was called in a couple years later, '98, '99, as a computer expert. I checked the victim's computer. Before the murder, there was a computer right next to the bed, on the side next to where the victim was found. After we got the case, we checked that computer to see access times. There was one file in there that was last modified about four hours after the murder occurred. It was a high score on a game. One of the four names entered for the high score said, "HI JOHN." The victim's name was John.

John was murdered at about midnight. The "Hi John"

was entered at about four A.M. The sheriff's police didn't arrive until about seven A.M., shortly after the girlfriend called
them.

This case is still cold, mostly because there are judicial issues with computer evidence right now. But the theory is, the
girlfriend killed John around midnight, cleaned herself up,
disposed of the gun in the lake that is nearby, came back,
cleaned everything up, and sat down at the computer and
played a game. The body's still in bed, right next to her.
She's sitting at the computer, saying hi to the body.

That case is still open.

FORENSIC INVESTIGATOR

What Makes a Case Grow Cold

Problem number one is actually finding the physical evidence
from the crime. The problem is, in a lot of police agencies,
what's happened is, even though they *should* have kept any
material relating to a murder case, they should have kept it
forever because there's no statute of limitations on murder,
but, in reality, there are all kinds of pressures on the detectives to get rid of stuff. They get pressured on "Hey, all this
money we're spending and all this space we're using storing
evidence." And the bureaucracy keeps sending them paper:
"Can we destroy this? Can we destroy this?"

That's what happened in the LAPD. They would keep
sending detectives these sheets with lists of cases, indicating
what year it was, and say, "Please indicate if this evidence
should be destroyed or kept." You have to assume that in at
least some cases, the detectives who worked on them moved
on to other cases or retired and probably their supervisors
kept getting these lists, and they could see the old case numbers coming up over and over and they probably signed off
on some, saying, "Yeah. Destroy it." Because they didn't

want to see it anymore. There are large numbers of cases
where the evidence just isn't available to us anymore.

PROSECUTOR

"Cold" case usually implies "old" case, something from 1995 or
earlier.

Well, tell you what, we didn't really start using DNA until
1990, 1991. Before that, they didn't really have very many
serological techniques; we could put a suspect in certain
groups, but nothing that could really identify somebody
with. And even before that, the late seventies and midseventies when crime labs really took off with government funding, there was very little that could be done with clothing,
with bloodstains.

A lot of times evidence wasn't properly packaged. Say
you've got biological samples—anything with DNA potential: body fluids, semen, or blood—if, for example, it's
thrown into a plastic bag and left there in high heat, high
humidity, even just a couple of days, thrown into the trunk
of a patrol car or thrown into a property room where it's not
air-conditioned and then brought into the lab—the crime lab
technicians may open that days later and find it's covered
with mold. Microorganisms—yeast, mold, bacteria, fungi—
are ubiquitous on the face of the earth and on our bodies;
they're on our clothes. They're trying to survive, and they
can't move very easily, so when they're presented with a
great, rich food source like blood on clothing, they just want
to go crazy. And if they're given a high humidity environment, which is very good for them, they will break it down
very quickly.

Degradation not only occurs because of microorganisms
attacking substances, but due to the passage of time. Ul-
traviolet light will break down the samples. If an article of
clothing has been in a property room for twenty years as
an unsolved case, it's not that it wasn't packaged properly

back then. It wasn't packaged according to what we know now.

FORENSIC SCIENTIST

If good groundwork wasn't laid right after the crime, it's not gonna work years later. Even if the crime was done twenty-five years ago, if there were good detectives originally, and they kept the evidence, and they interviewed the right people, and did thorough documentation, a lot of times you can go back and look at it, twenty-five years later, there might be some piece of evidence you can test to corroborate something the original detectives found. And then it all makes sense.

PROSECUTOR

Why do cases go cold? Sometimes it's time. It's time. I remember, I went to a talk one time given by this old Detroit detective sergeant. And, you know, Detroit's pretty hectic. He said, "I was a traffic cop. And when I'd stop a speeder, I'd look up, and here's about six more speeders going by me. And when I became a homicide guy, I'd have a homicide scene, and I was gonna work it, and I'd walk in the door the next night, and I'd have *another* homicide." Sometimes you can't control it. You've gotta have enough manpower. And the city can get whacked by homicides. You know—the Bloody Weekend. Time. A lot of it is time. And certain cases lose.

COLD CASE SPECIALIST

What Can Revive a Cold Case

The ability to solve homicides has a lot to do with the time you spend on the case. When I was head of the cold case squad, what I would encourage the commanders in the areas to do was, if they had a case they thought was solvable, and if they had detectives that had been working on it, have them come over to the cold case squad for a month or so and just focus on that homicide. I sent three detectives to be certified crime analysts, and they would review cases for potential solvability factors: What is the physical evidence? Could it be retested for DNA? Who is still around that we can talk to? Has anything changed in the relationships the suspect has? Are there any new leads?

COLD CASE COMMANDER

Solving cold cases: a lot of times, it calls for creativity. You have to be able to take a different view of the murder. Think outside the box, as the cliché goes. Take a different route. Because, obviously, the route that the original investigators took wasn't very productive, because it's a cold case.

An example of outside-the-box thinking: In 1995, a young lady in her midtwenties contacted one of our detectives in cold case about her mother's disappearance. She was just a child at the time. She had a vague recollection of her mother and father fighting—*all the time.*

There was a specific instance, right before her mother disappeared in 1964, where she remembered her father digging in the backyard, right outside the back door to the house, the sliding glass door.

One of our detectives had seen some reference to a ground-penetrating radar. There's a guy someplace in Colorado who runs this operation. NecroSearch is the name of the company. He came out to the former house with this sled-mounted radar that he would pull back and forth across potential burial scenes.

No luck in the backyard. But they pulled it across the concrete slab outside the back door, the sliding double door? And—bingo!

All that the ground-penetrating radar tells you is that the underlying earth has been disturbed; it's not in its original condition. It'll show you, eventually, the outline of a grave. A soil disturbance.

So we brought out the old concrete saws, dug up the slab, and lo and behold—here's a skeleton. Still wearing stockings with a garter belt, which enabled us to make this a pre–panty hose incident, which was consistent with the victim's age and the daughter's recollection of the mother's disappearance.

The father had always told his daughters that the mother had left him and he didn't know where she was. Through a lot of work, our detective located him and he was arrested, convicted, and sentenced to death.

This young woman had been haunted by this for thirty years.

When the father was being sentenced, the judge asked if he had any comments to make. And the guy said, "You know, it's just not *fair* that after twenty-five years, I should be sent to prison for this. It's *just* not fair."

COLD CASE SPECIALIST

DNA and Cold Cases

In the old days, you'd have a homicide, and, a lot of times, there was nothing you could do about it. Your main suspect won't talk. The only witness is the victim, and he's dead.

Maybe the suspect raped the woman before he killed her. You've got the semen. Or maybe there's a speck of blood, or a trail of blood. So what? You've got this common blood type. Big deal. The guy is included with fifty percent of the population. The prosecutor says, "What am I gonna do with this? Nothin'."

All that has changed with DNA.

HOMICIDE DETECTIVE

DNA is a gift to cold cases. It's an absolute gift. If the evidence still remains, the police return their attention, not because of any new investigative leads but because of "Hey! We still got some blood from that crime scene before they had DNA."

Or fingerprints: Now there's the IAFIS (Integrated Automated Fingerprint Identification System), instead of just AFIS (Automated Fingerprint Identification System), which gives you so many more capabilities. So now we can apply new technology to the old cases.

PROSECUTOR

Dr. Margaret Eby was the provost at the University of Michigan, Flint. She was famous for organizing a Bach Festival in Flint every summer. She was well known in the academic community.

She lived in a gatehouse on the old Mott estate. Mott was the founder of General Motors and, at one time, was the richest man in the United States. After his death, his wife lived on at the estate, and Dr. Eby rented the gatehouse

In 1986, my homicide team got the call that there was a murder on the Mott estate. This was the year that Flint had sixty-three murders, the highest ever. All I could think of was, "Oh my God, somebody's killed Mrs. Mott!"

We got there and found it was Dr. Eby. This gatehouse was a beautiful two-story brick building, which she probably rented for the prestige of saying she lived on the Mott estate. She was found lying on her bed, nude. She had just about been decapitated. Lot of wounds to her breasts, also. Nothing fatal, small stab wounds. Torture-type marks. We also noticed that she had been bound at the wrists with some type of plastic telephone-type cord. The blood was on the headboard and above the headboard, on the wall. He had struck an artery. The bed itself was soaked. But right next to her, were her clothes that she had worn that night, not even touched. Magazines at the foot of the bed weren't moved.

She didn't struggle. We could see that. This man had taken control of her, tied her up, and she wasn't able to fight back at all.

Nothing in the house was taken, that we could find. She

lived alone, so it was hard to determine what had been taken. Her purse was lying on the dining room table on the first floor of the house; her keys were still there.

We split our duties up. Our sergeant was the officer in charge. I was his second, the scene officer. I would do a narrative of the scene, writing where all the evidence was and then direct the collection of the evidence. Then I had a person assigned right with me who would do a scale drawing of the entire house. Then the next detectives were the interview detectives, who would do all the interviews, all the footwork, and run license plates and things like that for us.

We called the Michigan State Police Crime Lab and we backed right out of the house at that time. We backed right out, not to disturb any evidence. Then I worked with them, doing the same thing as we do in the narrative: Describe everything.

During the search of the house, we found where a person had cleaned himself up, on a porcelain sink in an upstairs bathroom, off her bedroom. And there was some blood that he missed. It was quite diluted, because he had obviously tried to clean himself. We also discovered that there was probably a fingerprint on the cold water faucet. You could see a partial print, just enough so they didn't want to try to lift that print at the scene. We took the faucet with us, submitted it to the crime lab, and sure enough, they were able to get a fingerprint from it.

So that's all well and good. Up to a point. Everybody leaves. Headlines in the paper: "Murder on the Mott Estate." The media was hounding everybody in the department.

The investigation focused in on an acquaintance of Dr. Eby's, who had recently visited, and then moved to the D.C. area. For years, that's who we all thought did it. Now, this fingerprint was still there. It didn't match the suspect's. The fingerprint was sent to Michigan's AFIS. Everybody assumed that Michigan was connected to the FBI's database. We weren't. So that print only stayed in Michigan. So, all these years, that print is in the system, just waiting for a match. But just in Michigan.

Years go by. It's a case where, every once in a while, something will come in on it, and we run on the information. Meantime, my lieutenant retires, the sergeant in charge retires, I now have a hundred homicides under my belt, so it falls to me. I'm the last detective there that had anything to do with the case. Nothing came of any of the leads.

In the spring of 2002, the cold case squad calls me in and wants me to work with them because of my familiarity with the case. We go back and do the same things we did in 1986: talking to her friends, people she had been with the night of the murder, the party she had been to earlier. Some of these people have died; some have moved out of state.

But now DNA is real good. It was always thought that the DNA that we found on Dr. Eby at the scene was not good. Her killer turned on her electric blanket while she was in bed. Everybody assumed . . . The crime lab said, "We don't think the DNA from the semen is any good; we can't make a match, because it was probably destroyed by the electric blanket."

But it wasn't. We took it back, sent it to the state, which in turn sent it to CODIS (Combined DNA Index System), which is the national database for DNA.

And my God, we got a hit. We got a hit on a murder in Romulus, Michigan, where Detroit Metropolitan Airport is.

In 1991, a Northwest Airlines stewardess, Nancy Ludwig, was murdered in almost the same fashion Dr. Eby was. This lady was younger; he wasn't able to subdue her as quickly as he did Dr. Eby. This lady fought back, so she had several other defense injuries on her hands from the knife. But she was almost decapitated also.

This was in the Hilton right off the airport. She had just flown in that night from one flight. She was a fill-in. Nobody heard about her staying at the Hilton. She didn't show up for her flight the next day. Somebody finally checks the room and finds her there. The night before, a male flight attendant staying at the same motel, looked out at the parking lot and noticed a man carrying Northwest Airlines luggage to his car, an orange car. He assumed it was a flight attendant.

Right after it happened, Dr. Eby's son read about it in the papers, got in contact with the Romulus Police Department, and said, "This sounds just like my mother's murder in Flint back in '86." So two detectives, one from Flint and one from Romulus, make phone contact, but that's as far as it goes. If they would have looked at each other's photos, they would have known it was the same killer. But they never did.

We've now got a hit. We know our person has killed two women in almost the same fashion. Now, every person we talk to, good friend, enemy, anybody, female even, we ask for a DNA buccal swab. Because this task force is with the state police, and they're in charge of the crime lab, we're getting priority. And we're getting our information back within days.

Both cases have gone cold. But after we get the hit, we sit down with their stuff; they sit down with our stuff. And there's a guy at the crime lab who looks at the fingerprint again and realizes that it only went to AFIS, never to the FBI. He submits it to the FBI.

And we get the fingerprint hit then, to a Jeffrey Gorton. It's from a Florida arrest, from 1986. This man had been breaking into trailers in Florida and stealing women's underwear and bras. They catch him and he's fingerprinted. He has one arrest in Florida, so he moves back to Michigan and starts working for his father's sprinkler system company. It so happens that the sprinkler system company services the Mott estate.

In November 1986, four days before the murder, he was one of the people at the estate, shutting off the system because it's getting cold and the system could freeze. The controls for the system are in the basement of the gatehouse. Okay?

Now, we're pretty sure this is the person. His fingerprint's there. He had access. He probably would have seen Dr. Eby. She didn't have curtains on her bedroom window. There's a theater across the parking lot and people often reported seeing her lying in the nude. Service people did, too. She wasn't afraid of her body, let's put it that way.

We really think Jeffrey Gorton is the killer, but we've got to get his DNA to match. The cold case squad calls me up and says, "We're gonna go sit on Jeffrey Gorton's house tonight. Do you want to be there?" We sat there; we're just waiting to get his DNA.

The next night, the undercover officers follow him to a skating rink. This man is married and has children. He's at the rink with his three children. The officers wait for him to buy a soft drink. He uses a napkin with his soft drink. As soon as he walks away from the table, the undercover officers grab the Styrofoam cup he was using and take it right directly to the Michigan State Crime Lab. That night, we had a match.

We got a search warrant for his house. He's arrested in the meantime. Outside his house, he has a car that's under a tarp. It's an orange car, matching the description the Northwest Airlines flight attendant gave back in 1991. It doesn't run, but it's under a tarp. In the house, we find thousands upon thousands of women's underwear, bras, things like that. *Thousands.* There are over a hundred stuffed between the mattress and the box springs of the bed. I don't know how his wife never knew that. There are garbage bags in his basement, filled. Some of them have tape with the address written on it, where he'd gotten it from.

They arrest him. The only thing he said was he had never been in Dr. Eby's house. Fine, that's all we wanted, because how did this print get there if he was never in the house?

They start going to these women's houses and they said, "Oh my God, yes. I remember my underwear being missing, but I thought I lost it." And they were all customers of this sprinkler system in Flint. And sprinkler systems' controls are usually in basements, so that's how a lot of things went missing, we figured.

But we never figured out how he picked out the flight attendant he murdered. And if I do one thing the rest of my career, it's going to be to sit down with Jeffrey Gorton and ask, "How did you pick Nancy Ludwig? How did she become a victim of yours?"

He's not talking to anybody; all we know is he walked out with her Northwest Airlines luggage.

We went to trial in 2003. The first one was in Wayne County, for the murder of Nancy Ludwig. I testified in that. He was convicted of first-degree murder. The second trial was scheduled for Genesee County, Flint, and on the eve of the trial he said he wanted to plead guilty to first-degree murder. His penalty is life without parole; he'll never get out of prison.

This case shows how terrific DNA testing is now. And that the CODIS database is unbelievable.

Here was a guy whose only arrest was for stealing underwear. This arrest was for— He walked up behind a woman in a store. She was wearing a skirt. He reached under her skirt, knocked her down, pulled her underwear off, ran out of the store. Now who would have thought someone like this would do murder? You know?

HOMICIDE DETECTIVE

DNA is terrific. But DNA by itself isn't enough. If you do DNA test-ing, what leads you to believe that you'll ultimately find the suspect, just because you've got the DNA? That doesn't make your investigation any better. What makes these investigations better? Why are these cold cases relevant now? The DNA database.

Now, you not only have the DNA profile on a piece of paper. What you do is, you put it in the database. Now, you have the potential that *this* is going to match other crimes. Maybe in the five years since the crime, the reason you haven't caught this guy is he's been locked up for five years! You know that if he's in the database.

And *that's* why cold cases are now a relevant proposition. It's no longer, why are we throwing good money after bad, when we haven't gotten any new leads? Now, how do we throw good money—i.e., DNA testing money—at this case because now we've thrown good money into the database.

The whole dynamic changes. The whole thing changes. The DNA database has breathed new life into cold cases.

PROSECUTOR

DNA and Unsolved Sexual Assault Cases

This rape case turned out to be the first cold hit out of the Mil-waukee County DNA database in 1997. This case was one where—one of *so many* of our sexual assaults—where, because of the brutality of the sexual assault, and because the assailants committed it in such a fashion that the victim was too frightened even to look at them—and the victims are told, "Don't look at my face. Don't look at my face."—you knew that there would have to be some miracle, almost, to catch this person because she's never gonna pick anyone out of a lineup, or even give us a description to go on.

What happened to this girl— She was nineteen years old, she was at work, took a bus home, and got off the bus. This was at night. She was walking to her house, which was about five blocks away. She was walking, and she noticed two guys were behind her. She felt that something was wrong, and she crossed the street. And they crossed, and she *knew* something was up. She crosses back again to the other side of the street, because there's a telephone over there and she runs to it to call 911.

But before she could even get the phone receiver off the hook, they're both on top of her, they both have guns, they both tell her, "Don't look at us. Just do what we say."

And they took her behind a couple buildings, to a back alley. Back there was probably one of the most *brutal* sexual assaults I've ever heard of. They stripped her. One stood behind her, as she was bent over, and assaulted her, penis to vagina behind, as the other stood in front of her, penis to mouth. And they both did this. At some points, the person behind her would remove his penis from her vagina and stick the gun barrel up it, and then take that out, and then put his penis back. Just a godawful, brutal assault.

All the time while the oral assault is going on, the person in front has a gun to her head: "Don't you look at me. Don't say anything."

When they finish with her, they throw her to the ground, kick her a bit, laugh at her, and take off. She gets up. She was pretty close to St. Joseph's Hospital, to run there. The person in front of her had ejaculated in her mouth. She spat that out on the cement of the back alley. Gets to the hospital, calls the police, the police come, they go back to the scene.

She shows them what happened. They find what they believe to be semen on the cement where the person was behind her because she said that she believed he ejaculated on the cement. Then she pointed out where she spat out the semen. So that was collected by the police. She couldn't give descriptions of these guys, had no idea.

And we knew then that we're not going to solve this case, unless, you know, you get awfully lucky. I guess, maybe a confession, or someone squeals on them. The chances of solving it were very, very remote when they got away so clean and the victim has no idea who they are.

Again, this is '97. DNA data banking is really in its infancy. And we had just started up.

At that time, our data bank of convicted offenders was only about four thousand. That was all. Today, it's eighty thousand in Wisconsin. This was an unsolved sexual assault with no witnesses, except this young woman, who could not see her attackers.

But we did have two sources of semen. They were able to get a good profile out of those and put them in the data bank. And a year later, we got a hit out of the data bank on the guy who stood behind her and ejaculated on the sidewalk. A perfect match with that. After our victim's assault, he had committed an offense, I forget what it was, it fit under our collection laws, so his sample was taken when he got to the confinement facility and that was put in the data bank. And the police did a terrific job of investigating and were able to find out who his associate was. And when we did a search warrant to get the associate's buccal swabs, he matched the semen that the girl had spat out.

This case was cold. It was freezing cold. It was solved through DNA and police interviewing. But without DNA, that case would never, ever have been solved. There's no other way to catch these guys.

PROSECUTOR

When we get these cold hits and can identify the rapist, what we hear from victims over and over again is—We might call them up five, seven years later and say, "Hey, that guy who raped you. We just caught him in the data bank. And he's been in prison for the past five years." And the first reaction generally is, "You mean I don't have to look over my shoulder anymore?" And that gives some closure. It's like, "I didn't *have* to worry all these years and, thank God, I'm not going to any more." And now she can follow him, and his life in prison. And we proceed with this new case, hopefully give the guy additional years.

The other great thing about these cold hits is that many, many times it's a vindication for the victims. Because sadly enough, many times they're not believed—by their family, or by the police, whoever's in their life at that time, boyfriend, significant other, husband. Sometimes they aren't believed. Say you're raped in an alley, people wonder, "What were you doing in that alley?"

Prostitutes can be raped. Drug addicts can be raped. People who put themselves in very dangerous situations—they all can be raped. High school girls may not be believed because they're out past curfew, they've made a mistake, they've done something stupid and foolish and they get raped, and they're told, "You're saying this now because you're late for curfew and you don't want to get in trouble." All sorts of things come up where there's doubt cast upon these victims.

And then you get the cold hit out of the data bank and catch the person and find out he's a serial rapist. Wonderful vindication and validation for them and a tremendous amount of relief. Sometimes they've been second-guessing themselves for years: "Should I have done something different?" Then you find out that this guy was just a creep and there's *nothing* you could have done. DNA validates what the victim has been saying. Being able to get these cold hits—it's been wonderful for victims, especially of sexual assaults, but for all victims. It's been wonderful for them.

PROSECUTOR

The Need to Confess

Time has a way of changing the heart. Time has a way of chang-ing people. Somebody might have been a hell-raiser and now they're saved; they found some type of religion and they just want to get what they did off their chest. Or somebody was in a relationship and now they're not. Now they're free to speak about the person they were terrified of.

It solely depends on time. And it solely depends on how people change over time. Time is your best friend.

COLD CASE SPECIALIST

I absolutely agree with that. New technology gets a lot of atten-tion. It's splashy. It makes good news copy.

But the fact of the matter is, the best thing we've got going for us in the investigation of cold cases is the passage of time. Relationships change. Feelings between people change. People who had romantic connections at the time—you know, feelings change. "Hell hath no fury," as the saying goes.

HOMICIDE DETECTIVE

This is key. You've got an old case. Let's say you've got a suspect on it. The best thing you can learn is that the woman he was living with, or his significant other at the time—they're no longer together. Maybe he beat her up, ripped her off, or cheated on her, or whatever.

My partner and I are firm believers that people always want to tell the truth and they'll tell somebody. So if somebody does something real wrong, they're always going to tell their best friend or their significant other. It happens. Oh, yeah. Absolutely. *Always.*

So that's what we like to do. We like to go back and interview the people the suspect may have talked to. It doesn't have to be a woman or a boyfriend or girlfriend; it could be like a good friend of theirs or a family member that they split up with. We get a lot of information by going back to people.

HOMICIDE DETECTIVE

Wiretaps can come in handy. That's one of the tricks of our trade. Once you have something, maybe a result from DNA or blood work or from trace evidence, or maybe there's an old boyfriend or girlfriend that's finally ready to spill the beans, you can have someone wear a wire to get things confirmed. That's how they've solved a lot of these old child molestation cases. You have someone who was molested as a child wear a wire and confront the priest or the uncle or whoever and see if they admit it. Or you have somebody confront the suspect or stimulate the suspect or his crowd and find out what they start saying to each other immediately after somebody gets arrested or something gets out in the press about the case. There's always that. And it's legal.

COLD CASE COMMANDER

I will bet you a crisp hundred-dollar bill right now. Here's the bet: The bet is that you, personally, cannot think of one thing in your life that you did that you think was seriously wrong, and it gnawed at you. I bet there's not *one* thing that you did in your whole life that you never, ever told another human being. You wanna bet?

You *have* to. You *have* to tell someone. There's an inherent need to tell. You want to cleanse your conscience.

Don't ever tell your girlfriend. Because, eventually, there's a chance you could break up and she's gonna tell on you. It happens all the time.

HOMICIDE DETECTIVE

What gets these guys many times, especially with gangbanger or reputation crimes, is, if you're trying to be a badass, it doesn't do any good if nobody *knows* you're a badass. So, frequently the guy will brag about the crime to somebody. And somebody will eventually get back to the police and say, "You know, I was talkin' to Joe So-and-So, and he said he did that one." That's the nature of the beast.

COLD CASE SPECIALIST

Interviewing Skills

We used to visit people locked up in the penitentiary, okay? A lot of detectives would say, Well, they're in the pen; they're not gonna say anything.

But you know what? We had a guy that we went to talk to. He was convicted of murder, sentenced to like fifty years. Information came to us that he was involved in an *additional* murder. So we went out to Statesville to talk to him, and he gave it all up. So you never know.

COLD CASE SPECIALIST

We've had guys on Death Row that have confessed to things. And they'll say, "What took you so long, man? I've been waiting for you for nine years. What've you guys been *doin'?*" They kind of like resolving things.

HOMICIDE DETECTIVE

When you call on the guys in prison, you do it just like a conver- sation. We say, "Hey, we haven't talked to you for a while. How ya doin'? What's new?" We don't sit in judgment. I've always said I have more respect for a person if they give up what they did. If they tell you what they did, you have more respect for that person rather than one that doesn't.

I know it sounds obscene, but sometimes you start having, uh, positive feelings about the guy. Now I'm kinda empathizing with him. I understand what he's goin' through. I understand why he may have done it. I don't agree with it, but I can understand it.

The best detectives *I've* seen— We've handled cases where a doctor's a suspect. Or a lawyer's a suspect. And these detectives can talk to them one on one. And then you get some low gutter-rat dog rock-head that did a murder and they talk to *them* one on one. The same way.

HOMICIDE DETECTIVE

A lot of times you go to jails and talk to inmates that have con-
tacted you, saying so-and-so told them about a crime. With
that, you have to be very, very careful. Unless you have some
solid information, you have to be very, very careful with
what certain people tell you in jail. Because a lot of times,
people in jail do what I call "ear hustling." What they'll
do—they'll be sitting in a rec room and they'll be listening
to the conversation of other people and they'll send you a
letter telling you they have certain information. That's where
interviewing comes into play. I can get them a polygraph
test; I can sit down and make a determination whether
they're lying to me.

They do ear hustling. They figure if they cooperate with
the authorities, it can shave some of their time off. They can
make a deal.

COLD CASE DETECTIVE

When you do cold cases, it has a *lot* to do with psychology. It has
a *lot* to do with being a good listener. It has a *lot* to do with
being a good observer. I'll give you a case in point. We had a
twenty-eight-year-old case, where a young female at the age
of fourteen committed a heinous crime by killing her mother.

We get the investigation twenty-seven years later. The
sons of the victim came in and said, "Listen. We know you
guys got a cold case squad. We need someone to tell us what
happened to our mom." At the time of the murder, the
fourteen-year-old daughter was the oldest. The other children in the house, the two sons, were very, very young at
the time.

The sons said they had assumed through the years that it
was a boyfriend who was responsible for it. And we knew,
based on the original interviews, that this wasn't an intruder.
We knew that somebody in the house had done it. We
weren't sure if all three children had got together and made
this plan to kill their mom or was it just one.

We went back and read the statements the daughter gave police back in 1971, '72. She was evasive in a lot of her answers. And we were able to analyze the statements of her brothers and others who personally knew her. She wasn't being totally honest. The beginning of her story didn't make sense. The middle of it didn't make sense, nor did the end of it make any sense.

Plus, in the interview with her, I was able to tell from her physical behavior that there were some things going on with her that she didn't want us to know. I've been trained as a forensic psychophysiologist and a lie detector examiner. Psychophysiologist—that's just a fancy way of saying I'm trained in observing people's behaviors during conversation. And through this observation, I'm able to tell—just from a person's reactions—whether or not they're being truthful or deceptive when they answer questions. Human beings are like leaky faucets. A lot of times, we give information nonverbally that we don't even know that we're giving.

At some point in the interview, she surrendered her trust to me, and she told me, "Okay, you got me. I shot my mother. I did it." She went on to explain to me *why* she shot and killed her mother. Basically, she was jealous of her mother's relationship with the boyfriend.

She killed her mother with a handgun. Twenty-seven years later, at age forty-two, she confessed to my partner and me.

I gave the information to her brothers, and, for a week or so, they were pissed off at me, but then they came around to it.

COLD CASE SPECIALIST

This call came into cold case from a correctional officer in New Jersey whose brother had gotten killed in Newark. Her brother had been dead for nine, ten years, and she hadn't gotten any answers on it.

It was a freaky thing. While she was working her tour at

the prison, there was a female that was in there. She learned
that the female was from the same area where her brother got
killed.

So, she was questioning the female about the people in the
area and stuff like that. Then she mentioned her brother's
name. And they started talking about her brother without
this female *knowing* it was the corrections officer's brother
she was talking about. She never let on to that.

So, during *that* time, there was *another* female in the
prison who personally knew the corrections officer's brother.
And without knowing it was the corrections officer's brother,
she said to her, "Yeah, he was killed and I was involved with
it."

The officer took that information directly to the police.
They looked into it and they came up with nothing. In fact,
I don't really think they believed her.

Several years later, my partner and I got involved with the
case when she came back. We went out and found the two
females that she was talking about.

The first female, the one who told the corrections officer
she was involved, denied any involvement. The guy who
ended up being the killer was her common-law husband. We
made a determination that her bragging she was involved in
the killing was probably just jailhouse talk and she wasn't involved with it. But she said, "Look. I know where a body is
buried." It turned out that the same people who killed the
corrections officer's brother were the same people who kidnapped this other guy, robbed him of like five kilos of cocaine, and buried him in a basement. These were two drug
dealers. The one guy paid the other guy to do the murders.
All this came out of our interviews.

The only thing we had on the primary killer was we had a
female who told us, "Yeah, I know him, but I don't like him.
He stuck a gun in my mouth. He threatened to kill me." We

convinced her to go press charges on him for that. This way, we'd have something to bring him in on, as opposed to just going out and snatching him up for a murder.

So we went out and got him for putting a gun in a female's mouth. We talked to him for several hours and he confessed to that. After that, you know, we took care of him, fed him, and stuff like that. And the next day, you know, we started questioning him about the corrections officer's brother. Questioned him for several hours about that, and at some point in time, he gave a confession about that. We took care of him again, and after we fed him, we came back to him about an hour and a half later and then we started talking to him about the person that they kidnapped and buried in the basement. It took us several hours to get a confession off of that. So we spent a *lot* of time with this guy. We had him, like from four thirty-five in the morning to maybe two o'clock the *next* morning. You know what I'm saying? It's grueling. For everybody. Absolutely.

The guy in the grave in the basement? The motive was— This one guy had five kilos of cocaine. They tricked him into believing that they were looking to buy five kilos from him. And he delivered it to them. And two days before the guy even got to where he was supposed to deliver the drugs, they had dug his grave already. They had a predug grave waiting for him.

COLD CASE SPECIALIST

We got a case going back fifteen years from an interview. When we were on the federal task force investigating the El Rukn crime operation in 1991, we started interviewing all these guys for murders. There were about seven hundred murders. They came up with this murder from July 4, 1976. Guy named Sam Calhoun. Was on the Ten Most Wanted List. One of the guys we interviewed said, "Man, he's down South somewhere, driving a cab."

This analyst on the task force, Leslie, ran all the southern states, using that name. She came up with five or six states. The credit for that case goes to her; she spent *hours* on the computer, running names, running nicknames, variations on his name. That's tedious work, but that support is so important.

My partner and I collected the guy's prints and we faxed them to all six states. It turns out he's in the penitentiary outside Pensacola, serving time for a robbery. He'd been in and out of the joint, but each time, by the time the prints got checked, it was months later, and he was released.

So we went down to interview him, the two of us. And the first thing he says to us, "Man, what took you so long?" And then he goes, "I used to call my mom all the time, figuring you'd be wiretapping my phone, and I'd move. I was always waiting."

He gave it all up. He gave it *all* up.

And that was a triple homicide and a woman raped. He and another guy were gonna stick up a dope house, then they ended up raping the woman inside. They ended up killing her. They killed a guy in there, too. And their next victim was the lookout kid in the alley.

They shot this kid, he was about sixteen years old, who came up to them originally: "Hey, look. This guy's got money. They've got money and dope in this apartment. I'll be the lookout." So then they said, "Okay. But you stay out in the alley."

So now they go in and they rape her. They kill her and the guy inside. They take the money. And then what happens was, now they're in the alley and they're looking at the lookout and they're gonna go and pick him up, right? So they look at each other and they said, "Man, I don't think we can trust this guy." So they run him over! With a Cadillac. At least it was a *pink* Cadillac. They killed him.

But the funny thing about it was, now they go back, they

start with the money they got, the proceeds, they go buy some booze, they go back to their buildings, and they're having a card game like on the second or third floor or whatever. They never opened their mouths about the murders, but now they've been drinking. They're at this card table. It's late at night, Fourth of July. And this one guy starts, "Man, you shoulda seen what Calhoun did, tonight." And Calhoun says, "Man, I told you not to say anything." And Calhoun shot him. The guy Calhoun shot dived out the window. So Calhoun killed his partner. So our guy, Sam Calhoun, he walks out. He goes home to Mama, to his mother, and says, "Mama, I'm goin' down to Florida. This ain't a very good Fourth of July for me."

Fifteen years later, we get him. When we went to pick him up, finally, for the extradition—we were bringing him back to Chicago to stand trial—we got up to the United gate. And they were on strike. So the guy goes, "Sorry. Mr. Calhoun can get on the flight, but you guys are bumped." So, Calhoun, being the cool dude that he is, he's our friend by now, he steps to the side of the counter—he knew not to take too many steps away from us—and he says to us, "Hey, guys. I'll wait for you at the other end. I'll wait for you at O'Hare."

I say to the ticket agent, "Sir? Can I get your business card?" I get his business card. "Sir, you are now in charge of Mr. Sam Calhoun." I go, "Sam! Tell him what you did." So now Sam starts laying out to the ticket agent how he killed these people, shot this woman in the back of the head after raping her, ran his lookout guy over . . . and the ticket agent's going "Ohhhh . . . I can get *all of you* on the next flight! I'll get you on the next flight!"

HOMICIDE DETECTIVE

There are some cases that should *stay* cold. I'll give you a true case in point. Back in 1955, a man was murdered in Newark. He had a little girl that was about five at the time. As she got older, she wanted to know what happened to her dad, because no one ever told her. Of course, she heard about our cold case squad. She came in, and I interviewed her.

I did some additional investigation and I found a folder. And finding a folder from 1955 was an investigation in itself. After finding that folder, I was able to read all the information that was recorded back in 1955. I was able to read all the police reports, everything the detectives had done, all the statements the witnesses gave. I was able to analyze those statements. I determined that the stepfather of this woman was the person who killed her biological dad.

Now, the unfortunate thing about that was the stepfather had since died. Her mother had since died. What happened back then was, the mother was having an affair with the stepfather when she was married to the biological father. The father would not grant her a divorce. The stepfather, during that time, was in the navy and he was staying at a navy base in New York. He traveled over and he and the biological father got into some sort of verbal confrontation. He left. He didn't kill him then.

The wife was the only one who knew that this navy guy had a safety key—you know like those hideaway key boxes under his car? That key was gone. The mother was the only one who knew he had it. The navy guy had the key to get into the apartment from the mother. And what happened was, the father was beaten to death in his apartment. The day after he was buried, the navy guy marries the mother and becomes the kid's stepfather.

And all through the years, there was a dark family secret. And everybody was telling the daughter about her stepfather, this and that. She remembered one time her mother threatening the stepfather that she would go to the police. By the time we got the case, all the players—the father, the mother, the stepfather—were dead.

The daughter didn't like what I told her. I said to her

from the beginning, "Listen. I can only go where this investigation will take me. And I may get information that you may not want to hear. But that's the only thing that I can do."
She said, "Okay, I'm okay with it." But when I gave her my findings, she was really hurt. She was sorry she found out.

COLD CASE SPECIALIST

Forensic Anthropologists on Discovering Bodies

I worked on a case in '95. A woman had disappeared three years earlier, on a Friday night. She was known to have been with her former boyfriend that night. He was a suspect in her disappearance.

Two years later, a third party emerged. He went to the police and told them a horrific story, told them that the three of them on the night she disappeared, in 1993, went down to the suspect's grandparent's house for a weekend of sex and drugs, basically. And the former boyfriend murdered her.

And then the two friends took great pains to get rid of the body. They dismembered it in the shower stall in this house, and then they put the remains in plastic bags. Most of it was never found. But some of the remains, according to this witness, were taken up to the witness's family cottage on the edge of a small lake in northern Michigan.

He led police and me to the cottage, to the exact place where a hole had been dug two years earlier. And he said they'd built a large fire there, in a fire pit, threw in the bags full of remains, and had this large fire for a number of hours. Some of the materials in the fire pit were removed; some of it was dumped in the lake. The fire pit was filled in. If he hadn't pointed it out, two years later, when we went back, we wouldn't even have been able to recognize that there had been a pit there.

So what I did was an archeological-type excavation of that

area. I removed four cubic yards of dirt, and found eight
pieces of bone that obviously had been burned and, put under a microscope, were shown to be human. Those remains
and one drop of blood that was found in the party house
constituted the entirety of the woman victim.

The informant came forward because he wanted immu-
nity from prosecution. He didn't get that, but he got a
lighter sentence. The former boyfriend of the victim got life
in prison.

In May of '85, people found a skeleton buried just to the side of
their house. They had a little garden next to the house and
they wanted to expand it. So they started digging and they
found a blanket. They pulled the blanket up, and some
bones came out. This was in a rural area in Southern Illinois,
where it's pretty common for people to bury their pets in the
yard. The family assumed it was somebody's dog, until they
found the jawbone.

The people who found this had been living in the house
for five years. They bought it from the previous owner, a
woman living there with three kids. A year before this lady
sold the house, she claimed that her husband went out for a
loaf of bread and never came home. It was like, "He's a
bum. He left me and the three kids. He deserted us."

We were suspicious that the skeleton was the husband,
Cody. The skeleton was wrapped up in two blankets. The
right side of the skull had this massive fracture. Horrible.
The back and left side of the skull were intact, but the right
side was just crushed.

I asked the current owners, "Have you changed the carpeting in the living room?" "No. It's the same carpet as when
we bought it." "Do you mind if I take a small carpet sample
in a corner? You won't even know it's missing." "Go ahead."
So I went and cut out a couple of threads from the carpet,

you know, the tufts. And I submitted it to the Illinois Crime Lab to see if they could find carpet fibers on the two blankets that would match. And they did.

There were a bunch of those maple seeds that fall off trees—people call them helicopters?—in the blankets. I sent those to the Illinois State Museum in Springfield to see what time they fall off trees. We knew that Cody went missing in May. The scientists that looked at them said they typically fall off maple trees in April or May every year.

I glued the guy's head back together. The way we identified him— He had a lot of cavities, no fillings. He hated dentists. And he had bone x-rays from a back injury. We did video superimposition. What you do with that, you take a known photograph of who you believe your victim is and you put a video camera on that picture. You take a second video camera and put it on the skull and then, with a switching device, you superimpose one over the other. If everything lines up, like the eyes, the teeth, you can make a physical match. This guy had this big, horsy grin in the picture, so we could literally overlay his teeth in the picture on the skull. It *was* Cody.

We took the wife to trial. The first trial ended up in a hung jury. She finally confessed to a lesser charge. Her story: Cody didn't work. He claimed he had a bad back. He laid around all day and drank beer, didn't do anything.

She went in one night, she said, he was asleep on the couch; the kids were asleep. She went in and she hit him about fifteen times with a cast-iron skillet. Just kept hitting him. Then she went and got two blankets from the front closet, laid them in front of the couch, rolled him off onto the floor, and used the blankets to drag him out in the yard and bury him. That's how the blankets picked up some of the carpet fibers.

There was a family that was fixing up an old house that they had bought five, ten years earlier. They had turned it into a beautiful house. The last stage was to put a concrete floor in the basement and replace the coal furnace, and stuff like that.

As they were digging out the dirt there, they found a shoe—didn't think that was too unusual. But then there was a leg attached to it, so . . . The police called us, and we excavated it as if it was a grave outdoors. When we excavate a grave, it's not just "Let's figure out what a body is doing in there." Or people talk about, you know, "We've got to dig to the body." I consider that the fill in the grave, even if it's five feet deep, that fill has been modified by humans, and, as such, it becomes physical evidence. So, even though it's dirt, it has to be preserved carefully, documented, analyzed, all that.

So, we're looking at the contour of the grave and we're looking at the edge of the grave. Because as you're digging into the dirt, the impression of whatever tool or instrument you use is left behind. We were looking for what instrument was used. In this case, it was a spade.

Once we exposed the body carefully, mapped it in, you could see how the individual was placed in that grave. The pants legs were up to the knees. The shirt was up to the chest. So you could see that the guy was dragged by his feet into the hole.

The previous owner was in the grave. His wife and daughter put him there. This guy traveled a lot, so nobody really noticed in the neighborhood that he was gone. He had been in that basement for about fifteen years and the groundwater had come up over his body.

From analyzing the bones—some of the bones were degraded—but we saw some stab wounds from knives in his back. From the scapula, you could see the imprint, or the defect, from the knife. The ribs below that were fractured, so the impact was very hard. You get an idea that—probably the wife here hit him as hard as she could and broke his ribs and put that knife into him. And then we saw shotgun pellets that were still embedded in his neck vertebrae. You could also see pellets' impact on his hyoid bone in his neck and on his humerus. From that, you could draw a line as to the diameter, and get an idea of his distance from the shotgun.

The reconstruction was: He was in bed, wasn't watching, she came up from behind, stabbed him as hard as she could, multiple times, and he fell off the bed and was probably crawling away, and she took the shotgun and hit him right in the neck.

Then they dragged him into the basement by his feet, for the most part. Pretty good reconstruction from a close examination of physical evidence.

When I excavate a grave, my goal is to show that body in that hole as the last image that the perpetrator would see prior to throwing dirt on the remains. I want to reconstruct it as close to that moment in time as I can. So I can say when we present it in court, "Here is the grave that they've dug. You can see some of the impression from the shovel. You can see how deep it is, how the walls slope. And then they throw the body in." They must have some picture of that; it must be imprinted on their minds, before they start throwing the dirt in. With our maps, with our photographs, I try to reconstruct what they saw at that moment in time.

The Tenacity of Investigators

This case goes back to July 1957. It's the LAPD's oldest cold case. A man went to a Lover's Lane, where he found four teenagers sitting in a 1949 Ford, one of those big, bulgy monsters. He robbed them at gunpoint, tied them up with torn pieces of their clothing, and taped their eyes and mouths shut. Then he drove this car, with the four teens still in it, to a more secluded place. He raped one of the girls in the front seat. He tells them all to undress and he leaves them stranded. He takes their car.

Shortly thereafter, he runs a red light in this stolen car. Two officers from the city of El Segundo, which is near where LAX is today, not knowing that this was a real bad guy, stopped him. They were talking to him and starting to write him a ticket. Two other officers came by, but they get waved off by the original officers, "Nothin's going on here. Everything's under control." These two guys leave.

About a minute after that, these guys get a call, "Officers shot." He shot both the officers who stopped him three times. The stolen vehicle was abandoned four blocks away.

And he just got away.

The initial investigation, back in 1957, was good police work. They recovered two bullets from the car, where one of the officers had fired at him as he escaped. They did eyewitness composite drawings from the teenage victims who described him as a white guy, Southern drawl, and from the police officers who had driven up and seen the guy. They got two partial fingerprints from the steering wheel and another print was obtained from the chrome strip of the stolen car.

Two years later, 1959, a man finds the frame of a revolver in his yard that the guy had tossed. In 1960, again in the same yard, the man's son found the cylinder of a revolver. The ballistics people— Inside the cylinder were six expended shell casings and the ammunition inside was consistent with the ammunition used to kill the officers. It was a consistent match with the projectiles recovered from the bodies of the officers.

They traced the gun to a Sears in Shreveport, Louisiana. They found the gun was purchased there in July 1957 by a guy who wrote his name as G. D. Wilson, with a fake address in Miami. They investigated the surrounding area of the Sears and found that someone identifying himself as a George D. Wilson stayed at the YMCA close to the Sears where the murder weapon was purchased. They took the gun registration card to the Y—the card was mostly print writing. But the investigation dead-ended there.

LAPD cold case reopened it in 2002. They decided to take the partial prints and combine them into a print composite. They scanned that into AFIS and they were notified that there was a possible match to this person, Gerald F. Mason, not that far off from the name he gave at the Sears. He fit the physical description given by the victims and the officers. The reason his fingerprint was on file was because of a commercial burglary and forgery in South Carolina that he went to prison for in 1956. He had no other known contacts with law enforcement. At the time of his arrest in 1956, he was residing at a YMCA in South Carolina. There you go: known to frequent the Y.

They got his prison packet prints which still existed— thank you, South Carolina—and compared them to all three latent prints from the stolen vehicle. It was a match. They went back and looked at the registration card from the Shreveport Y and they compared it with a known sample of his handwriting from his driver's license registration card from 1999. That had his signature, as well as his printed name. They compared the printing of the "Gerald F. Mason" with the printing of "G. D. Wilson" on the YMCA card and there were distinct similarities, so that the handwriting analysis experts said these were probably written by the same person. They compared his 1956 mug shot photo with the composites from the witnesses, and it was similar. The guy looked sort of like the guy who played the Beaver on *Leave It to Beaver*.

And then they did eight photos that they showed to one of the police officers, now retired, who had seen the guy, and he picked him out. Remember, they got the call of two officers shot just moments after they had seen the guy. He said, "If I had seen the person in this photo forty-five years ago, I would have arrested him for the murder of my fellow officers."

Everything matched: the gun, the ballistics, the Southern accent, the physical description, the handwriting and printing, the fingerprints, three witnesses' positive identification—that was it. They got him. This case had everything *but* DNA.

So far as we know, this guy had lived an absolutely clean life since 1957. Living in South Carolina, running an auto parts shop or something like that, and he was like Mr. Good Neighbor. The neighbors were like, "But he's so wonderful! He helps us out! There must be a terrible mistake!"

No. No mistake.

PROSECUTOR

We had a cold case involving a quadruple murder. In the early nineties, a woman and her three children were murdered in their home on the South Side of Chicago. It was over a bad dope deal that the murdered woman's boyfriend was involved in.

Investigators found blood at the scene that didn't match up with any familial relationship. They had the DNA profile worked up. It wasn't in the system, so they went over the files again. They went out and reinterviewed people. And the guy who turned out to be the murderer, he'd been interviewed initially because he knew the victim's boyfriend. When the homicide detectives first interviewed him, they saw a scratch on his hand and they questioned him about it. He said he'd cut his hand at home. They interview his girlfriend. Sure enough, she corroborates that story. And all they had at the time was his blood type. And this suspect dies in about '96.

In 2002, our cold case guys go back and rework everything. They take the blood evidence and now they can do a DNA profile. Now they go back and reinterview everybody.

The girlfriend admitted that she lied about him cutting his hand. He's dead now, so it doesn't matter.

Here's the thing: He was dead, but he had a brother, who probably wasn't the best citizen of all, either. They went down and talked to the brother, who voluntarily gave a buccal swab. They matched his swab with the DNA profile, which showed it belonged to a family member of the suspect. Then they had to exhume this guy's body to make a positive. And we got it.

COLD CASE COMMANDER

I think there are more murderers living among us than people re-alize. There are a number of cold cases where the suspect may only have been convicted of some fairly lightweight thing, but when they get the DNA match, they discover that these people have committed rapes and murders.

Probably many, many people have gotten away with murder. Maybe they were looking to steal something and somebody surprised them in a home burglary, and they get away with it. Maybe it's a situation where they wind up in a fight with somebody and they don't expect to kill the person, but they do. Or there's just one person that they really, really want to kill, and once that's over, they don't have to kill anymore.

They get away with it. And nobody ever knows who killed this person.

PROSECUTOR

Cops don't forget those old murders. They don't forget them.
Ever. I have dozens I still think about.

You know, every victim's a true victim. But let's say—kids. You really get emotional, you know. You try and detach yourself, but the poor kids don't have a chance at all.

We've had cases with— Let's say you get to your pension, you're getting Social Security. You've never been in trouble. And one of these morons thinks you've got some money in the house and goes in and kills you. Things like that always stay with you. Always.

HOMICIDE DETECTIVE

When cold case squads came up, every detective worth his salt had already saved his old files, the ones that didn't clear. And they'd go to cold case and say, "Can you look at this?"

Even retired guys call up our squad now. "Would you look over this? When I had this, we were *this* close. Do you think, maybe DNA?"

COLD CASE/DNA SPECIALIST

This is what I always tell people, especially suspects that I be-lieve are involved with a homicide. I tell them, "There are 365 days in a year. *One* of those days, you're gonna screw up. And I'm gonna be right there, or some other detective is gonna be right there, to prove that you screwed up. And we're gonna get you."

HOMICIDE DETECTIVE

I'm a great believer in going back to crime scenes. I go back to them, even years later. There's just something about being there you can't get from pictures or reports. Maybe you'll pick up a sense of what happened. Maybe you'll pick up on something new, sort of on the periphery. You never know.

COLD CASE COMMANDER

On Fate

The people who should be worried are the guys who think they got away with murder. Maybe it's a murder from a long time ago. Now they're starting to breathe a little easier. They shouldn't. Sooner or later, they're gonna get that knock on the door that they've been dreading for the last twenty years.

CRIMINAL PROFILE

When we catch up to them, they always seem—relieved. Even when they've gotten away with murder for *years*. They've been waiting for you. They've been waiting for that knock on the door.

HOMICIDE DETECTIVE

Nine

CRIMINAL TRIALS

When I first started working in the crime lab, a scientist who had been there a long time told me what happens when you take forensics into a courtroom. He said, 'Well, it's kind of like the circus. Our job is to build the tent. And then they send in the clowns.' All we can do is build the best tent possible, and what happens from there on out is beyond our control.
—Forensic Scientist

We see homicide, every day, day in, day out. I just can't get over it. It's so astonishing to see the frequency of homicides. That in itself astonishes me, that they *are* so frequent. It happens so frequently that—phew! Am *I* normal, or what?

You know, I'm fifty-two years of age. I've spent fifty-two years' worth of weekends in my life. And at the end of every weekend, I come back to work on a Monday without having committed a homicide over the weekend. Now why can't other people do that?
—Prosecutor

THEY CALL IT THE CHAIN. IT STARTS THE MOMENT THE FIRST responding officer enters a crime scene. The chain weaves through processing, investigation, and crime lab work, extending all the way to trial. In this chain of evidence, the way all the links hold together, the way the jury considers whether some of the links may be missing, or misshapen, makes or breaks the case the detectives and prosecution have forged.

Jurors can actually see parts of the chain: autopsy and crime scene photographs, videotaped interrogations, blown-up fingerprint impressions, tire tracks, and fired cartridge comparisons, for example. But most of the chain is carried into court on the testimony of witnesses and investigators. And as physical evidence becomes more and more crucial in determining guilt or innocence, forensic scientists do most of the heavy lifting.

It's a pretty daunting task. Men and women who spend most of their days doing solitary microscopic examinations—like the DNA analysts who must keep monastic silence in the lab for fear that a spray of epithelial cells from an errant "hello" might contaminate samples—are pushed into performance mode when they enter a courtroom. They must explain complicated procedures against a backdrop of juror expectations largely shaped by TV crime shows and high-profile criminal cases. And they must maintain their scientific objectivity through attorney cross-examination and gamesmanship.

This chapter looks at what it takes to prepare for trial and testify at trial from the perspective of detectives, forensic scientists, prosecutors, and defense attorneys. The chain that ends in a verdict starts with the thoughts of a homicide detective just called to a scene.

The minute you get that phone call, especially with homicides, you start planning. What am I going to encounter? What are my resources going to be? What is the defense going to use to try to screw me on this thing?

You do your investigation with the defense in mind, if you're experienced, because you realize, I've got to minimize the weak points of this case. And they've *all* got them. Every case has got weak points.

For example, there was a young woman, county employee, pretty young girl, and she had gone through a number of unsavory relationships. She was raising a young daughter. Several years ago, she was getting ready to throw a party for the basketball playoffs; the Lakers were playing back then. She invited a guy she just met at a store, he seemed very nice, over to the house to watch the game with a group of friends.

As luck would have it, her friends backed out, they didn't show up, leaving her alone with this guy. She was so concerned about him, based on her past experiences with men, that she said, "Look. Would you mind emptying your pockets before you come in?" He goes, "Sure. Fine."

She had a pretty little daughter, about eight years old. Little girl went to bed about ten o'clock. This guy murdered and sexually assaulted the mom. When the little girl came out and found her mother lying naked on the floor, with this guy still there, she said, "Help me pick my mom up. I need a drink of water." He tried to strangle her. He raped her also. This is an incredibly emotional scene. These are the kind that can get you.

One of the things the defense is going to do is try to muddy up the mom: "Look here. She brings this guy she doesn't even know back to the house." That kind of thing.

So what we did, when we took our crime scene photographs, in the kid's room—she was such a great mom, she had all these inspirational sayings and things like that hung up—I made sure those got into the crime scene photographs, close-ups of those. So I could say at trial, "Wait a minute. No. *Here's* the kind of mom she was."

When you go to court, you bring your victims back to life again.

HOMICIDE DETECTIVE

Because of O. J. Simpson, you can do the best possible job at a crime scene of collecting evidence, interpreting evidence, doing crime scene reconstruction—you can do all that, and even if you do an *incredible* job, somebody's going to be a Monday morning quarterback in court and tell you how much you screwed up. So, a lot of times, we go through the crime scene and just periodically [say], "Okay. Stop. Have we done this? What have we *not* done before we leave this room?" There's a lot of second-guessing yourself at scenes, thinking ahead to court. The problem is, you could just stay there forever and constantly second-guess yourself.

CRIME SCENE TEAM SUPERVISOR

The days of police getting to court and just reporting on an inter-rogation or a confession are pretty much over. You want to videotape everything so that the jury can see exactly what happened. If you don't want to videotape it, you shouldn't be doing it.

HOMICIDE DETECTIVE

We videotape all of our interrogations in the station to show in court. Our interrogation rooms are set up with little, un-obtrusive cameras. They go through a little hole in the wall, probably about the size of a pencil eraser. And then they go into a room where we have another detective in there, monitoring, making sure the tapes run right. We're using two tapes simultaneously in case of a glitch with one of them.

It's really good, because sometimes, you know, as a super-visor, I'd go in there and I could watch what the guy was saying and maybe get the detective out and say, "Wait. Did you notice this, or did you notice that?"

And while the detective's gone, incidentally, we have a lit-tle telephone in the room with the suspect. We don't say any-thing about the telephone; it's just there. As soon as the detective leaves—once again, the dumb ones are the unlucky ones—people grab that phone. "Hey! You gotta get that god-damn knife out of my dresser drawer!"

And it's gorgeous on videotape.

HOMICIDE SQUAD SUPERVISOR

How Forensic Scientists Prepare for Trials

The climax to your work is testifying in court. To put it plain and simple: Anybody can come in and learn how to process evi-dence, not everybody can do the comparisons and identifica-tions, but the end result is testifying in court. If you can't testify in court, you're basically useless. To put it plain and simple: You are useless. It all comes down to the nutshell, and the nutshell is testimony.

LATENT PRINT SPECIALIST

Forensic scientists and technical experts have to be able to go into a courtroom, articulate their findings, think on their feet, be fair, be objective, be unbiased, and withstand the vitriol of defense attorneys. That's a pretty tall order.

FORENSIC SCIENTIST

When you're being trained to work in the Illinois crime lab, you take a continuing course called Courtroom Demeanor. After about three months, you might have one mock trial during your supervised casework so you can practice speaking in a public forum. That breaks the ice. Down the road, you get into presenting evidence. Then you get into cross-examination.

At the very, very end, is your final mock trial, where you're evaluated by a panel of instructors and supervisors who grade you on your performance: How well do you answer questions? Were you technically accurate? How well did you perform on the stand? How did you deal with stressful situations?

And those are all thrown at us so we can be prepared for court. A lot of testimony is— You're out there and you don't know what they're gonna ask.

LATENT PRINT SPECIALIST

I teach courses now for the new people in crime labs who haven't testified in court as yet, on courtroom demeanor, dress, eye contact with the jury.

What you wear to court, as a scientist, is important. I think that juries have an expectation as to what a scientist looks like. To me, if you wear, say, a paisley tie, colorful and a little flashy—that's not the kind of pattern I recommend. I recommend a geometric pattern to ties for men because they're predictable, they're repeatable, and that is exactly what scientists are. We're interested in predictability in experimentation, reliability of instrumentation. And so the tie becomes an expression of who the individual is.

We train the scientists: Make eye contact. That is a *huge* thing. Listen very intently to questions. You don't cut off either of the attorneys when they're asking the question. Make sure you hear the question well. And then, as you answer, you go from juror's face to juror's face to juror's face, making eye contact, letting them know that you're not focused on the *attorney* when you're answering a question.

FORENSIC SCIENTIST

Attorneys will do things to disrupt your eye contact with the jury. They'll do things like walk as far away from the jury as they can to ask the questions, in hopes that you'll start having a conversation with the attorney, instead of focusing on the jury.

Let's say I'm testifying for the prosecution. The prosecutor will bring his podium right to the corner of the jury box so you can't help but look at the jury. The defense attorney will maybe stay at the table so that you have to look over at him or her to be polite. I had one who dragged the podium. He did it in kind of a subtle way, so I'm not sure it was obvious to the jury. It was like he kept adjusting it, and he kept adjusting it farther and farther away from the jury. So what I did was turn my body to the jury and look over my shoulder when he was asking his questions. But that comes with being completely aware of the setting in which you're delivering your opinion.

FORENSIC PSYCHOLOGIST

In court, the way you talk, even the cadence of your voice is im-portant. Whether you talk too quickly or too slowly, whether you pause, whether you do a lot of "ahs" or "ums," or some kind of process of delaying a response while you think about it. That's good to do.

It could even be things like adjusting your glasses and asking the attorney to repeat a question. That can be effective. I've seen it done to a high art. I've seen some professor types, where they will have their glasses on, and you will see them, when they're asked a pointed question, actually remove the glasses and ponder that for a second, and then lay the glasses down before they even begin to answer the question.

Very, very effective. It lets the jury know that a lot of thought has gone into giving the answer. Jurors are sometimes literally on the edge of their seats, waiting for that answer from that individual.

FORENSIC SCIENTIST

You've got to be able to make your testimony as clear as possible, without distorting it. You can have a Ph.D. in molecular genetics or biology get up there and very quickly lose the jury. Generally, you want to make complex scientific concepts as simple as possible. You don't want to lose them in the details.

That's something that a good defense attorney often will do. They may drone on and on and on and get into the most esoteric part of your testimony in cross-examination because they want to leave the jury wondering: What was *that* witness all about?

FORENSIC SCIENTIST

I've given a workshop several times for psychologists about testifying in court. I call it "Like Lambs to the Slaughter." Because here are these helping professionals, who go into court trying to be helpful and just get—slaughtered.

That's why testifying has become a specialty area in all the sciences. You know, some nice anthropologist from a university who has never been in court, if he or she doesn't have some idea of what they're getting into, they're just going to be *shellacked.*

You're trying to be helpful and trying to present information. First of all, you won't be allowed to do it the way you want to, because you have to answer questions. And you can be cut off at any point. Heaven forbid you start a sentence "Yes, but . . . ," because they'll stop you right after the yes.

All the rhetoric. The "Isn't it possible?" questions. There's a constant: If something *is* possible, you have to say yes and hope that the other attorney will pick up on it because, for the sake of your argument, you can't commit perjury, you know. Or when you're being asked questions like "Well, you didn't even *care* about this record, did you?" or "You didn't *like* my client!" or "Isn't it true that . . . ," when something is just blatantly untrue.

It can become a show. You have to stay focused on what you're doing and not get beaten around by the process. You have to keep clearly in mind what your opinion is and not get sucked up into the rhetoric and the desire to defend yourself.

FORENSIC PSYCHOLOGIST

Really, I'm nervous probably every time I go to court. I've testified as a forensic scientist about twenty-five times. The moments before I get on the stand? It's a little unnerving. I mean, there are butterflies. You're going over your notes. You *don't* want to make mistakes. You're about to go on stage.

LATENT PRINT EXAMINER

Behind the Trial: Motive

A real trial has a drama far exceeding anything you'd read in fic-tion or see on TV. There's nothing more powerful than a real-life case. These are real people that hurt. You see the families that are left behind. They have an expectation from the criminal justice system that the right thing is going to happen. The defendant sitting there; his family is occasionally in the courtroom. The *power* that all this brings to a real courtroom.

The mystery behind the trial: *why* somebody does something, for example. Frequently, not as a wonderful dramatic moment, but from arguments over stupid things, somebody looked at somebody wrong. And that ends up in a murder.

PROSECUTOR

We had a case where a woman was killed because she had bad breath. Another one: Two rocks of cocaine that the defendant had handed over to prostitutes weren't returned to him. Many of the reasons for homicides are so frivolous. To even give them as a motive in court seems ridiculous.

Sometimes we don't know *what* the reason is. People don't just come out and tell you, "Oh, yeah, I did it because of this or that." Sometimes they never explain why they did it,

And we never really know the reason.

PROSECUTOR

I defended a case stemming from this: A girl is mad at her boyfriend. He had been in prison on a drug offense, he's on parole, trying to get custody of his child back. She decides she's gonna rat him off.

She knows about a murder that happened ten years before that nobody has solved. Investigators got a videotape of a person in a football jacket that goes into a Shell gas station/mini-mart type thing. He's got a hat on. You see the guy go in to buy something, then five seconds later, he comes out. You hear an argument on the videotape and then you hear *boom-boom-boom-boom-boom-boom*. There's a shooting. A guy is killed.

Everybody says, "Well, it's the guy that had the jacket and

the hat." But, visually, you can't tell who it is. The hat has fallen off at the scene, so they have that.

So ten years later, this girl calls up police and says, "Hey, my boyfriend's the one who committed this murder at the gas station." This girlfriend was just making the whole thing up. They charge him with this cold case murder. I end up getting appointed to defend him.

I go to the defendant and tell him, "We've got this hat that fell off during the shooting. Should we have it tested?" I tell him about the DNA. "Okay. Go ahead."

Sure enough, the DNA on the inside of the hatband isn't his. So he gets acquitted.

Basically, he was with the group of people that did the shooting. It was like rival gangs and stuff. He not only knew it wasn't his hat, but he knew who did it, a friend of his. They never did prosecute that guy, though. Because all the eyewitnesses said it was my client. And if it weren't for DNA, this guy could easily be in prison, because his girlfriend had it in for him. Evil. Just evil.

DEFENSE ATTORNEY

Forensic psychiatrists sometimes talk among ourselves about whether we've actually met people whom we considered evil.

I interview people pretrial to assess whether they're fit to stand trial or to see if they might fit an insanity defense, which is extremely rare. The two ends of the spectrum with defendants are people who never had a chance, or people who are irredeemably antisocial. Generally, what you feel is empathy. Some crimes you can't get yourself there in your imagination. But most you can. The "us versus them" thing breaks down right away.

But evil? I've interviewed thousands of criminal defendants, but I've only met a couple that made me think I was talking with someone truly evil. What it felt like to me was not the presence of something, but the absence of anything human. And I didn't have empathy for them, because I was scared to death, to tell you the truth.

One I will never forget. I was interviewing this guy after an attempted prison break. I knew he was in prison for murder, but that's all I knew about him. I walked into the room and the hair on the back of my neck stood on end. And I thought, "What's up with *this*?" It was really weird. I attributed it to *me*: What *is* this? And I sat down and started talking to him, and I can't articulate it, other than to say, we're having a conversation, he's kind of cooperating, he's giving me information, and I felt like I was talking to an empty shell inhabited by something pretending to be human.

He wasn't saying terrible things. I mean, I've heard horrific stories and not had this reaction. By his account, he was a serial murderer, but I've met other serial murderers and not had this reaction. You know in horror movies where you have replicants, things that look human, but aren't? That's what it's like with these people. But you have to remember, there are very few of them.

FORENSIC PSYCHOLOGIST

Forensic Science Testimony in Court

Our toxicology section provided testimony in court on the kid-napping and sexual assault of a twelve-year-old. The victim claimed that the suspect had forced the victim to take these pills, commonly known as Soma, which is a muscle relaxant.

We had *just* developed the test to detect Soma at the time in our toxicology unit. The trial had already started. The defense was contending that this didn't really happen and the child was lying, the way that the defense tends to treat minors.

The trial was already underway when we were able to get this test done. Once we reported the test results, the defendant decided to plead guilty and take his chances. Our testimony ended up being pretty critical evidence to prove the veracity of the victim's story. This was a gruesome case. We were very happy to help.

FORENSIC TOXICOLOGIST

One of the best examples of forensic science solving a case, and of the crucial importance of a forensic scientist's testimony in court, was a murder trial that I prosecuted a few years ago.

A real estate agent lived by himself, had kind of a modest little home in Burton; Burton is kind of a blue-collar type of town, adjacent to Flint, Michigan. He was viciously murdered one morning. He was robbed. His car was taken. They took a VCR and some jewelry. This wasn't some millionaire real estate guy; this guy lived in Burton, for crying out loud.

Some local kids were eventually found driving his car. Their clothing was taken; statements were taken from them. One young man pled to reduced murder two. The other young man, he was only seventeen, went to trial. This young man was familiar with our victim. He had mowed his lawn.

The crime scene itself became the most important piece of evidence in that trial. The victim was beaten to death— pummeled—with what we believe to be the murder weapon, which was a small monkey wrench that our defendant apparently carried on him quite frequently. That weapon was never found. But we did find the outline of the weapon, in blood, on the carpeting of the victim's bedroom. Blood was all over the walls of the victim's bedroom. He had a painting of *The Last Supper* right next to his bed; it had a big blood spray pattern on it.

The forensic work on this was really important because this was a beating death, where you've got a lot of blood being shed. And one of the ways that we linked the defendant to the crime scene was that one of the shoes he was wearing had the victim's blood on it.

Probably one of the big *gotcha!* moments that I've ever

had in a trial was in this one. In Michigan, the prosecutor turns over all information we have to the defense, so there are no real surprises in a trial, normally.

The defense knew that we had sent his shoes to the crime lab, where they found blood on one of the shoes. The lab then took DNA and compared it and determined that the defendant had the *victim's* blood on the shoe.

The defense tailored their argument to point to the codefendant. They said that the codefendant did it all, and the defendant who was on trial, simply walked in, was confronted by this awful, bloody, brutal scene, and turned around and left. He was horrified: Oh my gosh! And then he got into the victim's car and drove off. Wasn't so horrified that he couldn't steal the victim's car, deciding that the victim wasn't going to use it because his head had been severely damaged.

The science of blood spatter became very important here, because the argument that the defense attorney made was that the event was over and the defendant simply had some blood on his shoe that he had brushed up against.

Our chief witness was a serologist and nationally recognized expert in blood spatter with the Michigan Crime Lab. He had examined the defendant's shoe and determined that there was a bloodstain on it. And, according to this witness, the dynamics of blood—how the blood gets on something—tells you a great deal about the event and the person who was wearing that item of clothing, what *they* were doing during the event.

In this particular case, according to the laws of physics, the blood spatter that was on the shoe could only have been made if the defendant, as our expert said, was present "during a blood-shedding event." The physics of a flying blood drop was such that, considering how it was deposited on the shoe, this blood droplet hit the shoe, leaving a round droplet, meaning that it was flying at a certain angle. This told us that the victim was alive or being attacked at the time the defendant was *in that bedroom.*

This blood spatter expert had drawn up some relatively simply diagrams to show the difference between if a blood spatter happens and hits at an angle, or if it simply drips down, because the defense attorney tried to switch gears—it was a damn good lawyer that was defending this guy!—said, "Well, maybe the defendant was present and some blood dripped off of the wrench the other guy used to beat the victim." And our expert came back with, "No, actually, if you look at the way the blood spatter—it left a round spatter as opposed to an elongated spatter. If it had simply dripped straight down, it would have left an elongated trail with a tail. And this was a relatively round spatter."

That was the pivotal moment, that the blood that was on that shoe was a flying drop. That encapsulated the weakness in the whole defense. The defendant didn't come in to the scene later. He was there during the blood-shedding event.

It was one of those moments where you could just kind of feel the wind coming out of the defense case. The defendant ended up being convicted. This is one I'll remember for a long time.

PROSECUTOR

I consulted with, and ended up being kind of cocounsel with, the defense on a case where a guy was accused of beating up a lawyer. The guy was sort of a nut. He liked to sue people. The charge was that this guy went into the office of a lawyer who had rejected his case and, literally, beat the hell out of him. I mean, the lawyer ends up in the hospital, he's got brain injuries, it's a brutal crime.

The lawyer's secretary says, "I think it may have been this old client." She said she got kind of a fleeting glance of the guy. So they get a real questionable ID.

The guy was actually convicted. But we got a new trial

granted because the first lawyer didn't look at any of the forensic evidence. So I get hired by the new lawyers to look at the case and look at the DNA evidence.

The client is kind of . . . kooky. He thinks everybody's in a conspiracy, didn't quite trust his own lawyers, so I'm trying to talk to the guy saying, "This is good." He doesn't know what DNA is and refuses to give a sample. We actually have to trick him into giving us a sample by having him lick an envelope.

The key piece of evidence turns out to be a watch that investigators found in the attorney's office. It's not the attorney's watch. It's a broken watch and it's got blood spatter on it. Nobody's ever looked at this piece of evidence.

So I go and look at all the evidence and I tell the lawyers, "This is going to be the key to the case, because there's all kinds of what they call 'habitual wearer' DNA on a watch."

And there were also specks of blood on the watch, presumably from the beating of the lawyer.

We sent it to a laboratory. This is the kind of marginal evidence that is very hard to get a result on, so I always try to get a good lab to do it. We work out a deal with the prosecution, get a joint test done with a DNA expert whom they've used any number of times.

The DNA guy gets wonderful results, a *beautiful* DNA profile. They get the wearer of the watch. There are subsamples that are mixtures of the lawyer and the other person. And it turns out it's not our defendant.

So Unknown Subject Number One is all over the place. We actually get a light switch swab that the lab got a result on. It was real clear.

But the prosecutor *still* goes to trial on the case because of the secretary's identification. And he attacks the DNA expert on the forensic science, right on the witness stand, and really pissed him off. He said, "Look, I work for your office all the time. Why are you doing this to me?"

The prosecutor is in *disbelief* over this watch. He's looking for other explanations.

The case is going to trial. The prosecutor comes up with this theory before the trial, that the watch belonged to a nurse. This was the story. The lawyer who was beaten had represented the family of a nurse who was killed in a medical evacuation flight that crashed. And the family was going to sue somebody. Somehow, the lawyer had ended up with the personal effects of what this nurse was wearing. And the prosecution claimed that, during the struggle with whoever was assaulting the lawyer, the box containing the nurse's belongings somehow got overturned and the watch happened to fall on the floor during the argument. So they come up with "the dead nurse theory."

This all comes up right after the DNA results, and we're right up to the start of trial. One of our lawyers is all frantic: "Oh my God, what are we going to do? This completely undercuts us." I said, "Don't worry about it. The lab tested this particular genetic marker, known as amelogenin, which tells you whether it's male or female DNA. What is on the watch is all boy DNA; it's not girl DNA." This undercuts the dead nurse theory and completely deflates the prosecutor.

The kooky guy gets acquitted. The lawyer didn't die. He eventually recovered, but he had pretty much no memory of what happened. They haven't caught the real assailant yet.

DEFENSE ATTORNEY

I had a hair case. The whole conviction was relying on my testimony that I found the victim's hair in this guy's car. She had no association with him. He raped her, and the hair was going to be the match between the two.

I'm explaining all the characteristics of hair, going through what you look for, how this can be used for comparison purposes. For some reason, and I don't know why, I kept staring over in the jury box at the one individual who was bald.

The jury picked up on it. They started giggling. The prosecution was kind of smiling. I didn't know about it till I was done testifying and the prosecutor said, "Why did you keep staring at that gentleman?" I'm thinking, "Wow! Here I was staring at that poor guy, talking about hair loss and what you can tell from hair and this and that." It was like, "Sorry, sir, that you don't have any. But if you did . . ."

So I left, not knowing if the jury heard anything I said or if they were just watching me stare at the one bald juror. It was just bad.

HAIR AND FIBER EXPERT

Trial work is literally like a play. Each play is different, depending on the facts of the case, depending on the strength of the case, and depending on the jury that's ultimately chosen *and* the judge and the defense attorney. And you're going to awaken emotions in your jurors, depending on your witnesses.

PROSECUTOR

A Dramatic Courtroom Ploy

I've served as an expert witness in forensic geoarcheology in a number of trials. In one of these trials, there was this rather unsavory character who stole bodies from the Roosevelt Lake area of central Arizona. His specialty was trading in naturally desiccated human mummies that had been buried in caves and alcoves. Because of the region's dryness, these mummies and the accompanying grave goods had been preserved for hundreds and sometimes thousands of years.

And he would sell these bodies to individuals who thought they were cool things to sink into a table or a bar, under glass, or to decorate their offices.

He was ultimately caught, as the result of a very elaborate two-year sting operation, in which various law enforcement officers posed as potential buyers. They got him trying to market the remains of a very young girl who had died about twelve hundred years ago and whose body was in a spectacular state of preservation. We were able to recover just enough sediment, from her body and the clothes that wrapped it, to link it to a place on federal property and to bring him to trial for this.

The guy's public defender thought that the gravity of the crime had been vastly overstressed by the prosecution. He thought that, if the jury were confronted with the actual evidence, they wouldn't convict him of anything.

And so, not reading his jury very well, which consisted of eleven women and one man, he brought into court one of the bodies that the defendant had sold to an undercover agent. This was a little girl who was about three years old and who looked like, except for the slight drying of her skin, like she might have died yesterday—eyelashes still in place, hair combed, wrapped in a little blanket, with little toys. The defense attorney had the body introduced as evidence in the court, which was the first time a human body had ever been used as evidence in a court case in the United States.

The minute the jurors saw it, they were prepared to kill him. So he was done, toast, finished. The prosecutor leaned over and said, "Is this guy insane?"

FORENSIC GEOARCHEOLOGIST

Forensic Experts on Attorneys

It's frustrating as hell to deal with attorneys because you've got to wait till they finish their questions. And sometimes they don't know what question to ask.

There is something very wrong with our system when the *one* person who has all the information from all the sources concerning a particular death is the person *least* qualified to evaluate it. I mean the scientific information, not the legal information. How many attorneys have a science background? How many of them know anything about biology? How many of them have a medical background?

Damn few. They're all political science majors.

MEDICAL EXAMINER

I can't tell you how many times a lawyer has said to me, and they *all* think they're the first one: "Okay, you're a scientist. You're gonna have to explain this DNA stuff to me. I went to law school because I wasn't ever any good at science." And they think it's funny.

DNA EXPERT

Attorneys have to get rid of their habit of thinking, "Okay. I've got this expert witness. Go!" If you've never done a DNA case before, or any case with heavy forensic evidence, don't think that you're going to go into trial, the morning that you're putting on your expert, and just wing it. You really need to spend time *ahead* of time learning and asking your expert to explain how the testing process worked or what the test is capable of doing and what it can't do, because your witness is going to be challenged on cross-examination. So, if you can get some of those things out in the case in chief, that can reduce the sting of it.

DNA EXPERT

I've had lots of experience, when I worked in the lab, with attor-neys expecting that the scientists were going to get up on the stand and say, "I did the test. And the defendant is guilty."

That's the big difference between science and law. Scientists have nothing to do with guilt or innocence. And they *shouldn't*.

As scientists, we are advocates of no one. Even if you're

hired, especially in a state crime lab, by the prosecution, you're not a prosecution expert. You are an advocate of the science. You testify to the results. "I tested this, I tested this; these are the results, these are the results." And that's where you stop.

It's the lawyer's job to use that piece of evidence and fit it in the puzzle and say, "This guy had motive. This guy had access. His DNA was at the scene." The lawyer puts it together and leads the jury down that path. And, obviously, the other lawyer's job is to attack that.

CRIME LAB DIRECTOR

The whole system is built around reasonable doubt. If they can ask a witness a question that makes the witness look like they don't know what they're talking about, or even just a question to fluster the witness, two hours of testimony can be completely shot. And the last thing the jury can remember is "That witness didn't know the answer to that question," so everything else comes in doubt.

FORENSIC PSYCHOLOGIST

Terminology can get you in court. The example that I use is the term "blood spatter." Probably half the people who talk about it say "splatter," which actually seems to make more sense, but that's not the term.

We had a detective who was in court, an experienced detective, but new to Homicide. He was testifying about the scene and he used the term "blood splatter" about a half dozen times. And the defense, when he finished his cross-examination said, "No further questions. Oh, yes! Your Honor, please. Just one more. Ah, Detective, isn't the term 'spatter,' not 'splatter'?" And the detective said, "You're right, Counselor. I did misspeak myself. That's an error. It *is* 'spatter.'" And the defense attorney said, "Oh no, no, no. The mistake is all mine. I thought you knew what you were talking about. No further questions." And that's what the jury heard.

HOMICIDE DETECTIVE

Prosecutors prosecute. And defense attorneys defend. It sounds stupid to say, but it's their job, and each side has tunnel vision about what they're doing.

One time I was testifying as a prosecution witness in the trial of a sixteen-year-old girl charged with first-degree murder as an adult. If she were convicted, she would go to prison for life without parole. And I said to the prosecutor, a female prosecutor I'd worked with several times, we were friendly, and I said to her during a break, "Oh, man. Mandatory life's a long time when you're only sixteen." At which point, she *snapped* at me and said, "Well! The *victim* has no life at all!" And I thought, "You know? Prosecutors prosecute." There wasn't a lot of room there for sympathizing with the perpetrator.

And the flip side of that is defense attorneys *defend*. What drives defendants absolutely nuts, however, is how both sides will chat and laugh with each other during breaks. I've had defendants say to me, "What are they *doing?* They're supposed to hate each other!"

FORENSIC PSYCHOLOGIST

Forensic Scientists on Juries

When I first started, if you went into court and testified that two objects were fired from the same firearm, that was good enough. You used to go into court and testify about what you had seen with your naked eye. Just your word as the expert was good enough.

Probably because of the introduction of the *CSI*-type crime scene shows and also because of the real-life courtroom dramas that have played out, like, O. J. Simpson, today more and more cases require some type of documentation that can be shown in court.

Today, the jury wants to see what we saw. Not that they would necessarily understand what we're seeing, but they know it's out there, they know it's available, and they'd like to see it, too.

FIREARMS EXPERT

We see much more scrutiny in terms of testimony because of all the celebrity trials that are out there.

They not only educated the public, but also educated all state's attorneys, all public defenders, all private attorneys, in how to cross-examine or ask questions of scientists.

It's more difficult now than before all these trials. Times have changed.

FORENSIC SCIENTIST

The "*CSI* effect": I think the old cliché of "the good, the bad, and the ugly" really refers to it quite well. The general population, the people who sit on juries, are much better informed because of it. The jury's level of understanding has increased. They're familiar with terms like gas chromatographs, mass spectrometers, DNA—because of *CSI*. That's the good part.

The bad part is the expectation, many times, of the jury that, if you don't have forensic evidence, then you don't have a case. But it's not uncommon to *not* have forensic evidence. Even though you collect everything at a crime scene, sometimes there's just nothing there.

And the ugly part is that, if you don't have forensic evidence, there have been occasions where the juries have refused to find the individual guilty, even though you had the classical case against him. There was no forensic evidence to associate the defendant with the crime. But there was a lot of good investigative information that was developed by the investigators that said that this was the guy who did it. And the jury refused to convict. As one juror said, "Well, they didn't have any forensic evidence, so he couldn't be guilty." They turn a blind eye to good evidence if it's not forensic evidence.

CRIME LAB DIRECTOR

Jurors have a whole set of expectations because of *CSI*. And sometimes they have unrealistic expectations. There have been cases where juries have voted one way and then come back and said that they voted that way because we thought that such-and-such an analysis should have been done because they saw it on *CSI*.

FORENSIC SCIENTIST

Oh, it's just terrible. It's gotten to the point now where when we [forensic scientists] get on the stand, we have to spend the first fifteen, twenty minutes *un*educating the jury about *CSI*. The prosecutor will ask us a series of questions designed to do this. They'll go, "Did you get DNA off this?" "No, I did not." "Did you try?" "No, I did not." "*Why* didn't you try?" "Because—*yada yada yada*." "Did you get fingerprints off everything?" "No." "When you *get* fingerprints, are you able to identify the suspect all the time?" "No, you don't."

Because the jury has seen *CSI* and they think that that's the truth. So when they get on a jury, they go, "They didn't do this. But they do this on *CSI*. So this must not be the right person."

LATENT PRINT SPECIALIST

The public perception is a little skewed. The public now thinks, "Okay, you catch somebody and within five minutes you can have one hundred percent accurate DNA testing that says it's this guy. It's a no-brainer. What's the problem?"

CRIME LAB DIRECTOR

I've testified in a few DNA sexual assault cases where the defendant could not be excluded from the DNA sample, but some additional DNA was found, and I've tried to explain what the potential sources of that could have been. It could have been an additional assailant. It could have been contamination when the evidence was collected. That's not proper, but even if there's somebody else's DNA there, that doesn't negate the fact that the defendant was also there.

The defense side would get up and try to confuse things: "You don't know that it's him. You can't say with a certainty that it's him because you found all this other contamination." And they try to make contamination seem as if it was on purpose.

But that's easily diluted if the prosecutor says, "You said it's possible. But with all the evidence and the cases you've seen before: Is that probable?"

And based on your expertise, you can say, "No. It's highly unlikely." But if the prosecution doesn't give you the opportunity to answer that, the jury is left with "You've got all this stuff! And it's all mixed together! And she's saying it's him, but it could be—all these other things!" I can imagine, if I was a juror, I could be there scratching my head, going, "Gee! It sounded really convincing when she was the only one talking, but now, you know, it could be this! And how are we supposed to decide?"

DNA ANALYST

I worked on a case and testified in court, as medical examiner, that I think really shows how good an investigation can be and how smart juries are.

There was a warehouse that dealt in audio-video supplies. A man driving past one weekend noticed it was open and decided to go in and say hello to his friend, who owned the warehouse. He goes in and, to his horror, finds there's a fire in the place. He picks up a fire extinguisher and starts dousing the fire and suddenly realizes that he's dousing a person who's on fire. Can you imagine? You go to say hello to a friend and you end up in a scene like that? He calls the police.

The investigators call the prosecutor and the medical examiner. What we had was a person who had been bound and gagged and set on fire. He was totally burned. His wife couldn't identify him.

We were able to identify him through his antemortem dental records. We x-rayed him and matched the postmortem and antemortem dental records. There were no fingerprints. During the autopsy, my findings suggested that this person was hit in the head, so that he was stunned. I also could tell that there had been an attempt to strangle this person. How did I know that? Because I found some very interesting patterned contusions on the neck. There were two very well-defined, pinpoint imprints on his neck at regular intervals.

I told the investigators, "I'm looking for a metallic object that would leave these imprints." They went back to the scene to find anything that matched. First, they sent me a very heavy linked chain from the scene. That didn't match. Then they sent me another chain made out of curved metal wires about two or three millimeters thick. The links had two cut ends, about eight millimeters from each other. Those wires matched the imprints in the neck.

My surmise was that the person had been subject to strangulation with that metal-link chain, and when the attempt was not successful, the person was hit on the back of the head with some metal object so that his skin was split in the back of his head. Once he was stunned like that, then I think the assailant had all the time in the world to hog-tie him up and set him on fire.

This is where the investigators from the prosecutor's office come into play. The assailant had tied the victim up with those plastic ties they use to bunch wires together.

The investigators not only took possession of the gasoline can and those plastic ties during the autopsy, but they traced the manufacturer of those plastic ties, and then traced them to the store where they had been sold. Lady Luck smiled on the investigators because the assailant paid for the plastic ties with his American Express card, believe it or not. So that is how our investigators hit pay dirt, by tracing the buyer of those plastic ties. From my point of view, I think that was pretty nifty work on their part.

They traced him all the way across the nation to California and brought him back. He was a very young man who had been paid to murder the owner of the warehouse.

It came to trial. The jury was absolutely wonderful. When I put this to the jury: Simple logic. You cannot tie up a person who is already on fire. You cannot hit a person in the head who is already on fire. You cannot strangle a person who is already on fire.

So I said the logic was that an attempt was made to strangle him first, which didn't succeed, so he had to be hit in the head and stunned. And then that gave the opportunity for his assailant to tie him up. And he was set on fire last.

The jury was very smart. They accepted it without one word, even with the objections of the defense counsel. He was protesting, "I object, Your Honor!" "I object, Your Honor!" The judge was very nice. He said, "Let the expert give his opinion because I think it is germane and pertinent to the way this event happened." Very nicely we established that fact and we convicted. It was a huge, big feather in the cap of the investigators in the prosecutor's office. They really excelled.

I think the defense was very, very clever in what they did. From day one of the trial, they made sure that the defendant's wife sat in front, holding a young infant in her arms.

She was present at trial every day. And I think that influenced the jury not to give him the death penalty. The guy got away with a life sentence.

MEDICAL EXAMINER

Forensic Scientists on Other Forensic Scientists

One of the dangers I see in forensic science is that people sometimes start to believe their own hype. Because you go to court, you're recognized as an expert; people pick you out because you're in the know, so they come to you and they want to know what's really going on. It *does* start to work on you after a while. And you have to be very careful because sometimes it's easy to start to fall into that slot where you start to believe that you're *really* as good as the attorney says you are.

This can affect your testimony. It has. It doesn't happen very often. I think we all go through it a little bit, but you learn to deal with it. You recognize that this is not a good place to be, and so you back off, and you go back to doing what you do, and that is science, real science.

But sometimes people, in an effort to be the hero, or in an effort to be recognized as the best, they start to overemphasize things, or to overtestify, or even to basically *lie*.

LATENT PRINT SPECIALIST

As a scientist, whenever someone tries to tell me precisely what happened in a blow-by-blow description, I am very skeptical. Because science is not certain. Only a charlatan is certain. And I've had more than one occasion to use that line in court. Juries understand that, too. They really do.

The more dogmatic someone is, the more careful you should be about accepting what they have to say. Intellectual dishonesty is not confined to one profession. You have to

watch yourself continually to make sure you don't start doing that.

FORENSIC PATHOLOGIST

There's a problem with jurors just accepting experts' testimony
based solely on the fact that they're experts. Say you get a little old man, gray haired, white lab coat. Even before he
opens his mouth, "This is a Ph.D., *blah, blah, blah.*" The jurors almost don't even listen. It's like, "Whatever this guy
says, it's got to be right."

DNA EXPERT

A Defense Attorney on a Wrongful Conviction Based on Junk Science

There was a very high-profile case that was decided on very
questionable bite mark evidence. I worked on the defense after this initial verdict; the case ended up extending from
1991 through 2002.

On New Year's Eve in '91, a woman who managed a bar
in Phoenix closed the bar down for the night. In the morning, the first workers to come in find this woman in the
men's restroom, naked, spread out, with her clothes strewn
around the restroom. Her tank top is cut right up the middle
with a knife. It's a real brutal, brutal crime.

They make an arrest the next day of a retired air force guy
and current postal carrier named Ray Krone. They bring in a
local dentist to look at a photograph of the victim's body at
the scene. He said, "I think there's a bite mark on the breast.
I think the guy may have crooked teeth." If the skin is flexible, this mark could be made with any kind of teeth.

Nonetheless, the detective hears from one of the victim's
friends that the victim kind of liked Ray Krone. They look
through her address book and they see Ray Krone's name
and phone number. The detective goes to Ray's house the

day after the murder and talks to him. Ray's got kind of crooked teeth, so the detective decides, "Those are the teeth."

On the way in to the station for questioning, the detective stops off at a convenience store and gets some Styrofoam plates. At the end of the interview, they take the Styrofoam plate, have Ray bite on it, take it to the dentist and the guy says, "That looks like a match."

Boom. Ray is charged with capital murder. The trial lasted only seven and a half days. At trial, he had a great alibi witness who testified at trial that he was with Ray New Year's Eve, watching bowl games at his house. "Ray was with me. He went to bed at eleven; I went to bed a little later." The murder happened at two A.M., so the prosecutor says, "You don't know he didn't go out and commit this murder and come back." They never found any evidence at his house.

Ray was convicted of first-degree murder because of a Styrofoam plate. All they had was a bite mark. After the first trial, in '93, the defendant's family contacts me, since I've done work in DNA evidence. I look over the evidence and all the other forensic work they did, and I thought all this was completely misexplained in the trial. I go to talk with Krone, he was on Death Row in Arizona, and he seemed like just a regular guy. He's just saying, "Help me. I didn't do this."

I always ask clients, "Do you want to do some DNA testing?" He said, "Do all the DNA you want." Usually, when they're guilty, they're not that encouraged by DNA testing. So it's always sort of a litmus test for guilt.

I thought, "Gosh. The record looks like all they have is this bite mark testimony." The prosecution had one bite mark expert from Nevada, who says you can make a positive identification from a bite mark, that it's better than a fingerprint, which is not the truth. He told the jury this in the trial. I'm thinking, "No wonder this guy got convicted."

We also got some DNA from a third party at the scene.

There were blood spots from the scene on the jeans the victim was wearing that didn't belong to the victim, nor to the defendant. But we couldn't identify whose they were. The DA argued that the victim must have borrowed some jeans that had some blood stains on them. One of the little old ladies on the jury said, "How do we know? Maybe she got the jeans at a rummage sale." That was the mentality I was dealing with.

I was convinced that the blood belonged to the true suspect. There were pubic hairs on the victim that didn't belong to Krone. In the first trial, the experts said they *did* belong to Krone, but it turned out that was wrong.

We went to trial again, and he got convicted again. There were three or four experts on each side. It was a battle over bite marks. The jury was out for a long time. They played around with all the evidence. They had models. There was a bite mark on the woman's breast, which was a key piece of evidence. They had actually taken a mold of the breast and the teeth, so the jurors worked with the models and they said it did look like it could fit. They convicted him again. The judge felt, although there were a lot of questions, he didn't give Krone the death penalty, because he thought he might be innocent. So he saved him from Death Row on that basis.

My defendant goes back to prison. All the appeals are denied. I'm still working on the case. New DNA technology was coming on line. STRs are now being used. We petitioned the court to do the new STR testing, where you can detect minute amounts of DNA. We actually get the judge to order that, if they get an unknown profile, that they run it in the DNA database. That takes about two, three years to get this all worked through the courts.

So, in late 2001, early 2002, they get a genetic profile from saliva that's on the tank top the victim wore. The tank top was cut in half by the knife that killed her, and then right on the left breast area where the bite mark was, were some stains that we had identified as being saliva. She was a waitress, so there were a lot of them.

With the new DNA testing available for the tank top, I insisted we use the police department crime lab so that the prosecution couldn't complain about where the work was done. They tested the tank top. They get an unknown profile and it matches the DNA from the blood on the jeans, so we know we're dealing with the same person.

Then they run the new profile in the CODIS database, and they get a hit. They get a hit of a perpetrator who lived across the street from the bar who was in prison at the time the test was run on a child molestation offense.

The prosecutors don't believe it. They think the crime lab made a mistake. They tell them to rerun it. They're in total disbelief.

The police went and talked to this guy in prison. His first story to police was, "No, must be a big mistake because I was in prison at the time that the crime occurred." So the cops say, "Oh, okay, must be a mistake."

I knew it wasn't a mistake because when they do a database hit, there's no chance that two people are going to be the same in the database. And the chances of hitting the guy that happens to live across the street from the scene of the murder, from everybody in that database throughout the nation—there's no way that's going to happen.

We checked his records. He *wasn't* in jail when he said he was. He was arrested about thirty days after the rape-murder in the bar.

After the detectives found *that* out, they went back. Now his story was, "Oh, I've never been to that bar." And they believed him.

Krone's been in prison ten years now. Two trials, high-profile. The detectives scoffed at the notion he was innocent. I basically said to them, 'You convicted an innocent person here, you SOBs." They even did a program for national TV in which they showed how great they did, called *Arrest and Trial.* It was like, "We caught Mr. Krone. We put him in prison. And aren't we great." This is about a year before the new testing.

My cocounsel and this old-time homicide guy in San Diego who really knows how to talk to people, they go and talk to the new suspect, Phillips, in prison. First, he says he never went to the bar. And the homicide guy gets him to talk, "Well, you know, we're just trying to figure out why your DNA was there." The suspect starts to break down a little bit and he says he was really drunk, he was in the bar, he had a blackout, he doesn't know what happened, but he wakes up the next morning, blood all over him. He turns on the TV and he sees that every station is covering the bar scene after the body was found. And he says, "Oh my God, what did I do? What did I do?"

Basically, he admits being there, but he doesn't remember what happened. But everything from the scene—the knife that was used had been cleaned and was hidden underneath the trash can liners in the trash can, for example—points to a very methodical murder. Somebody had the ability to think and reason that did that. But that was his story. And we had it on tape.

The prosecutors still didn't believe it. This was a huge story, and if you have a really innocent person, I've found the media totally gets behind putting pressure on the system to do the right thing. I've found if the morning paper puts a case on the front page, it'll be on the evening news. It works very well. So, now the prosecution is giving news conferences defending why they won't let this guy out of prison.

They go back and retest all the evidence. A number of fingerprints had been taken from the crime scene. Now they find that some of the prints match the new suspect.

Finally, the shoe drops, and they say Krone is innocent. They let him out of jail in 2002. He turns out to be the hundredth person nationwide exonerated with DNA evidence from Death Row.

The day he got out, there's my picture and Ray Krone's picture on the front page of all the newspapers. The first thing I thought of was the prosecutor, who I had fought on the case for seven years, a real SOB. I thought, "You know, this prosecutor got up this morning and he had his coffee and he opened up his paper, and the two people he hated more than anybody in the world are staring at him." He didn't have a good cup of coffee. That was a great feeling.

And the other guy, Phillips, has been charged. The case is set for trial. They're seeking the death penalty against *him* now.

"Let the Science Tell the Story"

Lawyers—on both sides—don't always let the science tell them what happened. Prosecutors don't believe the science if it doesn't fit their theory. And the defense attorneys don't believe it if it goes against *their* theory. Both prosecutors and defense attorneys filter everything through their belief structure.

DEFENSE ATTORNEY

I do a lot of postconviction work, where defense lawyers are representing somebody in prison and want advice on what to do on the evidence. I have this concept that I refer to as "post-traumatic Barry Scheck syndrome." Basically, the lawyers *believe* that their clients who are in prison are innocent and they want to do the DNA testing. And about half of the DNA tests, *at least,* come back showing that the convicted person *is* the person who did the crime.

But the defense lawyers have invested a lot of time in representing somebody, saying, "I believe this guy. He keeps saying he's innocent. He's got a story . . ." And they really buy it.

So, when the DNA test comes back, they don't want to believe it. They think, "God! There's gotta be something wrong here! I know he's innocent!" Because they all want to be like Barry Scheck. They want to free an innocent person. You get a little notoriety. And these attorneys just get really *depressed* when the DNA tells a different story.

So I have to do some hand-holding and therapy to the lawyers, saying things like, "You know, it's not uncommon. Don't feel bad. You still did a good job. It's not the right result, but it's still not a total loss." They never see it that way. They're just totally deflated. Post-traumatic Barry Scheck syndrome.

And then there are cases, of course, when they *do* have the wrong person, and then you have the prosecutors in total disbelief. In exoneration cases, the prosecutor is always the last person to believe that they've gotten the wrong person. He's the last man standing.

Cops do the same thing. You can talk to some good cops and, boy, they just think they've got this one guy that is *the* guy. I've had a number of these cases where they believe it's this one person. And it turns out, they're totally off. They've been working on this one suspect for five years. And the next thing you know, they come back and . . . I tell you, you talk to some detectives and their jaws are just on the table. It's just amazing.

The science is, basically, never wrong. It's the people that deal with the science that are wrong. If the science is done right, it is never wrong. I've learned that you've got to deal with the science and let it tell the story.

DEFENSE ATTORNEY

The police. The defense. The prosecution. We all have common interests. It's *not* the defense versus the prosecution. We all want to see that justice is done. The guilty party should be found and sentenced. And we all want to prevent the wrong guy from being sentenced to death or prison. I'm a defense attorney and I never thought I'd be friends with so many cops. You should see how excited these guys get about cold cases—not just finding the real killer, but freeing the innocent. We're all on the same side.

DEFENSE ATTORNEY

The ultimate expression of the system working as it should: a case that's well investigated, well defended, well prosecuted. When you have that, when justice is done, it's wonderful. It's just wonderful.

The popular picture of lawyers is not too good. But the truth is that most lawyers are very, very good. The police are honest. And juries are insightful and smart enough to figure the case out, and to apply the law that the judge gives them. And when it works, it's absolutely wonderful.

PROSECUTOR

A Prosecutor on the Moment When the Verdict Comes In

Think of what it's like to be an attorney in a homicide case. You had a well-tried case, where the case is not a slam dunk one way or the other. You're called to court, told that they have a verdict. And you sit there, with your officer in charge next to you, the defendant's there, the opposing attorney, and you watch the twelve jurors file back in and you're trying to read them. "Are they looking at the defendant? Are they *not* looking at the defendant?" It's a pretty intense moment.

There's *nothing* that anybody can write that can capture that moment when the jury returns for a verdict. When that jury walks in, it gets *real* quiet in the courtroom. When they've got a verdict, it is one of those moments that can last forever.

As a prosecutor, when a verdict of guilty comes in— You've worked so hard. You've invested so much of your heart into this case. I think relief probably is the first thing you feel, that it all worked like it's supposed to. There is some satisfaction, frequently tinged by a little regret.

You're sorry you didn't get to meet this person. In homicide cases, you're sorry you didn't get to meet this person when they were alive. Because you'll talk to their family and you'll wish you had known them. And it's too late then. And that's kind of sad sometimes.

In some ways, I know almost better than anybody else in the world—except for the defendant—what the victim went through. The final moments.

CAREER SKETCHES FOR CONTRIBUTORS TO *EVERY CONTACT LEAVES A TRACE*

J. M. Adovasio, Director, Mercyhurst Archaeological Institute, Erie, Pennsylvania; professor, anthropologist, and geoarcheologist. Adovasio received his Ph.D. in anthropology from the University of Utah in 1970. Since then he has served as a postdoctoral fellow at the Smithsonian Institution; professor and chairman of the Department of Anthropology at the University of Pittsburgh. Dr. Adovasio has conducted archaeological research in twenty-seven states and five foreign countries. His fieldwork includes the ongoing multidisciplinary investigations at Meadowcroft Rockshelter, Pennsylvania; Mezhirich, Ukraine; and Dolni Vestonice Pavlov, Czech Republic. During his thirty-seven-year career, he has specialized in the analysis of perishable material culture (basketry, textiles, etc.) and the application of high-tech methods in archaeological research. Adovasio is the author of the critically acclaimed nonfiction book *The First Americans.*

Ellen Aragon, Deputy District Attorney, Senior Trial Lawyer, Hardcore Gang Division, Los Angeles County District Attorney's Office. Aragon received her law degree from University of Southern California and joined the District Attorney's Office in 1985.

Christopher Asplen, Former Executive Director of the National Commission on the Future of DNA Evidence; prosecutor, partner in Smith Alling Lane Governmental Affairs, vice president of International Government Relations, Smith Alling Lane, U.S. Asplen began his legal career in 1989 as a local prosecutor for the District Attorney's Office in Bucks County, Pennsylvania, where he spent the next seven years. Asplen specialized in the prosecution of sexual abuse and sex crimes against children. In 1996 Asplen, then a senior deputy district attorney, moved to Washington, D.C., where he worked for the National District Attorney's Association, becoming the director of its newly formed DNA Legal Assistance Unit. Asplen joined the U.S. Attorney's Office in Washington, D.C., in 1998, prosecuting cases for the domestic violence and sex crimes unit. That same year, Asplen was asked to be the executive director of the National Commission on the Future of DNA Evidence, under the auspices of Attorney General Janet Reno. Asplen formed and served as executive director of the commission. In 2003, Asplen joined the firm of Smith Alling Lane, London, UK Asplen works in the government affairs group, specializing in forensic DNA.

SUSAN BALLOU, Program Manager for Forensic Science Research at the National Institute of Standards and Technology, Gaithersburg, Maryland. In 1977 Ballou received a bachelor's degree in forensic science from the University of New Haven, Connecticut. Ballou earned a master's degree in biotechnology from Johns Hopkins University in 2000. Ballou joined Connecticut's Office of Chief Medical Examiner as a chemist in 1997. She took a position with the Northern Virginia Division of Forensic Science in 1978 in the Virginia system, where she served as a drug chemist with diversification in serology, hairs, and fibers. In 1987 Ballou was hired as the sole serologist for the Montgomery County Police Department Crime Laboratory. She has written a chapter on wig fibers for *Mute Witnesses* and several papers regarding case analysis, ballistics, and computer forensics. Ballou came to the National Institute of Standards and Technology in 2000. Ballou was a member of Janet Reno's National Commission on the Future of DNA Evidence.

DR. JOHN M. BUTLER, Research Chemist and Project Leader, Human Identity DNA Testing, National Institute of Standards and Technology, Gaithersburg, Maryland. Butler received his doctorate in chemistry in 1995 from the University of Virginia. Butler conducted his research at the FBI Academy's Forensic Science Research Unit in Quantico, Virginia. Butler was recruited from the FBI lab to do postdoctoral work on a National Research Council Fellowship at NIST. In 1997 Butler was a staff scientist for Gene-Trace Systems in Menlo Park, California. In 1999, Butler returned to NIST as a research chemist specializing in forensic DNA. He has written *Forensic DNA Typing: Biology and Technology behind STR Markers,* considered the leading textbook in the field.

THOMAS A. BRETTELL, Forensic Scientist, Director, Office of Forensic Sciences, New Jersey State Police, Hamilton, New Jersey. Brettell also oversees the Equine Testing Lab in the Meadowlands, New Jersey. Brettell has a Ph.D. in analytical chemistry from Villanova University. Brettell began his forensic career as a forensic chemist for the state police in 1976. In 1980 Brettell was appointed technical director of the South Regional Laboratory in Hammonton. Brettell served as technical director for New Jersey's Central Crime Lab in West Trenton from 1982 through 1990, when he was transferred into the Chief Forensic Sciences Office. Brettell specializes in drug analysis and toxicology. Brettell became chief forensic scientist in 1998. In 2001 Brettell became director of the crime lab.

MICHAEL J. CAMP, Director, Division of Law Enforcement Services, State Crime Laboratory, Milwaukee, Wisconsin. Camp received a bachelor's in chemistry from Rensselaer Polytechnic Institute in 1966. He was awarded his doctorate in chemistry from the University of Wisconsin at Madison in 1972 and did postdoctoral work at Iowa State University. Camp joined the Wisconsin Crime Lab in Madison as a trace analyst in 1972. He also served as a member and leader of the crime scene response team. In 1976 Camp became an assistant professor of forensic chemistry and a coordinator of graduate programs in forensic science at Northeastern University in Boston. In 1981 Camp returned to the Wisconsin crime lab system as a trace analyst, this time in Milwaukee. Camp headed the trace analysis section at both the Madison and Milwaukee crime labs. In 1991 Camp became the director of the state crime lab at Milwaukee. Camp also teaches a class titled Criminalistics at the University of Wisconsin–Milwaukee.

CHIEF GEORGE E. CARPENTER, Wilmette Police Department, Wilmette, Illinois. Carpenter was awarded a master's degree in law enforcement administration from Western Illinois University (1984). He joined the Wilmette Police Department in 1973. In 1991 he was appointed chief of police.

DR. MARY ANN CLAYTON, Deputy Medical Examiner, Bergen County Medical Examiner's Office, Paramus, New Jersey. Clayton received her medical degree from Rutgers Medical School in 1981. Clayton's intern residency was in anatomic pathology and clinical pathology at St. Barnabas Medical Center in Livingston, New Jersey. Clayton was awarded a fellowship in forensic pathology at the State Medical Examiner's Office of Rhode Island in 1986. In 1988 Clayton joined the State Medical Examiner's Office in Newark, New Jersey, as a pathologist. Clayton joined the Bergen County Medical Examiner's Office in 1992 as deputy medical examiner.

SUPERINTENDENT PHIL CLINE, Chicago Police Department. Before being selected superintendent of police in 2003, Cline was chief of the Detective Division for five years. Cline has worked Violent Crimes, Street Gangs, and Narcotics during his thirty-year career. Cline joined the CPD in 1970, was promoted to detective in 1972, and was assigned to the Narcotics unit, where he served until 1977, when he was promoted to sergeant and assigned to the Tenth District. Cline returned to Narcotics later that same year, staying there until 1985, when he was promoted to lieutenant and assigned to the Twenty-first District. Cline became a detective lieutenant in Area Two Violent Crimes in 1986. In 1989, Cline was appointed a field lieutenant in the

Eleventh District. In 1993 Cline went to the newly created gang investigations unit. Cline was appointed commander of Area Five Detectives in 1994 and became commander of the Narcotics unit in 1998. In 2000 Cline moved to Organized Crime as deputy chief. In 2001 Cline was appointed chief of detectives. Cline became superintendent of police in 2004.

DETECTIVE EDWARD CONLON, New York Police Department 44th Precinct Detective Squad, New York, New York, author of the best-selling memoir *Blue Blood.* Conlon joined the NYPD in January 1995. In November 2001 Conlon was promoted to the detective squad.

CHIEF TOM CRONIN, Chief of Tribal Police for Coeur d'Alene, Idaho; FBI-trained Profiler; Commander, Forensic Services Division, Chicago Police Department (Ret.). Cronin joined the Chicago Police Department in 1969, working patrol in the Thirteenth District until 1971, when he became a crime analyst. In 1973 Cronin was promoted to detective. He was promoted to sergeant in 1977 and lieutenant in 1985. In 1985 Cronin was selected by the CPD to be trained in investigative profiling by the FBI's National Center for the Analysis of Violent Crime, a one-year fellowship with the behavioral science unit of the FBI. Cronin was promoted to captain in 1990. He was promoted to commander of the Forensic Services Division in 1998 until his retirement from the CPD in June 2000. Cronin became the chief of police for the City of Coeur d'Alene, Idaho, in July 2000. Cronin became the chief of police for the Coeur d'Alene Tribe in October 2003. Cronin retired in October 2005.

W. MARK DALE, Crime Lab Director (through 2004), New York Police Department; current faculty member, Department of Forensic Biology, State University of New York, Albany. Dale joined the New York State Police in 1973 as a patrol officer. In 1982 Dale became laboratory director with the New York State

Police Mid-Hudson Crime Laboratory. Dale retired from the New York State Police in 1996 and became director of the Washington State Patrol Laboratory System in Olympia, Washington. He returned to the New York State Police in 1997 and was reinstated as a state inspector in charge of the New York State Police Forensic Investigation Center and Laboratory System. Dale became director of the NYPD Crime Lab in 2002. Dale served as president of the American Society of Crime Laboratory Directors in 1994.

GRETCHEN DEGROOT, Technical Leader, DNA Analysis Unit, State Crime Laboratory, Milwaukee, Wisconsin. DeGroot joined the Wisconsin Crime Lab in 1986 as a lab technician. She has worked in the Milwaukee State Crime Laboratory's serology/DNA unit since 1990.

DENNIS C. DIRKMAAT, Director, Applied Forensic Sciences Department, Mercyhurst College, Erie, Pennsylvania. Dirkmaat is also an associate professor of anthropology in the Mercyhurst Archaeological Institute and a board-certified forensic anthropologist. Dirkmaat received his doctorate in anthropology from the University of Pittsburgh in 1990. Dirkmaat has conducted nearly two hundred forensic anthropology cases for over forty coroners, medical examiners, and state police, and has assisted the FBI.

FRANK C. DOLEJSI, Director, Bureau of Criminal Apprehension, Forensic Science Laboratory, St. Paul, Minnesota. Dolejsi joined the crime lab in Madison, Wisconsin, in 1968, where he worked in drug chemistry, toxicology, and serology. Dolejsi directed the serology unit from 1982 to 1984. In 1984 Dolejsi came to the Minnesota Forensic Science Laboratory as an assistant lab director. Dolejsi became director of the lab in 1997.

DETECTIVE DON ELFORD, Detective Division, Burton, Michigan (Ret.). Elford joined the Burton Police Department in 1980.

He served in the Detective Bureau from 1984 until his retirement in 2003. Elford specialized in crimes against persons. In 1990 Elford became a polygraph examiner and, besides working as a detective, administered polygraph examinations for Genesee County, Michigan. Elford currently works for the U.S. Department of Defense.

CAPTAIN GARY ELFORD, Grand Blanc Township Police Department, Grand Blanc, Michigan; formerly member of Cold Case Squad, Flint, Michigan. Elford joined the Flint Police Department in 1975 in uniform patrol. In 1983 Elford was promoted to detective sergeant. Elford worked in the burglary squad and the robbery squad. Elford moved to Homicide in 1985 and stayed there until 1998, with a stay in the sexual assault squad for nine months in 1990–1991. Elford was promoted to lieutenant in 1998 and served as an administrative lieutenant in the Administrative Bureau. In 2000 Elford retired from the Flint Police Department and was hired by the Genesee County Prosecutor's Office as an investigator and a partner in the Cold Case Task Force. Elford was offered the job of captain in charge of detectives in Grand Blanc Township in 2001.

PAUL FERRARA, Director of the Virginia Division of Forensic Science, Codirector of the Virginia Institute of Forensic Science and Medicine, and a Distinguished Professor of Forensic Science and Chemistry at Virginia Commonwealth University. He holds Ph.D. degrees in organic chemistry from Syracuse University and from the State University of New York, College of Environmental Science and Forestry. Dr. Ferrara was a member, coauthor, and consultant to the National Academy of Sciences, National Research Council Reports on the Use of DNA Technology in Forensic Science (1992 and 1996). He is a former member and chairman of the American Society of Crime Laboratory Directors—Laboratory Accreditation Board (1992–1996). In 1994 Dr. Ferrara was appointed by FBI Director Louis Freeh as a member of the FBI's

DNA Advisory Board. In 1998 he was named to the Commission on the Future of DNA Evidence. In 2001 Dr. Ferrara received the Briggs White Award, presented by the American Society of Crime Laboratory Directors in recognition of excellence through leadership in forensic science management. In 2002 Dr. Ferrara was appointed to Attorney General John Ashcroft's Initiative on DNA Laboratory Backlogs Workgroup.

KEITH FINDLEY, Defense Attorney Codirector of Criminal Appeals Project and Codirector of Wisconsin Innocence Project at the University of Wisconsin Law School, Madison, Wisconsin. Findley received his law degree from Yale Law School in 1985. Findley previously worked as an assistant state public defender in Wisconsin, in the Appellate and Trial Divisions. Findley has litigated hundreds of postconviction and appellate cases, and has appeared before the U.S. Supreme Court.

BARRY A. J. FISHER, Crime Laboratory Director, Los Angeles County Sheriff's Department, Los Angeles, California. Fisher has a bachelor's degree in chemistry from City University of New York (1966) and a master's degree in organic chemistry from Purdue University. He also has an M.B.A. from California State University (1973). In 1969 Fisher joined the Los Angeles County Sheriff's Department Crime Laboratory. He worked in most of the lab sections and supervised trace evidence and toxicology sections. In 1987 Fisher was appointed crime lab director. Fisher is a past president of the American Society of Crime Laboratory Directors. Fisher is the author of the highly acclaimed textbook *Techniques of Crime Scene Investigation,* now in its seventh edition. Fisher is past president of the International Association of Forensic Sciences and hosted the fifteenth triennial meeting of the IAFS in Los Angeles in August 1999, at UCLA. Fisher is a past president of the American Society of Crime Laboratory Directors and a past chairman of the American Society of Crime Laboratory Directors—Laboratory Accreditation

Board. He serves on the board of directors of the National Forensic Science Technology Center.

DONNA FONTANA, Forensic Anthropologist, New Jersey State Police, Hamilton, New Jersey. Fontana has worked as a forensic anthropologist for the State of New Jersey her entire career. Fontana joined the New Jersey State Medical Examiner's Office in 1981 as a forensic anthropologist. In 1992 Fontana joined the New Jersey State Police as a forensic anthropologist. Fontana served on the National Commission on the Future of DNA Evidence.

NORMAN GAHN, Assistant District Attorney, Milwaukee County, Milwaukee, Wisconsin. Gahn has been involved in the prosecution of sexual assault cases for the past fourteen years. He has been with the Milwaukee County District Attorney's Office since July 1984 after graduating from Marquette University Law School in Milwaukee. He has a bachelor's degree in psychology from St. Louis University and a master's in forensic sciences from George Washington University. Gahn has lectured extensively around the country on the use of DNA evidence in the courtroom. He is a member of the DNA Legal Assistance Advisory Group of the American Prosecutors Research Institute. Gahn was appointed in 1998 by the U.S. Department of Justice to the National Commission on the Future of DNA Evidence. Also in 1998, the Federal Bureau of Investigation formally recognized him as a pioneer in DNA technology in the courtroom. He is a recipient of the Profiles in DNA Courage Award presented by the National Institute of Justice, and was presented with the Voices of Courage Award in Criminal Justice by the Wisconsin Coalition Against Sexual Assault. Gahn is a recent recipient of a national award from the Foundation for Improvement of Justice in Atlanta, Georgia, for his role in promoting justice in America through the use of DNA evidence

LIEUTENANT COMMANDER VERNON J. GEBERTH (Ret.), New York Police Department, Bronx Homicide Task Force; author of

Practical Homicide Investigation. Geberth joined the NYPD in 1965. His twenty-three years with the NYPD included assignments as tactical patrol officer, detective, patrol sergeant, detective sergeant, patrol lieutenant, detective lieutenant, lieutenant commander (CDS), and commanding officer, Bronx Homicide. Geberth retired from the NYPD in 1987. Geberth served as investigative consultant, Lifecodes Corporation, from 1988 to 1991. Geberth is president of P.H.I. Investigative Consultants (started in 1987), which provides state-of-the-art instruction and consultation in homicide and forensic case investigations throughout the United States and Canada. Geberth is the author of numerous articles and several highly regarded and widely used books on forensics, including *Practical Homicide Investigation: Tactics, Procedures, and Forensic Techniques* and *Sex-Related Homicide and Death Investigation: Practical and Clinical Perspectives.* Geberth has a master's in psychology and is a graduate of the FBI's National Academy.

SERGEANT JIM GIVENS, Supervisor, Cold Case Squad, Phoenix, Arizona (Ret.). Givens joined the Phoenix Police Department in 1977 as a patrol officer. In 1982, Givens was promoted to patrol sergeant; then served as the front desk sergeant for the Phoenix Police Department. Givens then became detective sergeant in the property crimes detail from 1983 to 1984. Givens transferred to the sex crimes detail, where he supervised crimes against children through 1986, when he moved to Homicide. In 1987, Givens served as a street sergeant for three years, and then returned to the Homicide response squad. In 1992 Givens worked on forming the cold case squad, serving as its first supervisor, and was designated investigator for the special prosecutor. He was on disability leave from the force until 1995, when he resumed supervision of the cold case squad until his retirement in 1998.

GARTH GLASSBURG, Executive Director, Northern Illinois Crime Lab, Vernon Hills, Illinois. Glassburg has a bachelor's degree in biology from the University of Illinois, Chicago (1977), and a master's in biology from Southern Illinois University (1981). Glassburg joined the Illinois State Police, Bureau of Forensic Sciences, in 1986 as a forensic scientist, specializing in drug analysis. In 1995, Glassburg was made chemistry training coordinator for the Illinois lab. Glassburg became chemistry section chief in 1997. In 2000 Glassburg became the executive director for the Northern Illinois Police Crime Laboratory, which serves more than forty municipalities in northern Illinois.

ANN MARIE GROSS, Forensic Scientist 3 and Technical Leader, DNA Section, Minnesota Bureau of Criminal Apprehension, Forensic Science Laboratory, St. Paul, Minnesota. Gross started at the BCA Laboratory in January 1989. Gross worked in blood alcohol until 1991, when she transferred to the biology section, at a time when the BCA was starting DNA testing. Gross trained as a DNA analyst and spent three months at the FBI laboratory as a visiting scientist. Gross was involved in setting up the PCR DNA testing at the BCA lab.

SUSAN GROSS, Forensic Science Supervisor of the Chemistry Section, Minnesota Bureau of Criminal Apprehension, Forensic Science Laboratory, St. Paul, Minnesota. Gross's undergraduate degrees are in chemistry and psychology. She has a master's in forensic science. Gross joined the BCA in 1997 as a forensic scientist I in the drug chemistry section. In 1999 Gross joined the trace evidence section. Gross is also a member of the BCA's crime scene team. In 2004, Gross became forensic science supervisor.

DAVID HALL, Forensic Botanist and Plant Taxonomist. Dr. Hall holds bachelor's and master's degrees from Georgia Southern University and received a doctor of philosophy degree in systematic botany from the University of Florida in 1978. Hall holds certifications as a board-certified forensic examiner, an expert in botany, and a professional wetland scientist. Dr. Hall was director of the Plant Identification and Information Services at the University of Florida from 1972 to 1991. His responsibilities included teaching, plant identification, and biology of all Florida plants. He served as a senior scientist for KBN/Golder Associates from 1991 to 1997. He is a recognized expert in forensics and plant identification and has published ten books and over 135 articles. Agencies requesting his expertise for training and cases have included the FBI, Medical Examiners Offices, Florida Department of Law Enforcement, the Florida Water Management Districts, Florida Department of Environmental Protection, Sheriffs' Offices, and several universities. Hall currently owns and operates an environmental and forensic consulting firm in Gainesville, Florida.

FORENSIC DETECTIVE WILLIAM HAMILTON (RET.), Atlantic County Major Crimes Squad Atlantic City, New Jersey, Detective Hamilton joined the Atlantic City Police Department in 1971. In his twenty-eight years with the force, Hamilton served on patrol beat, radio car patrol, the police dive team, and the emergency response team. His investigative work included police photography, crime scene investigation, and fingerprint identification. Hamilton served as a detective in the Bureau of Criminal Identification, General Investigations, in the Detective Bureau, and on the Major Crimes Squad. Detective Hamilton retired in 1999.

DR. BILL HAMILTON, Forensic Pathologist and District Medical Examiner, Eighth District, State of Florida, Gainesville, Florida. Hamilton received his M.D. from the University of Miami (1975) and did his residency in anatomic and clinical pathology at Duke University (completed 1979); his forensic pathology fellowship was completed at the University of North Carolina School of Medicine, Chapel Hill, North Carolina (1978). Hamilton served as the medical examiner in Durham County, North Carolina, from 1977 to 1979; the assistant chief medical examiner, State of North Carolina, from 1977 to 1978; and the regional pathologist for the

North Carolina Medical Examiner System, Durham County, North Carolina, 1979. He was the associate chief medical examiner, State of Kentucky, from October 1979 through 1980. Dr. Hamilton has served as the associate pathologist, Alachua General Hospital, Gainesville, Florida, and as the district medical examiner, Eighth District, State of Florida, from 1981 to the present.

GLENN HARDIN, Toxicology Section Supervisor, Forensic Toxicologist, Bureau of Criminal Apprehension, Forensic Science Laboratory, St. Paul, Minnesota. Hardin has a bachelor's degree in chemistry and a master's in forensic science, both from the University of California at Berkeley. Hardin has been a forensic toxicologist at the BCA since 1989. He's been toxicology section supervisor since 1998.

ROCKNE HARMON, Senior Deputy District Attorney, Alameda County, Oakland, California. Harmon received his law degree from the University of San Francisco Law School in 1974. Harmon has been a deputy district attorney for Alameda since August 1974. Harmon developed a protocol to assist law enforcement agencies in solving cold cases through the use of DNA typing. Harmon handled DNA evidence in the O.J. Simpson trial as a member of the prosecution. Harmon teaches prosecutors about trial presentation of DNA evidence and investigators about the uses of DNA testing. Harmon was part of the Legal Issues Working Group on the National Commission on the Future of DNA Evidence. Harmon chairs the Forensic Evidence Committee of the California District Attorneys Association. Harmon received the International Homicide Investigators Association Award of Achievement in 2003.

NEAL HASKELL, Forensic Entomologist, Professor of Forensic Science and Biology at St. Joseph's College, Rensselaer, Indiana. Haskell received the first master's (1989) and first doctorate (1993) awarded in forensic entomology from Purdue University.

Haskell has done crime scene assessment, research, and lectures regarding forensic entomology. Haskell has served as a forensic entomology consultant on more than six hundred cases worldwide.

CAROL E. HOLDEN, Forensic Psychologist, Director of Evaluation Services, Center for Forensic Psychiatry, State of Michigan; Assistant Professor in Psychology, University of Michigan. Holden received her doctorate in clinical psychology from the University of Michigan in 1986. Holden joined the Center for Forensic Psychiatry in 1986 as a forensic psychologist. Holden became director of the center in 2002.

MAX HOUCK, Director, Forensic Science Initiative, West Virginia University, Morgantown, West Virginia. Houck received a bachelor's and a master's degree in anthropology from Michigan State University. From 1984 to 1985, Houck worked as an electron microscopy technician at Michigan State. Houck then became an applications specialist at Oxford Instruments, where he helped them develop products for the forensic market. In 1991, Houck joined the Medical Examiner's Office in Fort Worth, Texas as a forensic anthropologist and trace evidence examiner. Houck was the coordinating anthropologist for the Branch Davidian incident in Waco, Texas. Houck was assigned to the trace evidence unit at the FBI Laboratory from 1992 to 2001. Houck came to West Virginia University in 2001. Houck has coauthored and edited two books of forensic case reviews, *Mute Witnesses* and *Trace Evidence Analysis*, published by Academic Press.

MARK A. JOHNSEY, Master Sergeant, Illinois State Police Crime Scene Investigator and Forensic Anthropologist (Ret., 2001); currently, Legal Investigator, Lakin Law Firm, Wood River, Illinois. Johnsey joined the Illinois State Police in 1975 as a sworn officer; Johnsey also worked as a crime scene investigator and forensic anthropologist in the Division of Forensic Services.

Johnsey has processed between five hundred and six hundred death scenes. Johnsey served on the National Commission on the Future of DNA Evidence.

DETECTIVE ROLAND JONES, Robbery/Burglary, Area One, Chicago Police Department. Jones joined the CPD in 1994 as a patrol officer in the 23rd District. That same year, Jones served as a tactical officer in the 17th District. In 1996 Jones transferred to the 11th District, where he worked the West Side until 1999. Jones was then assigned to the special operations section, where he also served on the HBT (hostage, barricaded, terrorist) unit as a containment officer. In 2002 Jones was promoted to detective and assigned to Area One.

JOHN JUHALA, Commander, Forensic Science Division, Michigan State Police, Lansing, Michigan (Ret.). Dr Juhala received his doctorate in chemistry from the University of North Dakota in 1970 and has done postdoctoral research at the University of Illinois, Urbana-Champaign. Dr. Juhala joined the North Dakota Bureau of Criminal Investigation as a special agent in laboratory science in 1971. Juhala joined the Michigan Department of Public Health's Division of Crime Detection in 1972 as a lab scientist, where he specialized in arson analysis and drug analysis. In 1973, Juhala was appointed chief of the Bridgeport Crime Laboratory for the Department of Public Health. The Division of Crime Detection was merged with the Michigan State Police Forensic Science Division in 1977 and Juhala was named assistant lab director for the Michigan State Police. In 1993 Juhala was promoted to assistant division commander in charge of the Technical Services Division. Juhala became the division commander of the State Police Forensic Science Division in 2000. Dr. Juhala retired in 2002.

DENNIS M. KEATING, Forensic Investigator, Chicago Police Department and Illinois State Police (Ret.); currently, Firearms

Crime Analyst, Federal Bureau of Alcohol, Tobacco, Firearms, and Explosives. Keating has a bachelor's degree in criminal justice from the University of Illinois (1977), and a master's in science from Lewis University in Lockport, Illinois (1993). Dennis M. Keating joined the Chicago Police Department in 1965 as a police cadet; he later became a sworn police officer. Officer Keating was assigned to the Chicago Police Department's Crime Laboratory in 1981 in the chemistry section; he was promoted to evidence technician, forensic investigator, and firearms examiner. He retired from the CPD crime lab in 1996. Keating worked as a firearms examiner with the Illinois State Police from 1996 until 1999. Keating is currently working as a firearms crime analyst with the Federal Bureau of Alcohol, Tobacco, Firearms, and Explosives.

BRIAN KING, Deputy Chief, Wilmette Police Department, Wilmette, Illinois; former Task Force Commander, NORTAF (North Regional Major Crimes Task Force), Northern Illinois. Since 1987, King has served as patrol officer, detective, sergeant, commander, and deputy chief with the Wilmette, Illinois Police Department. King conducts criminal investigations training and homicide investigator training. He also consults in cold case investigations.

LIEUTENANT JOE LEATHERMAN, Latent Print and Crime Scene Section, Forensic Services Laboratory, South Carolina Law Enforcement Division, Columbia, South Carolina; First Vice President for South Carolina International Association for Identification (SCIAI). Leatherman joined the Richland County Sheriff's Office, Columbia, South Carolina, in October 1987. Leatherman ran the bloodhound tracking team. In 1991 Leatherman was promoted to Investigator and moved to the Sheriff's Department crime scene unit. Leatherman became sergeant in January 1997, and was put in charge of the crime scene unit. In January 2001 Leatherman joined SLED. He was promoted to lieutenant in 2004.

HENRY C. LEE, Chief Emeritus of the Connecticut State Police Laboratory, Meriden, Connecticut. Dr. Lee was the director of public safety for the State of Connecticut and was the former director of the Connecticut State Police Forensics Science Laboratory. Lee earned his doctorate in biochemistry from New York University in 1975. Lee has been with the Connecticut State Police Laboratory since 1975, when he volunteered his services to assist the Connecticut State Police in developing forensic laboratory services. Lee is the author of several acclaimed books on forensic science. Lee has investigated more than four thousand homicides and testified over one thousand times in court.

SERGEANT RICH LONGSHORE, Homicide Bureau, Los Angeles County Sheriff's Department. Longshore was with the Novato Police Department in northern California from 1966 to 1969. Longshore joined the department in January, 1970. Longshore worked in the Custody Division for two years, then worked South Central Los Angeles, Lennox Station. In 1975 Longshore was promoted to sergeant and was assigned to Lomita Station and then served as a training sergeant at the Police Academy. Longshore returned to Lennox, and then served as a SWAT team leader in the Special Enforcement Bureau for four years. Longshore was on the Special Operations Committee for the 1984 Olympics. Longshore then served in a headquarters assignment, the Internal Affairs Unit, and the Internal Investigations Bureau for the next seven years. Longshore went to Narcotics for two years. Longshore has been in the Homicide Bureau since 1995.

LIEUTENANT OF INVESTIGATIONS JAMES M. MACKERT, Organized Crime Division; Training Officer for Organized Crime Division, Chicago Police Department, Chicago, Illinois. Mackert joined the Chicago Police Department in 1994. Mackert worked in the Eighth and Ninth Districts before transferring in 1995 to the Eleventh District. Mackert served as a tactical/gang officer for nine years (with three months spent after 9/11 as an intelligence analyst with the Central Control Group). In 2004, Mackert was transferred to the Organized Crime Division's narcotics and gang investigations section, where he worked on several street teams purchasing narcotics and conducting long-term narcotics-related investigations. Mackert was promoted to detective sergeant early in 2005 and to lieutenant in August, 2005. Mackert has a master's degree in criminal social justice from Lewis University and a master's in public administration from the Illinois Institute of Technology. Mackert received his Ph.D. in education from Loyola University, Chicago, in 2005.

GREG MATHESON, Acting Laboratory Director, Chief Forensic Chemist I, Criminalistics Laboratory, Los Angeles Police Department. Matheson joined the crime lab as a forensic scientist in June, 1978. He worked in toxicology; the special testing unit (housing the gas chromatograph and mass spectrometer, in which poisons analysis, explosives, and arson materials were tested); filament examination; and the serology unit (Matheson became the supervisor of the serology unit in 1989). In 1994 Matheson was named one of the two assistant directors of the LAPD Crime Lab, in charge of the forensic analysis section, encompassing the major crime units: serology, DNA, trace, firearms, questioned documents, and the field response unit. In December 2003, Matheson was appointed acting director of the crime lab.

TERRY MCADAM, Supervising Forensic Scientist, Washington State Patrol Crime Lab, Tacoma, Washington. McAdam specializes in trace evidence, bloodstains, and general crime scene. McAdam began his career in the Northern Ireland Forensic Science Lab in Belfast in December 1977. McAdam worked there for ten years, in explosives and firearms, as well as in the blood alcohol, toxicology, arson evidence, and trace evidence sections. McAdam came to the Washington State Crime Lab in Seattle in October 1987 as a forensic scientist in drug analysis, where he worked for two years. McAdam then worked in trace evidence and crime scene. In December 1998 McAdam was promoted to supervisor of the trace evidence section in Tacoma, where he is also a member of the crime scene response team. McAdam has processed approximately five hundred crime scenes.

DETECTIVE SERGEANT WILLIAM J. MCINTYRE, Violent Crimes Unit, Atlantic County Prosecutor's Office, Hammonton, New Jersey (Ret.). McIntyre served four years, from 1974 to 1978, on the Northfield, New Jersey, Police Department as a patrol officer. In 1978, he joined the Litigation Division of the Atlantic County Prosecutor's Office as an investigator. McIntyre was senior investigator in the homicide unit and supervisor of the rape unit from 1980 to 1987. McIntyre was appointed senior investigator in the Litigation Division in 1987 and served there until 1992, when he became senior investigator of the Criminal Investigation Division, Special Operations Section. In 1994 McIntyre was promoted to detective sergeant in the Atlantic County major crimes squad. From January 1999 through July 2000 McIntyre was detective sergeant in the violent crime unit. McIntyre served on the National Law Enforcement Summit on DNA Technology. McIntyre, who started patrol in Somerset, New Jersey, worked homicide on the major crimes squad from 1980 until 2000, when he retired. McIntyre now presents training sessions nationwide in cold case evaluations. He also heads his own private forensic consulting firm, WJM Associates, LLC.

COMMANDER JOE MURPHY, Forensic Services Division; former Commander, Cold Case Squad. Murphy joined the CPD in 1970. In 1978 Murphy was promoted to detective and was assigned to Area One Homicide. Murphy became a sergeant in 1984, when he returned to the Detective Division as a supervisor. In 1988 Murphy was promoted to lieutenant and was assigned to the ATF Task Force. Murphy was named commanding officer of Area Two Violent Crimes in 1989, where he worked till 2000. Murphy was in charge of the cold case quad squad from 2000 to 2002. Murphy now serves as the homicide case inspector in the Detective Division.

JOHN P. NIELSON, Criminalistics Supervisor, Latent Print Specialist, State Crime Laboratory, Milwaukee, Wisconsin. Nielson began his career as a deputy sheriff in Iowa City, Iowa, from 1975 to 1983. He started studying fingerprinting in 1977 and became an identification officer in 1979. Nielson became a certified latent print examiner in 1981. Nielson joined the state crime lab in Milwaukee as a fingerprint examiner in 1983. Nielson has supervised firearms, documents, fingerprints, and photography in the crime lab since 1996.

LT. DAVE O'CALLAHAN, Detective Division, Robbery Unit, Chicago Police Department. O'Callahan joined the force in 1970. He spent the first part of his career on Chicago's West Side as part of a gang/tactical team. In 1977 O'Callahan joined the Area One Homicide/Sex Crimes Unit as a detective. O'Callahan was promoted to sergeant in 1986. O'Callahan was assigned to an ATF Task Force in 1987 and then supervised tactical teams in the Patrol Division. O'Callahan returned to the Detective Division, Robbery Unit, in 2003 and retired in 2005. O'Callahan now serves as Investigator, Special Prosecutions Unit, Financial Crimes, Cook County State's Attorney's Office, Chicago.

CAPTAIN RAY PEAVY, Homicide Bureau, Los Angeles County Sheriff's Department, Los Angeles, California. Peavy joined the Sheriff's Department in 1968 as a police officer assigned to the county jail, then was assigned to patrol at Lakewood Sheriff's Station, which policed six cities in Los Angeles County. In 1970 Peavy joined the Vice Bureau, where he worked undercover in West Hollywood. Peavy was promoted to sergeant in 1983, and was assigned to Lennox Station. He was then transferred to Marina del Rey. In 1986 Sergeant Peavy came to the Homicide Bureau as an investigator. Peavy became a lieutenant in 1988 and worked in a jail facility before being assigned to Alameda Station as a watch commander. Peavy returned to Homicide in 1993. In 2003 Peavy was promoted to captain of the Homicide Bureau.

DAVID B. PETERSEN, former Assistant Director, Minnesota, Bureau of Criminal Apprehension, Forensic Science Laboratory, St. Paul, Minnesota; former President of Association of Crime Lab Directors; forensic scientist. Petersen joined the Minnesota Forensic Science Lab in 1981 as an analytical chemist. From 1981 through June of 1986, Petersen worked in arson investigation, explosives analysis, and drug chemistry. At the same time, Petersen served as a member of the crime scene team. In June 1986, Petersen accepted a position with Hewlett-Packard Corporation as an instrument engineer. In 1989, Petersen returned to the Minnesota Forensic Science Lab, working in drug chemistry, explosives, and arson. From 1990 through 1997, Petersen served as a Crime Scene Team leader and as quality assurance coordinator for the lab. He then served as assistant crime lab director. In 2004 he was elected president of the American Society of Crime Lab Directors (serving until March 2005). In 2005, Petersen was convicted of a felony drug offense and served a six-month sentence.

DAVID PETERSON, Latent Print Examiner, Minnesota Bureau of Criminal Apprehension, Forensic Science Laboratory, St. Paul, Minnesota. Peterson joined the air force in 1968, where he served in Air-Based Defense and the Office of Special Investigations, which included crime scene processing. Peterson retired from the air force in 1989. Peterson worked in the private sector for a few years for Koch Industries and then joined the Wichita, Kansas, Police Department as a crime scene investigator in 1993. Peterson trained for, and became, the latent print examiner for the Wichita Police Department in 1995. Peterson joined the Minnesota Bureau of Criminal Apprehension in July 1997. Peterson has served as a latent print examiner, member of the crime scene team and crime scene team leader.

CHRISTOPHER J. PLOURD, Attorney, Certified Criminal Law Specialist, Forensic Evidence Consultant. Plourd is a sole practitioner in the Law Offices of Christopher J. Plourd, located in San Diego, California. Plourd specializes in cases involving forensic scientific evidence, particularly forensic DNA technologies. Plourd received his law degree from Thomas Jefferson College of Law, San Diego. He served as an assistant public defender, Imperial County Public Defender's Office, El Centro, California, from 1983 to 1986. Plourd was a staff attorney with Defenders, Inc., from 1986 to June 1988. He has operated his own law practice since 1988. Plourd was a member of the Crime Scene Evidence Collection working group for the National Commission on the Future of DNA Evidence. Plourd regularly lectures attorneys, judges, law enforcement officers, and law students on forensic scientific evidence.

NORMAN REEVES, Forensic Consultant, Bloodstain Pattern Analysis, Tucson, Arizona; Deputy Chief, Investigative Section, Gloucester County Prosecutor's Office, Woodbury, New Jersey (Ret.). From 1966 to 1974 Reeves served in the Pitman, New Jersey, Police Department as patrol officer, detective, and detective sergeant. Reeves served in Vietnam from 1967 through 1969. In 1974 Reeves joined the staff of the Gloucester County Prosecutor's Office, working as a county detective, detective supervisor, lieutenant of county detectives, captain of county investigators, and deputy chief. Reeves retired in August 1991 and began independent consulting in the field of bloodstain pattern analysis.

OFFICER TOM REYNOLDS, Police Forensic Investigator, Chicago Police Department (Ret.). Reynolds joined the CPD in 1966 and served as a patrol officer until 1971. From 1971 to 1979 Reynolds served as an evidence technician. Reynolds worked as a police forensic investigator from 1979 to 1999. Reynolds teaches Introduction to Forensic Science at Chicago State University and at Harold Washington College at the Chicago Police Department Academy.

KATHLEEN "COOKIE" RIDOLFI, Professor of Law; Director, Northern California, Innocence Project (NCIP), Santa Clara University, Santa Clara, California. Ridolfi earned her law degree at Rutgers University in 1982. In the 1980s, Ms. Ridolfi was a trial lawyer with the Defender Association of Philadelphia In 1991, she began teaching at CUNY Law School. Ridolfi teaches criminal law and criminal procedure at Santa Clara.

RICHMOND M. RIGGS, Prosecuting Attorney, Genesee County Prosecutor's Office, Flint, Michigan. Riggs attended Michigan State University and received his law degree from Thomas Cooley Law School in Lansing, Michigan, in 1981. Riggs was in private practice for four years, working on the Saginaw/Chippewa reservation in Mt. Pleasant, Michigan. Riggs joined the Genesee County Prosecutor's Office in 1986.

WILLIAM C. RODRIGUEZ III, Chief Deputy Medical Examiner, Armed Forces Institute of Pathology, Washington, D.C. Rodriguez received his doctorate in anthropology from the University of Tennessee in 1983. In 1984 Rodriguez was hired by the Caddo Parish Coroner's Office in Shreveport, Louisiana, as forensic anthropologist and deputy coroner. In 1987 Rodriguez became a forensic anthropologist and chief of operations for the Onondaga County Medical Examiner's Office in Syracuse, New York. Rodriguez joined the Armed Forces Institute of Pathology in 1990.

MARK RUSIN, ATF (Alcohol, Tobacco, Firearms and Explosives) Special Agent; Firearms Expert, Regional Coordinator for ATF National Integrated Identification of Ballistics Information, Tucson, Arizona. Rusin grew up on the South Side of Chicago. In 1980 Rusin joined the Las Vegas Metro Police as a patrol officer. Rusin became an ATF agent in December 1983, and was assigned to San Francisco, where he worked in the Metro gun squad and an organized crime squad. Rusin then worked in the Explosives Division of ATF Headquarters in Washington, D.C., as a project officer from 1989 to 1990. In December 1990 Rusin was promoted to group supervisor in Philadelphia. Rusin was transferred back to ATF Headquarters in 1992 to the Intelligence Division, where he was the International Alcohol and Tobacco Interdiction Coordinator. In 1995 Rusin transferred to ATF's Office of Inspection. Rusin became the inspector in charge of the Chicago Bureau in 1996 and then was assigned to the assistant special agent in charge position till 1999, when he was transferred back to ATF Headquarters, Special Operations Division, where he worked as the ATF representative to the White House. In November 2003 Rusin became ATF western regional coordinator.

DETECTIVE RASHID SABUR, Criminal Investigation Division, Homicide Squad, Newark Police Department, Newark, New Jersey. Sabur joined the Newark Police Department in 1987 and has served for fourteen years in the Criminal Investigation Division, where he spent three years investigating sex crimes and eleven years investigating homicides and cold cases.

NORM SAUER, Professor of Anthropology and Director of the Forensic Anthropology Lab, Michigan State University; Forensic Anthropologist. Dr. Sauer has been a member of the faculty at Michigan State since 1973. He received his doctorate in physical anthropology from Michigan State University in 1974. Sauer began doing forensic anthropology in the midseventies. He has worked on more than one thousand cases for the Michigan State Police, for medical examiners around the state of Michigan, for attorneys around the United States, and has worked with the FBI and ATF. Sauer is a member of DMORT, the Mortuary Operation Response Team. DMORT is a federal agency that calls experts to scenes of mass disaster to help identify victims. Dr. Sauer's work for this agency included assisting in the identification process for the victims of 9/11.

ROBERT C. SHALER, Director of Forensic Science, Eberly College of Science, Pennsylvania State University (from July 2005); Director, Office of the Chief Medical Examiner, New York City Department of Forensic Biology, DNA Lab (1990–2005). Shaler has a doctorate in biochemistry from Pennsylvania State University. In the late sixties Shaler was a biochemistry professor at the University of Pittsburgh, when he saw an ad in the *Pittsburgh Press* advertising Scientific Sleuthing classes taught by crime lab personnel. Shaler received a master's degree in forensic science and came into the state crime lab as a drug analyst in 1970. Shaler returned to the University of Pittsburgh Chemistry Department, teaching forensic chemistry in the midseventies. In 1977 he was hired by the Aerospace Corporation in Washington, D.C., to manage several contracts, including bloodstain analysis systems. In 1978 Shaler became the chief serologist for the City of New York in the Medical Examiner's Office. Shaler joined Lifecodes Corporation, the first American private forensic DNA laboratory, in 1986, where he was the director of Forensic Business Development. Shaler traveled the country, lecturing to police departments and attorney groups about the benefits of DNA testing. In 1990 Shaler returned to the Medical Examiner's Office in New York to set up a DNA testing lab, called the Department of Forensic Biology, currently the largest forensic DNA lab in the United States. In 1990, Shaler also started a crime scene reconstruction unit, called the Medical Examiner's Scientific Analysis and Training Team. For almost four years, Shaler was in charge of the team that used various methods, including DNA, to identify the remains of the people killed in the 9/11 attack on the World Trade Center. Shaler is the author of *Who They Were: Inside the World Trade Center DNA Story: The Unprecedented Effort to Identify the Missing.*

RONALD L. SINGER, Crime Laboratory Director, Tarrant County Medical Examiner's Office, Fort Worth, Texas. Singer has a master's degree in biological sciences. He joined the newly created crime lab of the Jefferson County Parish Sheriff's Office in Metarie, Louisiana, in 1972 as a drug analyst. In 1975 Singer moved into firearms and toolmark analysis and also began training in trace evidence. Singer served as crime lab director of the Jefferson County Parish Sheriff's Office from 1976 through 1988. Singer was invited to establish a crime laboratory for the Tarrant County Medical Examiner's Office in 1989. He has served as chief criminalist there since 1989. In 2000, Singer's position of chief criminalist was re-designated as crime lab director. Singer served as president of AAFS (the American Academy of Forensic Sciences) in 2004. Singer is currently president (his term extends from 2005 to 2008) of IAFS (the International Association of Forensic Sciences).

DR. SUNANDAN B. SINGH, Medical Examiner, Bergen County, New Jersey, Paramus, New Jersey. Singh graduated from Osmania University in Hyderabad, India. Dr. Singh worked as a family physician in a rural area of India for two years. He then did postgraduate training in pathology and bacteriology at Grant Medical College, Bombay University. After Pakistan and India went to war in 1965, Dr. Singh served as a captain in the Indian army until 1969. Dr. Singh completed his M.D. in pathology and bacteriology in 1970. Dr. Singh came to the United States to study and work as a resident at Harlem Hospital Center, affiliated with Columbia University, in 1971. Dr. Singh became a pathologist in South Jersey. Singh served as medical examiner in Camden County, New Jersey, from 1980 to 1986. Singh then served as an assistant medical examiner in the State Medical Examiner's Office, Newark, New Jersey. In 1992 Singh became the medical examiner of Bergen County.

JAMES SNAIDAUF, Group Supervisor and Forensic Scientist, Latent Fingerprint Section, Illinois State Police Forensic Science Center, Chicago, Illinois. Snaidauf joined the latent print section of the

Illinois State Police in 1995. In 2001 Snaidauf served as president of the Illinois IAI (International Association for Identification). In 2001 Snaidauf became group supervisor of the latent fingerprint section. Snaidauf is an adjunct professor in the master's program in forensic science at the University of Illinois–Chicago.

KARA STEFANSON, DNA Resource Specialist, Cook County State's Attorney's Office, Chicago, Illinois. Stefanson holds degrees in forensic science and criminal justice, both from Michigan State University. After graduation in 1992 Stefanson worked as staff serologist for the DuPage County Sheriff's Department Crime Laboratory. In 1998 Stefanson accepted the position of group supervisor, DNA analyst, Forensic Biology/DNA Unit, Illinois State Police Forensic Science Center, Chicago, Illinois. Stefanson joined the Cook County State's Attorney's Office in 2004. Stefanson has trained more than two thousand members of law enforcement, emergency room personnel, and trial attorneys in the field of forensic biology and DNA analysis.

DAVID DYER STEPHENS, Forensic Scientist, Serology and Trace, Michigan Department of State Police, Bridgeport Regional Forensic Laboratory, Bridgeport, Michigan. Stephens has a bachelor's degree in medical technology from Michigan State University (1983) and a master's in general administration from Central Michigan University (1997). Since July 1997 Stephens has served as a forensic scientist with the Michigan State Police, specializing in serology, shoe and tire impression comparisons, hair comparisons, fiber comparisons, blood spatter interpretation, and event reconstruction.

SERGEANT R. P. (RUSTY) SULLIVAN, Supervisory Sergeant, Crime Scene Unit, Investigations Division, Aurora Police Department, Aurora, Illinois. Sullivan served as dispatcher/ LEADS supervisor for the Village of Montgomery Police Department, Montgomery, Illinois, from 1979 through 1982. Sullivan served as a police officer in the villages of Sugar Grove and Montgomery from 1980 until 1985. In April 1985 Sullivan joined the City of Aurora Police Department and, in 1988, was assigned as an evidence technician. Sullivan is also a member of the investigative deadly force (officer-involved shooting) team.

ANJALI SWIENTON, Forensic Scientist, Attorney, and President/CEO of SciLawsForensics, Ltd., Germantown, Maryland. Swienton has a bachelor's degree in molecular biology from Johns Hopkins University, a master's in forensic science from George Washington University (1992), and a law degree from American University, Washington College of Law (2002). From March 1998 to November 2002 Swienton served as a senior forensic analyst at ACS Defense, Inc., a federal contractor at the National Institute of Justice, Office of Science and Technology, in Washington, D.C. Swienton is president and CEO of SciLawForensics, which is designed to help government agencies, private agencies, and educational institutions develop training tools for the criminal justice system, both from a scientific and a legal perspective.

STEVEN A. SYMES, Forensic Anthropologist; Assistant Professor, Mercyhurst Archaeological Institute, Mercyhurst College, Erie, Pennsylvania. Symes received his doctorate in physical anthropology in 1992 from the University of Tennessee, Knoxville, Tennessee. From 1976 to 1978 Symes worked as an archeologist with the South Dakota State Archaeological Research Center, Fort Meade, South Dakota. Symes worked on the Arikara Indian skeletal data collection at the Smithsonian Institution from 1981 to 1984. From 1985 to 1987 Symes was the head physical anthropologist for several U.S. excavations. Symes served as forensic anthropologist and morgue director for the Davidson County Metropolitan Nashville Medical Examiner's Office from 1986 to 1987. From there, he served as forensic anthropologist for the Shelby County Regional Forensic Center, Department of Pathology, University of Tennessee, Memphis, where he also taught in the Department of Pathology. In 2003 Symes joined Mercyhurst Archaeological Institute. He is on contract with the Newark, New Jersey, Medical Examiner's Office for toolmark analysis. Symes's expertise is in forensic toolmark and fracture pattern interpretation.

GEORGE TAFT JR., Founder and Director (Ret.) of the Alaska Department of Public Safety, Scientific Detection Laboratory, Anchorage, Alaska. Taft worked as a chemist with the Texas Department of Public Safety's Crime Lab in Austin, Texas, from the late fifties to 1984. Taft was promoted to director of the Austin Laboratory in 1980. In 1984 the State of Alaska recruited Taft to set up a new crime lab, which included overseeing the construction of the new lab, equipping it, hiring forensic scientists, and obtaining ASCLD (American Society of Crime Lab Directors) accreditation. Taft currently serves on ASCLD's Laboratory Accreditation Board. Taft also travels extensively, lecturing young people about forensic education.

ANN TALBOT, Bureau Chief, New Mexico Department of Public Safety (NM-DPS) Forensic Laboratories, Santa Fe, New Mexico. Talbot started as a serologist and trace evidence analyst in the Metropolitan Forensic Science Center, Crime Laboratory, Albuquerque, New Mexico, in 1979. Talbot also did toxicology, blood alcohol analysis, and controlled substances analysis. In 1982 Talbot started working crime scenes as a "secondary," whose responsibilities included photography and lifting latent fingerprints. Talbot worked on the bench until 1990. In 1991 Talbot was appointed director, Metropolitan Forensic Science Center, Crime Laboratory, Albuquerque. Talbot became the division director in 1997. In 2005 Talbot became the bureau chief of the NM-DPS Forensic Laboratories.

SERGEANT BOB VANNA (RET.), Chicago Police Department Marine Unit. Vanna joined the Chicago Police Department in December 1967 as a patrol officer in the Third District. Vanna worked on the tactical team (plainclothes) and the special operations group. In 1977 Vanna was promoted to sergeant. He served as patrol sergeant, tactical sergeant, special operations sergeant, and hostage barricaded and terrorism team sergeant. Vanna also worked mass transit and did motorcycle detail in a Chicago Housing Authority complex. From 1986 to 2002 Sergeant Vanna served on the marine unit, where he patrolled Lake Michigan and the Chicago River for the purposes of rescue, evidence recovery, and body recovery.

FORENSIC SPECIALIST MICHAEL A. WASOWICZ, Evidence technician, Skokie Police Department, Skokie, Illinois; detailed to the North Regional Major Crimes Task Force (NORTAF) as Supervisor of the Forensic Unit. NORTAF serves thirteen communities in the North Shore, Chicago, area and primarily investigates homicides and nonparental kidnappings. Wasowicz joined the Skokie Police Department in 1984. He has been an evidence technician for sixteen years. Wasowicz is certified by the International Association for Identification as a senior crime scene analyst and bloodstain pattern examiner.

MICHAEL C. WEIL, Computer Forensic Expert; former Department of Defense Computer Forensic Examiner. From August 1996 to March 1998, Weil was a policy researcher for the Illinois Office of the Attorney General, Policy and Program Development. Weil authored a grant for the development of the Illinois Computer Crime Institute, a statewide law enforcement computer crime investigations and training program. Weil became the senior forensic analyst for the Illinois Computer Crime Institute, Illinois Office of the Attorney General, where he developed and taught courses relating to internet investigations and computer forensics in 1998. From January 2002 to November 2002, Weil served in the Department of Defense Computer Forensics Laboratory, Counter-Intelligence/Counter-Terrorism Section.

Weil then worked in the data imaging and extraction section of the DOD Computer Forensics Laboratory as Section Chief. Weil served on the National Institute of Standards and Technology Computer Forensic Tool Testing and National Software Reference Library Steering Committee from April 2001 to October 2002. In January 2004, Weil joined a Chicago consulting firm, where he conducts computer forensic examinations. He currently serves on the Technical Working Group for Education in Digital Evidence and the Technical Working Group for the Investigative Uses of High Technology of the National Institute of Justice.

EARL WELLS, Director, Forensic Services Laboratory, South Carolina Law Enforcement Division, Columbia, South Carolina. Wells's undergraduate degree was in chemistry. Wells joined the Forensic Services Laboratory in 1969; he worked as a trace evidence analyst, started an Implied Consent Program for the State of South Carolina and also served as assistant director for the Forensic Chemistry Laboratory. Wells is a facilitator at the University of Tennessee's National Forensic Academy in crime scene and trace evidence. Wells has been director of the Forensic Services Laboratory since 1997. Wells served as president of ASCLD (The American Society of Crime Lab Directors) in 2005.

CHIEF OF POLICE CHARLES J. WERNICK, Illinois. Wernick joined the Evanston Police Department as a police officer in 1972. Over the next fourteen years, Wernick's assignments included the selective enforcement team, which concentrates on major crime patterns and the Juvenile Bureau (as an investigator). Wernick next joined the Detective Bureau, working on criminal investigations and serving as senior investigator for Vice and Narcotics. Wernick was promoted to sergeant in 1986. His duties over the next three years included work as Internal Affairs Bureau supervisor and as supervisor in the Detective Bureau, directing major case investigations. In 1996 Wernick was promoted to lieutenant, in charge of the gang and narcotics unit. In 1997 Wernick was appointed the operations commander for the North Regional Major Crimes Task Force. He became task force commander of NORTAF in 1999. Wernick became commander of police in 1998, in command of the Investigative Services Division. Wernick also served as evidence technician supervisor. Wernick became chief of police, Highwood, Illinois, in 2001 and chief of police in Northbrook, Illinois, in 2005.

JOHN H. WILLMER, Forensic Scientist, Firearms and Toolmark Identification Section of the Division of Forensic Science, Richmond, Virginia, Crime Laboratory. Willmer has an undergraduate degree in chemistry from Northern Michigan University. Willmer served in the navy in bomb disposal as a lieutenant during the Vietnam War. In 1973 Willmer joined the Michigan State Police as a trooper. Willmer joined the firearms/toolmark section of the Bridgeport lab, part of the Michigan State Police, in 1977. Willmer spent the next twenty years there as a firearms and toolmark examiner. He was also a member of the bomb squad for the Michigan State Police. In 1997 Willmer retired from the Michigan State Police with the rank of detective sergeant. That same year, Willmer joined the Richmond, Virginia, Crime Lab as a forensic scientist.

DEBORAH OMAN ZIMET, Assistant State's Attorney, Capital Homicide Unit, Broward County, Florida. Zimet received her law degree from Nova Southeastern University in Fort Lauderdale, Florida, in 1981. Zimet received a second law degree in international and comparative trade law from Georgetown University in 1985. Zimet did insurance defense work for two years and then came to the State's Attorney's Office in 1987. Zimet has been in the Capital Homicide unit for the past thirteen years.